Faulkner and Welty and the Southern Literary Tradition

Faulkner and Welty
—— *and the* ——
Southern Literary Tradition

Noel Polk

University Press of Mississippi / Jackson

www.upress.state.ms.us

The University Press of Mississippi is a member
of the Association of American University Presses.

"Scar" was first published in *Faulkner and War* by the University Press of Mississippi, 2006.
"Testing Masculinity in the Snopes Trilogy" was first published in *The Faulkner Journal* 16:3
    (2000–2001). I thank Dawn Trouard for permission to reprint it here.
"Faulkner in the Luxembourg Gardens" was first published in *Études Faulknériennes I: Sanctuary*.
    Ed. Michel Gresset. Rennes, France: Presses Universitaires de Rennes, 1996. I am grateful to
    Nicole Moulinoux for permission to reprint it here.
"The Ponderable Heart" was first published in *Études Faulknériennes V: Eudora Welty and the
    Poetics of the Body*. Ed. Geraldine Chouard and Danièle Pitavy-Souques. Rennes, France:
    Presses Universitaires de Rennes, 2005. I am grateful to Nicole Moulinoux for permission to
    reprint it here.
"How Shreve Gets in to Quentin's Pants" will be published in *William Faulkner: An Ecumenical
    Gathering*. Ed. Mario Materassi and Donald M. Kartiganer. Florence, Italy: U of Florence P,
    due fall 2008. I am grateful to Mario Materassi for permission to preprint it here.
"Faulkner and the Commies" and "Domestic Violence in 'The Purple Hat'" are first published
    here, by the kind permission of the author.
"Water, Wanderers, and Weddings: Going to Naples and to No Place" reconstitutes parts of "Going
    to Naples and Other Places in Eudora Welty's Fiction" (first published in *Eudora Welty: Eye of
    the Storyteller*. Ed. Dawn Trouard. Kent, OH: Kent State UP, 1989) and "Water, Wanderers, and
    Weddings: Love in Eudora Welty" (first published in *Eudora Welty: A Form of Thanks*. Ed. Louis
    Dollarhide and Ann J. Abadie: Jackson: UP of Mississippi, 1979).
"Reading Blood and History in *Go Down, Moses*" was first published in *History and Memory in
    Faulkner's Novels*. Ed. Ikuko Fujihira, Noel Polk, and Hisao Tanaka. Tokyo: Shohakusha, 2005.
    I am grateful to Ikuko Fujihira for permission to reprint it here.

∞

Library of Congress Cataloging-in-Publication Data

Polk, Noel.
  Faulkner and Welty and the southern literary tradition / Noel Polk.
    p. cm.
  Includes index.
  ISBN 978-1-934110-84-3 (cloth : alk. paper) 1. Faulkner, William, 1897–1962—Criticism
and interpretation. 2. Welty, Eudora, 1909–2001—Criticism and interpretation. 3. Literature
and society—Southern States—History—20th century. 4. Women and literature—Southern
States—History—20th century. 5. American literature—Southern States—History and criticism.
6. Southern States—Intellectual life. 7. Southern States—In literature. I. Title.
  PS3511.A86Z946353 2008
  813'.52—dc22   2007038113

British Library Cataloging-in-Publication Data available

For Nancy

Contents

PREFACE

These essays began as invited lectures given to specific audiences on specific occasions and designed to contribute to discussions of specific themes in Faulkner's and Welty's works. Some were written for and delivered to foreign audiences and then published in foreign journals and proceedings and so have been mostly unavailable in this country. Their occasional nature and the time limits necessarily imposed on panelists have allowed me to focus on what I find most fascinating in literary study, the smaller units of a literary work—from punctuation and other curious occlusions to passages and characters and episodes that often go unnoticed in the critical discourse—and their relationships to a work's "larger" themes, the interplay between the bricks and mortar and a work's grand design. I am very pleased that the University Press of Mississippi has given me this opportunity to collect them here.

I am grateful to Seetha Srinivasan, director of the University Press, for many years of friendship and support and for being a faithful publisher of my work, and to Walter Biggins and Anne Stascavage for their most necessary help on this volume. I also want to thank my colleagues at Mississippi State University, especially Rich Raymond, head of the English Department; Phil Oldham, formerly Dean of Arts & Sciences, and Gary Myers, now acting dean, and Peter Rabideau, Provost, for giving me the chance to be a member of the faculty at Mississippi State, and for their generous support in all things professional and personal. I thank Laura West, Managing Editor of *The Mississippi Quarterly*, and

Julie Harman, my research assistant, for their unflagging efforts in support of my work.

I am likewise grateful to many friends and conference organizers over the years who have been kind enough to invite me to participate in conferences and then generous enough to publish my work: Waldemar Zacharasiewicz, Richard Gray, Nicole Moulinoux, Mario Materassi, Rosella Mamoli Zorzi, Agnieszka Salska, Jadwiga Maszewska, Joseph Blotner, Peter Nicolaisen, Lothar Hönnighausen, Don Kartiganer, François Pitavy, Danièle Pitavy-Souques, and Dawn Trouard. Joseph Blotner, Richard Godden, Joseph Urgo, Tom McHaney, Pearl McHaney, Jim Carothers, Theresa Towner, Jim Watson, Peggy Prenshaw, Susan Donaldson, André Bleikasten, and Anne Goodwyn Jones have all likewise contributed greatly, formally and informally, to my understanding of Faulkner and Welty. The late James B. Meriwether in the best of times gave me a lode that I have mined for years. I'm also grateful to Nancy Jackson, for her hospitality and her computer.

Abbreviations

I quote from the Library of America texts whenever possible. To simplify references, I have adopted the system of abbreviations for Faulkner's texts that *The Faulkner Journal* uses.

FAULKNER:

AA	*Absalom, Absalom!*
AILD	*As I Lay Dying*
F	*A Fable*
FD	*Flags in the Dust*
GDM	*Go Down, Moses*
H	*The Hamlet*
ID	*Intruder in the Dust*
Jer	*If I Forget Thee, Jerusalem*
LA	*Light in August*
M	*The Mansion*
Mos	*Mosquitoes*
P	*Pylon*
R	*The Reivers*
RN	*Requiem for a Nun*
S	*Sanctuary*
SF	*The Sound and the Fury*
SO	*Sanctuary: The Original Text*
SP	*Soldiers' Pay*

T   *The Town*
U   *The Unvanquished*

Welty:
BI   *The Bride of the Innisfallen*
CG   *A Curtain of Green*
GA   *The Golden Apples*
LB   *Losing Battles*
Novels *Complete Novels*
OD   *The Optimist's Daughter*
Stories *Stories, Essays, & Memoir*

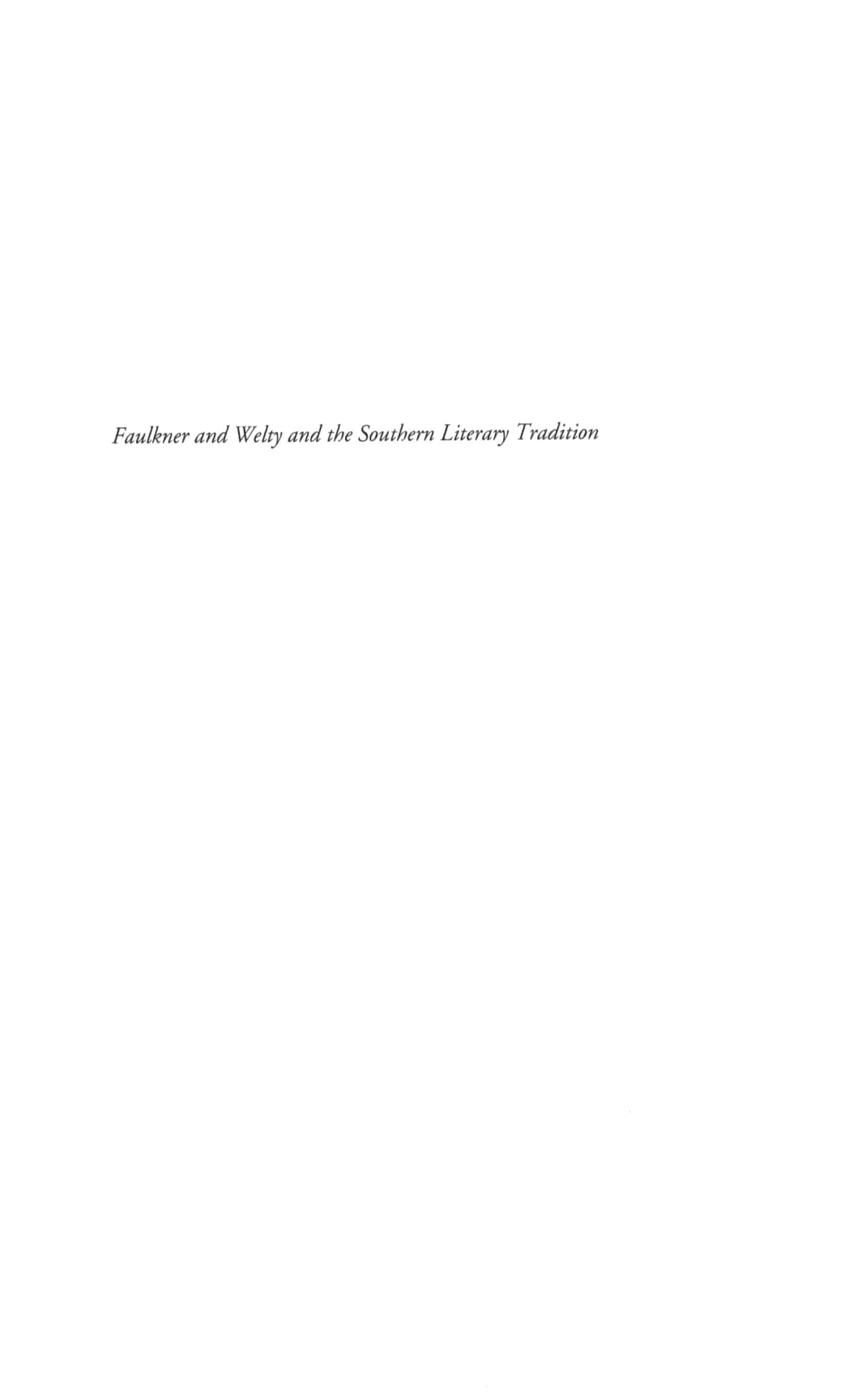

Faulkner and Welty and the Southern Literary Tradition

Faulkner and Welty and the Southern Literary Tradition

W illiam Faulkner's eye is a defining eye. Generations of post-Faulkner southern writers and readers have adopted his vision and so seen "The South" through his eyes rather than through their own or struggled against that vision, experiencing it as a barrier to be gotten around behind above or below in order to keep from seeing only the South that he saw. For so many writers in the South, especially those who want to be southern writers rather than writers, Faulkner's vision seems to have defined what can be seen, so that southern writers following him have indeed been in a double bind. But as large and encompassing as Faulkner's vision is, it is, finally, only a single vision, and he would have been less likely than anyone else to assume that his was the only one. Perhaps the problem is based in geography: writers from other parts of the world tend to speak of Faulkner as an opportunity instead of an obstruction, to speak of the ways in which he expanded the possibilities of fiction rather than of the ways in which he closed them off. But, then, not many writers in Latin America or Europe or Japan have had to worry about getting off the track when the Dixie Limited came roaring down at them.

Discussions of the relationships between William Faulkner and southern writers following him have been largely hamstrung because they are normally driven, willy-nilly, by questions of Faulkner's influence, questions with which interviewers have plagued writers who have had to operate in Faulkner's wake if not always in his shadow. I doubt that very many southern writers since Faulkner have not been compared to him in reviews and in scholarly writing, if only because reviewers have to compare books to something and partly because scholars who write literary history must perforce build on what has preceded: you can't write history in a historical vacuum. But because the questions assume the interviewees' positions as both junior and as inferior, the subsequent generations have spent far too much of their energy escaping and denying—*dealing with*—Faulkner's legacy, even if only in being conscious of reviewers' inevitable for-better-or-worse comparisons of their work with the tradition of "southern" letters that Faulkner so forcefully defined.

Their denials, of course, are the most compelling evidence of how completely inescapable he and his work are. The interviews and the criticism would suggest that as a generation they engage in a collective fretting, wailing, like Quentin Compson at the end of *Absalom, Absalom!*: "I dont hate him! I dont! I dont! I dont hate him!" On the other hand, it may be that what they are really saying is not *I dont hate him* but rather, *I hate that question. I hate it. Why do professors keep asking me that question?* It must be difficult enough for southern writers to grapple honestly with Faulkner's Founding Presence in the tradition, much less to have to respond to presumptive questions about an influence they don't necessarily completely understand or need to process intellectually, having books to write and better things to do.

But I seem already on the verge of defending Eudora Welty against some accusation or other. This defensive posture seems inevitable under any circumstance that forces us to consider *Faulkner and* whoever, just as we Faulknerians somehow always seem to wind up defending him against one charge or another of subordinance that govern discussions of Joyce and Faulkner or Shakespeare and Faulkner—which discussions are also nearly always driven by questions of influence or borrowing. It's as though critics must or anyway do always operate chronologically, following T. S. Eliot's "Tradition and the Individual Talent" and Harold Bloom's *The Anxiety of Influence*, without recognizing that writers don't necessarily operate chronologically and that what they derive from their predecessors may not be anything that they can or need to articulate or that critics can possibly understand. And, since Bloom deals exclusively with male writers and their oedipal struggles with their predecessors, it is certainly worth noting that women writers stand in an entirely different relationship to the "tradition" and that it would be surprising indeed if they dealt with it in the same way male writers do; we have fostered a good deal of misunderstanding of women writers, especially southern women and especially of Eudora Welty, by assuming that they do.

In point of fact, then, probably more critics than writers have been overwhelmed by Faulkner, more critics than even southern writers have felt that Faulkner alone has defined the terms by which we can talk about the South. Thus writers like Walker Percy and Barry Hannah, who deal with a more urban world than Faulkner does, a world more directly a part of their own experiences than Faulkner's, have occasionally had a hard time with many traditional critics who believe that they therefore represent a decline in "southern Literature," whatever that is. As Thomas L. McHaney has suggested, the old guard of southern critics wants to penalize southern writers who have indoor plumbing and give extra credit to them if they write about people who do not. Hannah has addressed the problem more or less puckishly in his fiction, wherein homosexual confederate soldiers and characters with mellifluous names like Roonswent Dover play havoc with traditional representations of southern heritage and lineage; and in such stories as "Bats Out of Hell Division," for my money the greatest story ever about the Civil War, he completely rewrites the way in which our southern Traditions about the Civil War get themselves transmitted—transmogrified and sentimentalized, that is—to all of us Civil War buffs and "posteritites," as his historian/soldier/narrator calls us. It owes more to *The Texas Chain Saw Massacre* and *Night of the Living Dead* than to Faulkner or Shelby Foote or Douglas Southall Freeman. Walker Percy spent more time than he should have wittily denying that he is a southern writer, only to have the venerable and much-loved Cleanth Brooks deny Percy's denial. Richard Ford is not the only southerner to write that all writers, even southerners, should be left alone to create their own categories of expectation.

Eudora Welty, quite simply, has mostly had none of this question: she has not even generally entertained the question of Faulkner's influence on her as worth her time. "It was like living near a mountain," she says, with characteristic and modest acknowledgment of The Presence in North Mississippi. Unspoken in her image, and perhaps even unthought, is the simple fact that what most often lives near a mountain is another mountain.

It is fairly easy to trace the points at which Welty's and Faulkner's lives intersected. It was not very often, even though they lived barely 150 miles apart. Faulkner initiated their acquaintance in a letter from Hollywood in 1943: "Dear Welty," he wrote, "You are doing fine. You are doing all right." He then named *The Robber Bridegroom*, and the "collection called GREEN something," and "The Gilded Six Bits"—a story by Zora Neale Hurston, which he had mistakenly thought was one of her stories, perhaps because Zora and Eudora rhyme. He told her that he thought of Djuna Barnes when he read *The Robber Bridegroom* but expected her to pass that. He asked about her background, then confessed that he hadn't read Green something yet, but "expect nothing from it because I expect from you. You are doing very fine. Is there any way I can help you? How old are you?" (Crane).

According to Welty, they met occasionally at Faulkner's home in Oxford, ate dinner, sang hymns, and went sailing, but never discussed writing or literature. She reviewed *Intruder in the Dust* in 1949 (*Eye* 207–11) and responded to Edmund Wilson's *New Yorker* attack on *Intruder* with a savagely funny indictment of Wilson's condescending presumption that Faulkner's southern material, rather than his intellect or even his hard work, was responsible for the quality of his fiction, and that Faulkner would have been a better writer if he had spent more time in such literary centers as New York talking to such writers as Edmund Wilson about literature ("Department"). Welty's response to this pomposity was, I think, the germ of her thoughts about the relationship between a writer's geographical place and the quality of the writing, thoughts that resulted in her well-known (and much misunderstood and much abused) essay of six years later called "Place in Fiction."

She reviewed Joseph Blotner's edition of Faulkner's letters in 1977 and used examples from his work as illustrations in several essays, among them "Place in Fiction," "Some Notes on Time in Fiction" and *Short*

Stories. Faulkner mentioned Welty only once more, in the late fifties, during his time at the University of Virginia where, when asked about her, he again mentioned *The Robber Bridegroom*. They met a couple of months before his death in New York, at a ceremony during which Welty presented him with the Gold Medal for Fiction of the American Institute of Arts and Letters. She wrote an elegant obituary for the Associated Press upon his death in July 1962.

So far as I can determine, this is the sum total of their public interaction. Privately, of course, we have no way of knowing what, if anything, they meant to each other. There's no evidence that Faulkner borrowed anything from Welty and, for all of her manifest reverence for his work, for all that she claimed to have learned from him, there is no more evidence that she ever borrowed a single line or character or scene from him, ever crossed the state line of his Mississippi save as a grateful reader—except when in *The Golden Apples* she has Virgie Rainey turn her back on a semblance of the Yoknapatawpha County courthouse (of which more shortly). Perhaps she made some conscious effort to honor the claim he had staked and simply avoided his territory. More likely, she saw a different landscape than the one he saw and so had no real need to mine his. But her work does respond to his in significant ways that suggest that her reverence was by no means unaware of his sources in a problematic tradition or uncritical of the implications of his accomplishment for those standing in a different relation to that tradition.

Welty and Faulkner have too often been lumped together by traditionalist critics who have wanted to see them as somehow both empowered and limited by their "place" in Mississippi; who have argued that their literary strengths lie directly in their roots in the South—indeed, in an entirely autochthonous relationship with the southern soil, in a relationship with the earth like that of Antaeus, the giant who lost all his strength and fearsomeness when Hercules lifted him off the earth—as though no southern writer could write wearing shoes or with clean feet. Such critics have found it necessary (or convenient) simply to dismiss the relatively few works that Faulkner and Welty had the temerity to set outside Mississippi, as though they had committed gratuitous acts of literary suicide. Welty, of course, has suffered most in traditionalist readings of her work. Even sympathetic and admiring critics have seen her fiction as a sort of genteel, domestic, non-aggressive, female, version of Faulkner and, to paraphrase her comment about Faulkner, we have generally asked her to stand on a lower step when posing for the group photograph ("Department").

Faulkner's work quite self-consciously addresses itself to epic issues, deals with them on an epic scale in an epic landscape: his language strains at its outermost limits to raise every event, every gesture, to its highest, most intense pitch of significance. The universe is his world; he moves fluidly and freely within it and he strides with the certainty of a colossus to get where he wants to go. His novels deliberately engage the "great" themes of western literature; they are rich in their analyses of culture and of human life in the twentieth century. The problems with this reading of Faulkner (as of other canonical male writers), as we did finally learn from feminist critics, are the operating assumptions behind traditionalist views, which hold as given that Faulkner's historically canonized themes and epic struggles are larger, more cosmic, more significantly responsive to crises in western culture and are therefore more important than the seemingly tamer, less grandiose, more domestic, work of Welty and other women writers.

Driven by these assumptions of what constitutes "great" literature, we have paid the wrong kind of attention to the surface geniality, the face of the familiar, of much of Welty's fiction and have missed how troublingly, how profoundly, she has opened up the atom of the domestic and found there another universe, her own, an infinity of space that affords her an absolutely original engagement with the world and, more particularly, with that western and southern literary tradition that has in fact both defined and delimited her, though hardly in the ways we have assumed (Mark). She slices away at the exteriors of a familiar only incidentally southern and takes us into the hardest to reach nooks and crannies of human life. She dissects our comfortable assumptions about family and community, about ourselves, and in doing so offers a more comprehensive because a more intensely local understanding of those traditionally cosmic concerns than Faulkner does precisely because she demonstrates how these "cosmic" concerns work on us, individually, in the most private, the least epical, but in some ways the most dramatic and most complex because the most intimate places of our lives.

Welty thus offers us alternative visions of our relationship with the cosmos, equally powerful visions that suggest other, equally potent options for understanding and responding to our worlds, options that may threaten us in ways that Faulkner's traditional vision does not. His world is tragic; things fall apart: breathing is a sight-draft dated yesterday: we live, we suffer, we die. But in Faulkner we mostly know who the enemy is, what the stakes are; we know that we must struggle and we know how. In spite of her vision of the universe's wholeness, however, Welty's world is considerably harder to negotiate than Faulkner's precisely because she knows that the enemy is not so easily recognizable: she knows that the real battleground is more nearly the minefield of our own back yards than of the "universe." For her, and for us as her readers, the enemy is terrifyingly close; it resides permanently in and is inextricable from those structures of family and community that traditional readings of southern literature always invoke as the enduring source of value in southern life.

One of Faulkner's most intimate works is the quasi-autobiographical "Mississippi," which he published in 1953 at a time when he was just about to begin an overtly political engagement with his native state, writing letters to editors and essays and giving speeches in which he argued against the racial status quo. "Mississippi" is an eloquent and moving record of his attempts to grapple with the specifically local problems and pressures his native land had caused for him, and of his reconciliation with past and present Mississippi.

The protagonist of "Mississippi" is Faulkner the citizen, not Faulkner the artist. He makes this distinction clear throughout by referring to the citizen in the third person—"he," "the boy," "the young man," "the man," "the middleaged," "the gray-haired"—and by refusing to speak of his career as a writer, although he never takes us very far from that career: "Mississippi"'s narrative moves easily between Faulkner's two Mississippis, as if to demonstrate just how thin the line separating them is.

"Mississippi"'s opening pages outline the state's history from its beginnings in "the alluvial swamps" and follows it through its prehistoric Indian inhabitants, its European settlers, the frontier, the cotton economy, the Civil War, Emancipation, Reconstruction, to the end of

the nineteenth century, when he, "the boy," is born into that powerful flood of specifically southern history. Though he will be a child of
the twentieth century, the forces shaping his life as a Mississippian are
very much those of the nineteenth: the boy hears about the Civil War
even before he hears about Santa Claus, and the first character he speaks
of from his childhood is Mammy Callie, the family nurse, an ex-slave
who refused to leave the Faulkners after Emancipation and who was to
survive into Faulkner's forty-third year, a constant reminder that the
Civil War and Reconstruction in the South are not mere historical circumstances but everpresent, daily realities. She plays a little game with
the family of constantly reminding them that they "owe" her eighty-
nine dollars in back wages, wages—the dollars, at any rate—that have
been offered over and over again and which she has refused to accept
(*ESPL* 16). This "debt" becomes Faulkner's gentle, unforced metaphor
for all that white Mississippi owes to its black citizens, that it will never
repay partly because Mammy Callie—the Negro—does not really want
the debt wiped out and partly because what is owed cannot really be re-
paid. Along with the chief protagonist, Mammy Callie is "Mississippi" 's
most important character. Her life runs through the essay as a moving
counterpoint to the boy's own maturation.

She sees the child into his life; "Mississippi" reaches its elegiac end
as "the middleaging" sees her out of hers, delivering her funeral oration
and "hoping that when his turn came there would be someone in the
world to owe him the sermon which all owed to her who had been, as
he had been from infancy, within the scope and range of that fidelity
and that devotion and that rectitude." Her death is the thematic climax
of "Mississippi," and in her life and death Faulkner encapsulates all that
his citizen protagonist has learned about his native state: how, that is,
one can be so completely a victim—of color, of law, of economics—as
Mammy Callie had been and still find room to love even that which had
victimized her, and how it might be possible for him, the middleaging,
both to hate the people and the system that had victimized Mammy
Callie and to follow her example in being able to find something to love,
even in her oppressors.

"Mississippi" moves to closure as "the man" returns from travel to
find himself "Home again, his native land; he was born of it and his

bones will sleep in it." His first articulation of his reconciliation with Mississippi recognizes that love and hate are not mutually exclusive: "loving it even while hating some of it." He hates the greed, the waste of the lumberman and the land speculators who changed the face of the landscape by cutting down the big trees for timber, moving the Big Woods farther and farther away from the areas he hunted in as a child. "But most of all," he writes,

> he hated the intolerance and injustice: the lynching of Negroes
> not for the crimes they committed but because their skins were
> black. . . . ; the inequality: the poor schools they had then when
> they had any, the hovels they had to live in unless they wanted to
> live outdoors: who could worship the white man's God but not in
> the white man's church; pay taxes in the white man's courthouse but
> couldn't vote in it or for it; working by the white man's clock but
> having to take his pay by the white man's counting . . . ; the bigotry
> which could send to Washington some of the senators and congress-
> men we sent there and which could erect in a town no bigger than
> Jefferson five separate denominations of churches but set aside not
> one square foot of ground where children could play and old people
> could sit and watch them. (37–38)

"Mississippi" concludes with Mammy Callie's death, the gathering of her children, her laying out, and the middleaging's funeral sermon, all of which build to the essay's final paragraph, Faulkner's second, more complex articulation of the relationship between love and hate: "Loving all of it even while he had to hate some of it because he knows now that you dont love because: you love despite; not for the virtues, but despite the faults" (42–43).

Even in this most personal and intimate, most domestic, of his writing, Faulkner's struggle is epic, a heroic confrontation between cosmic forces—love and hate; justice and injustice; life and death—that are eternally antagonistic to each other and to human peace: one lives only under the terms of existential combat. It's an intensely moral struggle, that puts humanity—*man* he would say—in an irresolvable universal conflict whose antagonisms are permanently fixed in the nature of things.

In Faulkner the best we can hope is to turn the tension itself into part of our weaponry, to counter force not with reason but with superior force: you don't love *because*, you love *despite*; you choose what you will struggle for and against and you wrestle to the ground those opposing forces that would have you doubt the meaning or validity of your choices. For Faulkner, then, even love is a matter of will, of main strength, a test of himself against the cosmos.

There is in all this, of course, a tragic heroism, attractive and indeed essential to those of us raised in his tradition. But the pyrrhic irony of Faulkner's victory—our victory, too, when we manage it—is that to assert victory is also to admit defeat: to win he must submit to the ought, the should, the moral imperatives that require him to love despite when he can't find a sufficient because, imperatives that derive from the value systems of the cultural tradition of which he is so vital a part. The victory thus requires him to suppress his own powerful emotions of despair and frustration in favor of the communal mandate that love is better than hate, reconciliation better than alienation. Put so baldly, of course, these sentiments are hard to argue with. Who wouldn't prefer the comforts of love and community to wandering alone in the existential waste land of the twentieth century? At the same time, their baldness permits us to see them also as platitudes which like all platitudes operate in the service of a cultural status quo, offering themselves up as Truths of the sort that reify and ensure a community's cohesion and stability. But such platitudes, uncritically enforced, take communities one step beyond stability into rigidity.

Faulkner's powerful conclusions in "Mississippi" also beg numerous questions that his fiction does not; indeed, most of his fiction offers very precise analyses of the dangers of cultural stasis. But even the fiction, finally, in its assumptions or perhaps assertions of its own universality, also begs many of the same questions about the hierarchical structures of community and about the profoundly different effects these structures have on men and women. In "Mississippi" and elsewhere, Faulkner takes for granted his own capacity—indeed his need, often articulated as an artistic credo: life is motion, stasis is death—always to keep in motion, to avoid the rigidity that platitudes can lead to. As a male, Faulkner bears a relationship different from women's to the tradition that valorizes "love" and "reconciliation," that prefers its own definitions of "justice" and "injustice," "family," and "community." As a man, like Welty's King MacLain, Faulkner can choose what he wants to love and be reconciled with. Women traditionally don't have that freedom: to them falls the dailiness of love and reconciliation, of cohesion, their practice rather than their rhetorizing; they perforce deal with those junctures where tradition and practice unravel, de-reify themselves in a scattering jumble of particles which the ordering tradition works, somehow, to hold together, with the glue of rhetoric that always leaves cracks. In "Mississippi," Faulkner takes no account of Mammy Callie's position in his reconciliation with Mississippi; to the extent that he does not he patronizes her in ways that he doesn't patronize the black characters in his fiction, especially Mollie Beauchamp and Dilsey Gibson, whom we have taken to be modeled on her. To be sure, Faulkner uses Mammy Callie here in the service of what he would doubtless call his larger purposes. Even so, even granting his absolute sincerity of intention, he does not, in "Mississippi," seem to understand the extent to which he imposes on her attitudes that she either might not hold or, and with despair one says it, might not have any choice but to hold; indeed, what were her options? Her love despite is of course better for Faulkner, but how is it better for her? What does she get out of it except the opportunity to love her oppressors? In which case love is, indeed, its own reward.

Thus it seems not only fair but necessary to ask just how and why love is better than hate, reconciliation better than alienation: for whom are they better, and at what cost are they bought? These are important questions in Welty generally, specifically in *The Golden Apples*, and central to that collection's magnificent final story, "The Wanderers" which, like "Mississippi," involves a homecoming and a funeral that forces a confrontation with the same loves and hates, the same challenges of reconciliation. Welty's responses to them, however, are quite different from Faulkner's. Virgie Rainey is "over 40" years old when she returns home. Like King MacLain, the heroic and fascinating wanderer of the town's romanticizing imagination, she too has been away from Morgana, for her own reasons and we do not know where or what she has been doing, and has some time before the story begins returned home. She is a subdued version of her "June Recital" self, the wild and free spirit who as an adolescent rejected the tyranny of Miss Eckhart's metronome; she is obliged now in her middleage to care for a senile and problematic mother, who forces her to submit to the deadening metronomic regularity of domestic life in Morgana, of which Miss Eckhart's hated metronome is the collection's metaphor. Her mother's first words to her when she walks through the door, after her long absence, are "You're back at the right time to milk for me" (545).

Welty's staging of the ritualized activities of Virgie's mother's funeral—the coming and going, the visits, the laying out of the body, the gestures of sympathy, Virgie's necessary (and unwelcome) commingling with all these figures from her life (none of whom, she notes, except Snowdie MacLain, has ever been to visit her or her mother)—is Welty's unrelentingly unsentimental and often savagely funny analysis of such communal rituals. The story's spine is Virgie's growing capacity to admit to herself just how and why she is different from, and also just how little she cares for or needs any of these folks, this "community," nominally and traditionally the center of value in southern life, including her own mother, all of whom Faulkner's tradition would demand her to love despite. In fact, in her mother's death Virgie discovers a wonderfully liberating and purifying capacity to hate, to be angry, which becomes her salvation precisely because it frees her from the need to love or even tolerate any of them, her own mother included, much less to continue to live among them.

Several times throughout the day of the funeral she deliberately shuns all contact: "Don't touch me" (524), she uselessly repeats to Cassie and others, who touch her anyway, in embrace or to pull her in one direction or another and ignore her demands to be left alone. Virgie's efforts to be physically separate from them reaches a moment of high comedy in one of the closing scenes in which Cassie—who wants desperately to force Virgie to feel about her mother as she, Cassie, feels about her own mother, a suicide—chases Virgie in her car, pulls up beside her and drives side by side out of town with her, shouting at her through the open windows to force a conversation that Virgie clearly doesn't want to have. Cassie insists that Virgie drive by her yard to see how she has spelled out her own mother's name in 232 Narcissus bulbs, to insure her return every spring (551).

Most of all Virgie wants to be free of her mother—an outrageous thing, by all communal standards. When Katie dies, Virgie notes that "The clock jangled faintly as cymbals struck under water, but did not strike; it couldn't." Here is no Faulknerian ding dong of Time and Doom, but rather a liberating pulse of time now become accommodating and friendly, fluid and non-metronomic: unclocklike, unTimelike. The clock jangles "faintly" not in alarm, but as a sign of some impending revelation, something just about to be understood; the "cymbals struck under water" (520) likewise suggest some stirring impulse of fanfare, of celebration, of simple unadmittable delight in her freedom that she is not, at this moment, prepared to let become conscious, but which will provide the specific energy for her reactions through the rest of the story. She realizes, at the moment of her mother's death, that she herself is "not much afraid of death, either of its delay or its surprise" (520), and she feels "a torrent of riches . . . flow over the room, submerging it, loading it with what was over-sweet" (520). Not her years of self-sacrifice but her mother's long overdue death releases her from the prison of home and family and community that her self-sacrifice has placed her in.

She endures the opening skirmishes with the visitors who come when they hear that Katie is dead. When in the evening they leave, they seem in their parting "to drag some mythical gates and barriers away from her view," making it possible for her to see what she has never been able to see: when she sees the "little last crescent of hills before the country of the river, and the fields" the world "shimmers" in the "lighted distance." The cotton fields still "look busy on Sunday; even while they are not being picked they push out their bloom the same." She sees, for the first time, a landscape artificially divided into families and property and seasons and even meteorological conditions: "the frail screens of standing trees still measured, broke, divided—Stark from Loomis from Spights from Holifield, and the summer from the rain (529)." Welty interrupts these meditations on these divisions with the appearance of Old Plez's ancient automobile, which appears to Virgie "cracked like some put-together puzzle of the globe of the world. Its cracks didn't meet from one side across to the other, and it was all held together with straightened-out baling wire, for today" (530). Like Plez's car, Morgana is a ramshackle vehicle, held together by no more of a force, no more of a reality, than the used baling wire of tradition.

Her mother having gone to the underworld, this Virgie/Virgo/ Persephone releases herself to the upper world, not in the spring for the plowing and the harvest, but in the fall—September, the month of Virgo—the time of harvest. She has reached her own fullness: at more than forty Virgie is at least pre-menopausal and so free, or nearly, not just of her own history (now that her mother is dead) but also of the metronomic cycles of her body that have bound her to time, to the rhythms of the earth, even to the natural rhythms of life and death. In an extraordinary passage, she goes down to the river for a swim:

> It was bright as mid-afternoon in the openness of the water, quiet and peaceful. She took off her clothes and let herself into the river.
>
> She saw her waist disappear into reflectionless water; it was like walking into sky, some impurity of skies. All was one warmth, air, water, and her own body. All seemed one weight, one matter—until as she put down her head and closed her eyes and the light slipped under her lids, she felt this matter a translucent one, the river, herself, the sky all vessels which the sun filled. She began to swim in the river, forcing it gently, as she would wish for gentleness to her body. Her breasts around which she felt the water curving were as sensitive at that moment as the tips of wings must feel to birds, or antennae to insects. She felt the sand, grains intricate as little cogged wheels, minute shells of old seas, and the many dark ribbons of grass and mud touch her and leave her, like suggestions and withdrawals of some bondage that might have been dear, now dismembering and losing itself. She moved but like a cloud in skies, aware but only of the nebulous edges of her feeling and the vanishing opacity of her will, the carelessness for the water of the river through which her body had already passed as well as for what was ahead. The bank was all one, where out of the faded September world the little ripening plums started. Memory dappled her like no more than a paler light, which in slight agitations came through leaves, not darkening her for more than an instant. The iron taste of the old river was sweet to her, though. If she opened her eyes she looked at blue-bottles, the

skating waterbugs. If she trembled it was at the smoothness of a fish or snake that crossed her knees.

In the middle of the river, whose downstream or upstream could not be told by a current, she lay on her stretched arm, not breathing, floating. Virgie had reached the point where in the next moment she might turn into something without feeling it shock her. She hung suspended in the Big Black River as she would know to hang suspended in felicity. Far to the west, a cloud running fingerlike over the sun made her splash the water. She stood, walked along the soft mud of the bottom and pulled herself out of the water by a willow branch, which like warm rain brushed her back with its leaves.

At a distance, two little boys lying naked in the red light on the sandbar looked at her as she disappeared into the leaves. (530–31)

This remarkably Emersonian passage's resonances with Faulkner's "The Bear" seem unmistakable. But Virgie is no transparent eyeball or Isaac McCaslin bemoaning the loss of the Big Woods. Far from contending with it or from seeing herself as in any way separate from it or even transparent in it, Virgie becomes the universe, the constellation Virgo; she melds with it, absorbs it, assumes her position in the larger, the truly "universal," scheme of things as unselfconsciously and magisterially as Botticelli's Venus.

This scene occurs early, hard on the heels of her mother's death. From which point Virgie gradually divests herself of all the impedimenta of her containment in Morgana—her childhood friends, the remnants of her father's family, who come only to funerals; her parents' generation, who've gossiped her into running away; the men she's worked for, slept with, including her sailor lover Kewpie Moffatt (whom she misremembers, with a puckish smile, as Bucky); Miss Eckhart and a countrywoman's dead baby, both of whom she remembers as she walks through the cemetery: and both of whom, she realizes and admits, she hates.

But free now to hate, she discovers that in fact she doesn't hate Miss Eckhart, and she understands that she has "never doubted that all the opposites on earth were close together, love close to hate, living to dying; but of them all, hope and despair were the closest blood—unrecognizable one from the other sometimes, making moments double upon themselves, and in the doubling double again, amending but never taking back" (546). Almost simultaneously with this revelation, near the end of the story, Virgie sits majestically alone, contemplating all her possibilities. The earth and sky gather around her, stopping their motion, in salute and approbation:

> it was ripe afternoon, and all about her was that light in which the earth seems to come into its own, as if there would be no more days, only this day—when fields glow like deep pools and the expanding trees at their edges seem almost to open, like lilies, golden or dark. She had always loved that time of day, but now, alone, untouched now, she felt like dancing; knowing herself not really, in her essence, yet hurt; and thus happy. The chorus of crickets was as unprogressing and out of time as the twinkling of a star. (546)

This is a paradigmatic moment in Welty, one which she will repeat, with variations, in the stories of her next collection, *The Bride of the Innisfallen*: a moment in which a lone woman comes to herself in a dark wood and responds not as to a moment of fear and perplexity but savoring it as an epiphany in which she discovers that she can be happy alone, she stops to luxuriate in her freedom.

In "Mississippi" Faulkner resolves his conflicts with his home, his place, by overcoming his hatred not with love so much as with the will to love, so that the exercise of love is an act of main strength that must subdue hate, suppress it as something inimical to love. Virgie overcomes the cultural mandate to love her family and friends by giving herself permission to hate them. She discovers that hatred purges and liberates in ways that love never can: hate does not require the suppression of what we love but love often tyrannically demands the suppression of the things we hate. The freedom to hate can thus bring us closer to the things we love because in the free exercise of both emotions we can come closer to our own true terribly complex selves: as Virgie comes to understand, hate and love, hope and despair, are not antagonists at all, as in Faulkner's vision, but closely connected, intimate, and essential to our human wholeness.

This is not a Eudora Welty that we are accustomed to or prepared to accept. We have preferred to think of her as a gentle purveyor of the domestic, the odd, the grotesque. We have been comfortable reading her through the critical language of southern literary studies that developed at about the time she began publishing. That language has never been large enough to contain either Faulkner or Welty but it has worked most perniciously to keep us from understanding Welty. By reading her through such so-called "southern" filters as place, humor, race, history, and the grotesque, our critical vocabulary, our cultural assumptions, have protected us from the parts of Welty's work that might unsettle and threaten us since they are actually subversive of those so-called "values" of family and community—"place"—that are so much a part of what we have been taught to think of as central to "southern" literature.

But we can no longer ignore what is so manifestly there in Welty's work. In *The Golden Apples* she re-writes southern literature, or at least provides us an opportunity to erase it and start over. The "community" of Morgana is a community only in the sense that a group of people live more or less together geographically. Mrs. Stark knows that one old woman owes another old woman a decent and respectable funeral (515) but nothing in the book suggests that anybody in this "community" feels any obligation to the living, to themselves or any other. Morgana, like the southern communities of our agrarian traditions, worships the metronomic rhythms of night and day, of lunar and menstrual and seasonal cycles. Instead of offering change and renewal, however, the rhythms of nature in *The Golden Apples* reify into forms of communal limitation, which Virgie and King MacLain have resisted but to which the community has prostrated itself because it cannot see beyond the next tick of the clock, the next five p.m. when the cows need calling and milking, the next spring when we must plant. As a "community," then, Morgana constantly turns inward, using its rituals of life, death, and June recitals not to regenerate but to replicate itself. Morgana is thus trapped in the deadening circularity of cycles: it worships its seasons, its rituals, its monuments, its cemeteries: finally, it worships death. Perhaps death is the only way out of the cycle: suicide is not unknown in Morgana.

Through no particular act of her own, Virgie no longer has to submit to these rhythms. Free of her past, she no longer has to replicate her life from one day to the next; she can now regenerate a free and independent self, one yet to be discovered or perhaps one that can be recovered from her "June Recital" adolescence. Looking outward, she exfoliates, enlarges and becomes the universe with which Faulkner so constantly and epically contends and to which the people of Morgana have long since surrendered. At the story's close, true to her last name, Virgie has brought rain to the waste land and she sits under a tree. The French origins of her name suggest that she has become Virgie *reine*, Virgie the Queen, the Virgin Queen, Aphrodite and Virgo on a stile throne, her back to the MacLain County courthouse—the house of the court, the royal palace of the King. As Danièle Pitavy-Souques has suggested, it could specifically be the Yoknapatawpha County courthouse to which Virgie and Welty have turned their backs (*La Mort* 47). It is certainly the symbolic counting-house of the political landscape of the southern literary tradition that Faulkner's courthouse so powerfully symbolizes. Her back squarely turned to that courthouse and that tradition, Virgie looks not inward but outward, facing the richly lubricious and delicious landscape of her own future: the landscape of possibility, not a landscape closed off and limited by history and economic realities. Indeed, when Virgie returns to Morgana she takes a job with a logging company, de-mystifying by destroying Faulkner's Big Woods, in effect saying to Isaac McCaslin, Come on, Big Boy, let's rid ourselves of these damned trees so we can see where we are, where we can go, and how we can best get there.

Virgie, her back to the courthouse, provides another paradigmatic moment in Welty, a repetition of the earlier one when the universe, time, stopped to acknowledge her freedom. It is a striking moment, difficult to understand because we are not accustomed to seeing women happy and alone, happy because alone. Likewise, and perhaps even more importantly, traditional readings of "southern" literature teach us to believe that change is loss and that what we lose is always more valuable than what we gain: all this because change always involves a direct assault on the "old verities"—the old verities, very because old, and always inextricable from our communal memories of a past that was somehow better than the present. We have thus too easily accepted a "sense of place" as a mantra of southern literary study, and have been reluctant to understand how often history, our sense of the past, of place, keeps the present in a deadening chokehold. I hasten to point out that though many of Faulkner's characters and critics make the mistake of idealizing the past so strongly as to resist change, Faulkner himself never does. He constantly argues that the capacity to cope with change is the test of maturity in an individual; but even these terms—cope and test—point to the intensity of the moral struggle that change entails for a people who invest their individual and communal lives, their places in time and space, in the values of the past, those "old" verities.

In this struggle, Morgana is undoubtedly a Faulknerian, a southern, community, precisely the community that Virgie, at the end of "The Wanderers," is poised to reject. She sees change not as loss but as opportunity: if she chooses, she can now step aside from history, as so many of Faulkner's characters want desperately to do but cannot. Virgie, refusing to be imprisoned in the past, faces a future limited only by the choices she can now make. She is willing to discover new verities, new configurations of social organization, that could give new and vital meaning to her life.

We are prepared to be thrilled and moved by the traditional visions of the William Faulkners. We respond to his colossus-strides across our universal skies because, as Roland Barthes said of wrestling, we want our heroes' sufferings to be writ large; we want our private agons to be reflected by and absorbed in those "universal" ones so that we can attach meaning to our own lives by virtue of that Cosmic Suffering in which we participate, as spectators, dramatically and empathetically. We are not so prepared to be discomfited and challenged by the quotidian world of Welty's fiction, wherein we are more likely to be participants than spectators. Her view fixes us at top dead center of the most intimate and complex parts of our daily lives—in a place that Faulkner, with all the clashing and clanging of his self-conscious commitment to Cosmic Significance, never puts us. Faulkner of course saw what he saw, as Shakespeare did, and we are immeasurably the richer for it. But he didn't see it all, nobody can, and like Shakespeare he saw what his tradition allowed him to see.

Eudora Welty's eye, too, is a defining eye, but it is also a subversive eye that looks at things other eyes don't know to look at or, worse, avoid. But hers too can be an enlarging and enriching vision, if we have the courage to see what she is showing us instead of what we want to see.

How Shreve Gets in to
Quentin's Pants

The occasion for my title occurs in *The Sound and the Fury* just after Gerald Bland, his mother, Spoade, Shreve, and two veiled young ladies encounter Quentin Compson in the clutches of the law and of an angry brother who wants Quentin pilloried for molesting his sister, whom Quentin has ostensibly been helping to find her way home. Julio, the brother, is as certain of Quentin's intentions toward his sister as Quentin is certain of Dalton Ames's intentions toward his own sister Caddy. It's part of an extended tumultuous episode of two or three pages of which we haven't yet taken the full measure.

When Shreve hears that Quentin is under arrest, he starts climbing out of Mrs. Bland's automobile, and Quentin notices that he is wearing "a pair of my flannel trousers, like a glove" (985). The final detail, the glove, argues pretty certainly how Quentin's tight flannels mould and magnify Shreve's genitals and how conscious Quentin is of them. Quentin claims that he doesn't "remember forgetting the pants" when he packed his clothes earlier in the day for shipment home—"I didn't remember forgetting them" is an extremely curious, even paradoxical, way of describing his packing: it's almost a double negative which, like double negatives, always mean grammatically the opposite of what a user is trying to say. Quentin may thus mean that he remembers very well that Shreve has his pants, and in any case the phrasing seems to be a rhetorical ploy by means of which he can distance himself from the trousers and what they now contain and from the question why they are on Shreve and not on their way to Jefferson. We can also tell something of the pants' impact on Quentin at this moment by his almost instantaneous deflection to Mrs. Bland's double chins, which he also claims to have forgotten, and, more importantly, to the two pretty girls also in the car who, though they are veiled, he believes regard him "with a kind of delicate horror" (985). Quentin forces his attention from exposed male sexuality to the double chins of a voyeuristic and pandering mother and then, finally, to the veiled heterosexual threat that the two girls represent. He may, of course, feel that they look on him with horror simply because they know that he's under arrest, but the impact on him, at this moment, of Shreve in his pants allows us to speculate that their horror, delicate or not, is grounded in his fear that they somehow intuitively know he is queer—maybe they have caught him looking at Shreve's genitals—and that their "delicate horror" is more nearly disgust. The girls' names—Miss Holmes and Miss Daingerfield—resonate thematically, indicting Quentin's own home and, by implication, heterosexual union: home, as Quentin has reason to know, is a dangerous place.

From a view outside his head, the ensuing scene is a broadly comic one, a kind of antic slapstick, a parade worthy of The Keystone Cops or Fellini. Looked at through Quentin's eyes, however, the scene is a dark tableau of all the sexual baggage he has brought to Cambridge from Mississippi. Quentin drags with him to the Squire who is to decide his case a network of characters who represent the array of his pathologies: Gerald and his mother, an oedipal couple that grotesquely parodies the murky oedipal issues in his own family; Miss Holmes and Miss Daingerfield; Shreve, whom Spoade calls his "husband"; an astonishing group of naked and half-naked boys who emerge from the surrounding shrubbery and woods almost like an hallucination; an angry brother who also wants to defend and control his sister's virginity; and, finally, the little girl herself, whom Quentin calls "little Sister," and who may be, in some way, Caddy's own young unsexual, pre-sexual, self, the Caddy that Quentin claims to want to preserve. Quentin drags all of these horrors to the judgment seat with him—a temporal judgment seat that foreshadows that ultimate Judgment Seat, which he plans to see before the day is out.

This portion of the scene follows a complex narrative orchestration of Quentin's past and present which braids together three different plots: the one involving Quentin and the little Italian girl; the one in which Quentin at first alone and then with the lost girl in tow encounters the boys first when they are fishing and then at the mill where they are skinny-dipping. Woven throughout the scene is Quentin's simultaneous memory of his sexual play as a child with Natalie in the barn in the rain, which Caddy interrupts: Quentin and Natalie are playing something like doctor in the barn, touching each other. Caddy's intervention turns the scene into a tempest of guilt and shame and retribution that ends when Quentin throws himself into the pig's wallow and then smears it all over Caddy. Fuguing in and out of that powerful memory of childhood innocence turned corrupt are Quentin's two encounters with the boys. Does the intertwining of the memory of Natalie with his attempts to help the little Italian girl find her way home allow us to wonder how pure Quentin's motives are—one aborted, perhaps abortive, youthful heterosexual encounter to be replaced by another with perhaps different results by which Quentin could establish his heterosexuality? Does he want to play doctor with his present little sister? Perhaps. He is interrupted this time too—not by Caddy but by the girl's brother, who stops him from what Spoade later jokingly calls Quentin's "nefarious work" (989).

At the first encounter, Quentin and the fishing boys banter pleasantly enough. They aren't catching anything, though, and Quentin overhears one propose that they go to the mill to go swimming (970). It's no accident of Quentin's peregrinations that he heads directly for the pond at the mill, in tow the little girl whose sudden appearance there spoils the boys' homosocial eden, though Quentin tries to assure them that "she's just a girl. She can't hurt you." Perhaps Quentin drags her there to veil his truly nefarious purposes, to get a look at the naked bodies of these boys; he is, after all, hyper-conscious of male bodies throughout. Perhaps, too, he drags her there precisely to grant himself the interruptus that Caddy had provided in the earlier scene.

If Quentin follows the boys to the pond to see them naked, he sees more than he bargains for. As the scene nears its climax, he suddenly sees "*him* coming up the path running" (983, my emphasis) but does not identify the "him." Then he sees "*another* man, an oldish man running heavily, clutching a stick, and a boy naked from the waist up, clutching his pants as he ran." "There's Julio," says the little girl, but we dont know which male she is referring to. The initial "him" that Quentin sees might of course be Julio, but we would expect Julio to be with the sheriff, who is clearly the other man. The other "boy, naked from the waist up and clutching his pants" as he runs, is clearly not Julio, since when Julio jumps on Quentin, the "half naked boy" begins "darting and jumping up and down . . . clutching his trousers." Further, the abrupt appearance of the sheriff and the "boy" in the same sentence may suggest that they have been together while the boy was naked. In the same sentence Quentin also notes and juxtaposes with the boy and the sheriff another astonishing figure, "another stark naked figure com[ing] around the tranquil bend in the path running and change direction in midstride and leap into the woods, a couple of garments rigid as boards behind it" (983). Apparently the half-naked boys are the fishing, skinny-dipping boys just out of the mill pond: Julio has queried them about his sister, been told which direction she and Quentin went, and taken off with Anse in pursuit. The boys get out, grab their clothes and try to dress while running so as not to miss anything; some don't quite get fully dressed. These boys, then, are avenging homoerotic furies who interrupt Quentin's heterosexual idyll with the Italian girl as Caddy had interrupted his play with Natalie. Both Caddy and the boys and Julio and the sheriff may drastically overestimate what Quentin's nefarious purposes are: but they may not. What's important, it seems to me, is what registers most potently on Quentin as this astonishing series of events takes place, including Anse's twice-noted phallic "stick" and the phallic "garments rigid as boards" which follow the latest naked boy into the woods. At the very least, if Quentin goes to the mill to see the boys skinny-dipping, he gets what he wants, in spades. These boys represent Quentin's suppressed homoerotic desires chasing him relentlessly and even bringing with them, as if to remind him how dangerous they are, the sheriff—the superego, the simultaneous agent of repression of that forbidden desire. The scene is a maelstrom of the homoerotic and of its possible consequences: Miss Holmes and Miss Daingerfield, veiled, look on him with a kind of "delicate horror," but that's certainly a mild response compared to the horror and loathing with which he certainly regards himself in such moments when the homoerotic descends upon him so publicly and so menacingly—and, given the police and the judge, so judgmentally.

During the scene that leads to Quentin's pathetic fight with Gerald Bland Quentin twice turns, shifts so as to repudiate Shreve's hand so publicly upon his knee. Moments like these provide us with a slightly different context against which to view two or three other passages in Quentin's section. The first occurs in the section's earliest pages. Looking out the window of his Harvard dormitory room, Quentin watches the helter-skelter rushing of students on their way to class. Spoade emerges from the crowd and disrupts Quentin's meditations, throws his poetic description of the scene, his elegant parallel structures and his compound and complex sentences, into a syntactical and sexual chaos: "and Spoade. Calling Shreve my husband. Ah let him alone, Shreve said, if he's got better sense than to chase after the little dirty sluts, whose business?" Quentin immediately deflects his thoughts toward the problem of his virginity as a heterosexual, about which he agonizes much throughout the day. At the end of the paragraph, however, he reverts to the homoerotic, repeating again Shreve's suggestion that homosexuality is better than "chas[ing] after the little dirty sluts," before remembering his response: "Did you ever have a sister? Did you? Did you?" (936–37). Since these words later precede Quentin's attack on Gerald Bland, we may suppose that Quentin's defense of Caddy's maidenhead is at least in part a denial of the homosexual: he is angry because Gerald can get laid in the right and proper normal way and he, Quentin, cannot.

Several things interest us here. First is the absolute crumbling of Quentin's syntax here and elsewhere, especially when the twin stalkers of the homoerotic and the heteroerotic collide and unmoor him from the grammar by which he maintains control over his disintegrating psyche. When he is most in control, his syntax is elegant, complex, beautiful; when he loses control of his thoughts, syntax more or less goes out the window and his thoughts turn to chaos. Toward the end of his section he loses complete control even of capitalization and punctuation and in its penultimate paragraph, Quentin's final conversation with his father, he loses even the capitalized "I", which has been a kind of totem ego for him. The syntactical breakdown when Spoade emerges into his vision suggests that Spoade really emerges from some undeniable claim on his deepest desires. Quentin immediately connects Spoade with what is so obviously a problematic relationship with Shreve. The recalled scene, especially Spoade's banter about the dirty little sluts, might argue that there is something relatively open among them about the homoerotic (perhaps they even live in a sort of homosexual community), but we can't tell how much of a wife Quentin is to Shreve, and of course Shreve and Spoade may be merely teasing Quentin about his inability to lose his virginity, which a real man would have lost long before reaching Quentin's age—or he would at least lie about it. Quentin seems to have been unable either to lose it or to lie.

Other scenes, briefly: watching Gerald Bland row the skull, Quentin meditates on Gerald's mother's braggadocio about Gerald's success with women. Mrs. Bland likes him, Quentin, he thinks, because he is at least a Southerner, but she doesn't like Spoade, "since she met [him] coming out of chapel one He said she couldn't be a lady no lady would be out at that hour" (947). Again Quentin's syntax breaks down. Most authors would have put a dash between "one" and "He" to indicate an interrupted thought, but Faulkner does not; the lack of such punctuation indicates how smoothly Quentin corrects his thoughts as they head in a forbidden direction before they reveal why Spoade was in the chapel at such a late hour and perhaps why Mrs. Bland is out so late. We may be certain that neither was there to worship. University chapels have always been notorious as homosexual gathering places, and that is what Quentin refuses to acknowledge; if Spoade has been there for a homosexual tryst, we may easily imagine a ménage-a-trois of Spoade, Shreve, and Quentin. Why Mrs. Bland is out that late at night is not clear either, but it's easy to speculate that she is checking up on the boys that Gerald hangs out with; perhaps she's suspicious of Gerald's sexual preferences and that is why she all but pimps for him with girls. What Quentin suppresses here may also help explain why Mrs. Bland goes to the proctor to have Quentin moved out of Shreve's quarters (958): she wants to protect Quentin—and Gerald—from that homosexual element.

One final passage is worth a word or two, Quentin's remembered discussion with his father about women, which occurs just after he and the little Italian girl leave the bread shop, and a garbled memory of his discussion with Caddy about her pregnancy, her "sickness": "Because women so delicate so mysterious Father said. Delicate equilibrium of periodical filth between two moons balanced. Moons he said full and yellow as harvest moons her hips thighs. Outside outside of them always but. Yellow. Feet soles with walking like. Then know that some man that all those mysterious and imperious concealed. With all that inside of them shapes an outward suavity waiting for a touch to. Liquid putrefaction like drowned things floating like pale rubber flabbily filled getting the odor of honeysuckles all mixed up" (975). This passage, one of the several most oftquoted and uneasily commented upon in all of Faulkner, may lie at the root of all Quentin's problems. In earlier passages he reports arguments during which his father accuses his mother of setting Jason to spy on Caddy and Dalton Ames. Quentin gets accused of spying too, but denies it vehemently; this passage gives us reason to doubt those denials. I propose that here Quentin remembers seeing Caddy and Dalton Ames having sex. Again syntax fails him: but we may make some sense of the passage. His memory of "feet soles with walking like" may suggest that he watched from a position where he could see their feet, Caddy's pointing upward, Dalton's between them pointing downward, all four sort of walking and moving "like"—Quentin begins a simile, but words, comparisons, simply fail him. Father has filled him with disgust for sex, women, the monthly cycle of "periodical filth." Female genitals shaped "suavely" need only a touch to turn them to putrefied liquid; men are always "outside outside" but always want to get inside inside. His final vision combines a semen-filled condom—"drowned things floating like pale rubber flabbily filled"—and the honeysuckle, a combination that forever weds honeysuckle with Caddy's sexuality, forever suffocates and overwhelms him. But he's watching Dalton too.

This is a Freudian primal scene, a child's first vision of parental intercourse, the beginning of Oedipal dynamics in a child's develop-

ment, presented here with substitutions as such scenes nearly always are
in Faulkner. In Freud, the Oedipus complex always involves an element
of the homoerotic—the viewing child wants to replace both parents in
coitus but may associate the act with violence and, if discovered watching, with increased shame and guilt that demand expiation. Dalton, not
Caddy, dominates Quentin's voyeuristic memory of them together. In
his quieter, more intimate moments, he allows himself to fondle Dalton's name, repeating it several times in triads almost like a chant, a love
song, caressing his face as much as words can: "Dalton Ames. Dalton
Ames. Dalton Shirts. I thought all the time they were khaki, army issue khaki, until I saw they were of heavy Chinese silk or finest flannel
because they made his face so brown his eyes so blue. Dalton Ames"
(947). He's got a crush on Dalton Ames that he cannot claim: and incest, horrible as it is, is more acceptable than homosexuality. Quentin's
pathologies in his family are clear: his father's lugubrious, viscous attitudes toward women; his constant whining about his weak position
in his family vis-à-vis his brother-in-law; Quentin's mother's whining
about everything, while appearing always so seductively in or ready for
bed. Nothing in Quentin's home can have given him a very healthy
model for marriage or heterosexual union; the only models are indeed
quite terrifying ones. But neither has anything given him permission to
pursue the homosexual. He is a man without a sexual option to give him
the identity that he so clearly craves.

I hasten to add, in closing, that I am not arguing that Quentin is a
practicing homosexual, though of course he might be; there is no such
evidence, but only this galaxy of troubling evidence that at very least
suggests how deeply the homoerotic urge and the fear of homosexuality
have attached themselves to his sensibilities and sensitivities and how
awful it is to feel pulled in that direction when his culture and his family assumes heterosexuality, problematic though it be, as the right and
proper end of a man. I'd suggest too an ontological dimension to Quentin's dilemma: the possibility that he is homosexual, his fear that he is,
works toward his decision to commit suicide much more profoundly
than anything else that has been suggested. He wants desperately to *not*
be a heterosexual virgin, but simply can't get there, as he puts it in this
anguished passage: "and I thought about how I'd thought about I could

not be a virgin, with so many of them walking along in the shadows and whispering with their soft girlvoices lingering in the shadowy places and the words coming out and perfume and eyes you could feel not see, but if it was that simple to do it wouldn't be anything and if it wasn't anything what was I . . ." (990). In his mind, in his culture, a boy who can't get properly laid with so many available girls around, is just plain queer: and he cannot be that—or, as it turns out, anything else.

To a certain extent, of course, Shreve's literally wearing Quentin's pants is a Faulknerian joke, of a piece with the one that drives the present-day narrative of the Benjy section: Luster's dogged determination to find a golf ball that he can sell to a golfer for a quarter and go to the show. Tom McHaney suggested, in conversation, long ago that not just Luster but all males in *The Sound and the Fury* are searching for lost balls. But neither joke is really as funny as it seems. Shreve might not be in Quentin's pants, but he's surely in his head, a far more terrifying place for him to be.

Faulkner in the
Luxembourg Gardens

O ne of the strangest twists in *Sanctuary* is its final scene, for which Faulkner quite unexpectedly drags us to Paris's fabled Luxembourg Gardens. It is a profoundly *rendered* scene, almost a *nature morte*, a poem profoundly *imagiste* whose unnarrated elegance gives it the same visual hold upon our imaginations as Ezra Pound's "In a Station of the Metro" and partakes of some of that poem's qualities of mood and scene. Perhaps most curious of all is that though it seems to dissolve before our very eyes, it is at the same time visually realistic and detailed, so finely chiseled as to be almost an object, a statue that both insists that we see it from all sides at once and refuses to let us see it whole.

Further, the scene is deliberately staged in this setting; we are not just in a garden, but in Paris, in the Luxembourg Gardens, for a final opportunity to gaze and wonder at the novel's oft-looked-at heroine, who sits by her immobile father, posing indifferently—or posturing—into her miniature makeup mirror, while at the same time back in the American South Popeye, her impotent ravisher, spends his last words on earth asking his hangman to fix his hair before he dies. In what we now call the "Original Text" of this novel, Popeye's execution frames the mordantly elegant paragraphs about Temple and her father. The scene is thus precisely the "dying fall" Michel Gresset has called it, and the Original Text ends literally with Popeye's "dying fall" through the hangman's trap door, hair straight: if he'd had a compact mirror, as Temple does, he'd have used it himself, but he has to rely on the hangman's eye. For Temple and for us the ending is a fading to a diffusion, a diminution to a silence that finally silences all that intrudes, like Horace's kingfisher, heard from somewhere afar off, upon the scene's quiet perfection: the "random shouts" of the children, the rattle and clutter of the old men and their clicking croquet balls, and the disquieting disharmonies of the Berlioz played by a military band, of all things, "like a thin coating of tortured Tschaikovsky" (398).

It is twilight, Faulkner's favorite time of the day, that liminal moment when light and dark are equally mixed and neither one nor the other. In the version of *Sanctuary* published in 1931, the paragraph describing Temple and her father ends the novel. In the Original Text, as noted, Faulkner concludes with the paragraph of Popeye's death in italics, a visual suggestion that his death at the end, like his presence at the beginning of the novel, occurs somewhere "beyond" the immediate linear narrative and probably outside of consciousness. Popeye's death occurs as a function of Temple's own disappearance here in the Luxembourg Gardens; it is a sort of objective correlative—or, italicized, perhaps rather a subjective correlative, if there is such a thing—to Temple's dissolution into the "dying brasses" and the "season of rain and death." As we shall see, what dies in Temple when Popeye dies is what he represents: her ambivalent attitude toward her own sexuality—her desire for it, her fear of it—, its place in a patriarchal culture that operates no less powerfully, in North Mississippi as in the France of kings and stained queens.

The Luxembourg Gardens, then, is a setting culturally at odds with the rest of the novel's location in the rural and unsophisticated North Mississippi and in Memphis, Tennessee. Paris, of course, is the very symbol of western culture, of all that North Mississippi is not. It is quite particularized as in the setting for the elegant novels of, say, Henry James and Edith Wharton. Twenty years earlier, Temple and her father might indeed have been characters in a James or Wharton setting, Americans in Paris, New World innocents encountering the corrupting intricacies of the old world. But part of Faulkner's point is precisely that the Paris of James and Wharton had, between 1914 and 1918, simply ceased to exist.

For most Americans in the decade or so following World War I Paris was not the Paris of James and Wharton but rather that of Hemingway and Fitzgerald and other expatriates: a loose, unstable confederation of French citizens with even looser morals, folks broken and resourceless after the war, who, at least as far as Americans were concerned, existed mostly to provide wine and food and other services to rich Americans. It was a city where anything could happen and often did, so that in the American popular imagination Paris was primarily a licentious city defined by the baser appetites it catered to, appetites trivialized but definitely symbolized by the idea of the "French post card" and other "dirty pictures" associated with Paris.[1]

Thus *Sanctuary's* final scene in Paris is oddly out of joint in a number of ways. Temple and her father and the Luxembourg Gardens could almost be figures in the frontispiece of a nineteenth-century novel. Indeed, in the Original Text, in a scene that anticipates the tableau in the Luxembourg Gardens, Horace watches Narcissa and Gowan walking in the garden outside Narcissa's home. He remembers his own discomfort with spring's "green-snared promise of unease" that he saw from his own window in Kinston and he wants to deny them their own bodies : "They should stroll along cloisters, marble, dead shapes. not among mutational greenery," he tells Miss Jenny. "They're incongruous. Flowered walks are for young people with shy, writhing. hidden hands, walking a little blind at an interval over-discreet, while they move with the decorous precision of two figures in the frontispiece of a nineteenth century novel. All he needs is a dyed moustache; she, one of those hermaphroditic dogs peeping above her shoulders where modern women wear artificial flowers" (*SO* 33). Except for Judge Drake's un-dyed silver moustache, Horace here in effect describes the scene in the Luxembourg Gardens and throws in one of Miss Reba's terrified dogs for good measure.

---

1. In *If I Forget Thee, Jerusalem* (1939), Harry Wilbourne declares that the State of love in America is such that "if Venus returned she would be a soiled man in a subway lavatory with a palm full of French postcards" (588). In *The Town* (1957) Montgomery Ward Snopes, "Atelier Monty," almost provides the materials for a scandal by showing at night in the back room of his photography studio the "dirty pictures" he brought home from France.

Much of the meaning of the scene in the Luxembourg Gardens lies in what we can call *Sanctuary's* "French connection." The tone of the closing scene, its icy reserve, its chiseled perfection, is quite different from his own experience of the Gardens when he was there in the mid-twenties and from the France of the popular imagination. His letters home reek of his absorption in and by Paris life and manners, by how cheaply and freely and well he could live there. The city's impact on him as a young man seems to have been complete and permanent and I have no doubt that he made his way back to the *Rive Gauche* every time he returned to Paris. Faulkner wrote to his mother from Paris in early September 1925 a letter which seems clearly, from our vantage, not just to anticipate but actually to announce *Sanctuary's* closing scene:

> I have just written such a beautiful thing that I am about to bust—2000 words about the Luxembourg gardens and death. It has a thin thread of plot, about a young woman, and it is poetry though written in prose form. I have worked on it for two whole days and every word is perfect. I havent slept hardly for two nights, thinking about it, comparing words. accepting and rejecting them, then changing again. But now it is perfect—a jewel. I am going to put it away for a week, then show it to someone for an opinion. So tomorrow I will wake up feeling rotten, I expect. Reaction. But its worth it, to have done a thing like this. (*SL* 17)

If any part of *Sanctuary's* origins lies in this "beautiful thing," then at a very basic level *Sanctuary's* return to Paris is a form of homage to its beginnings, to the clear sense of excitement, of accomplishment, that writing it gave him. If his letter home is any indication, the passage was an important breakthrough for his sense of himself as a writer, an important, perhaps crucial, moment in his career. Before this he had written derivative poetry and some prose sketches; he had thrown overboard one novel while crossing the Atlantic; and as he wrote this scene he was working on the materials for a novel to be called *Elmer*, which he never completed to his satisfaction. One might propose, then, that Faulkner seems to have dated the origins not just of *Sanctuary* but also of his career to those 2000 "perfect" words.

The scene in the Luxembourg Gardens is thus homage to his time in Paris and to that first rush of excitement and is as well a return, wistful perhaps, to the Paris of his youth. By the time he completed *Sanctuary* in 1929, he was four years older, a writer with a developing national reputation; his debts were piling up along with his prospects, and he was about to marry his old girl friend and inherit her two children. Biographers have frequently suggested that Temple Drake is at least partly a portrait of his intended bride; if so, it seems significant that Lee Goodwin's trial, at which Temple swears his life away, begins on June 20, 1929, the date of Faulkner's wedding. By the time he finally published a revised *Sanctuary* in 1931, he was six years removed from Paris, deeply in debt, very unhappy, and writing tragic masterpieces. Paris, that free and magnificent time in his life, was a fading memory. His attachment to the scene he wrote in Paris, then, may be no more than a personal gesture, a sense of return, a tribute: closure upon a life that would be no more.[2]

But he had taken France's language, literature, and culture to his heart long before he first visited it for the first time in 1925. Even as a child and a young man he was probably never very far from Paris in his imagination. His grandfather had a "reasonably diffuse and catholic library" that included complete sets of Balzac and Dumas and Hugo (*ESPL* 178). There is every reason to believe that he read avidly in these

---

2. In a patently autobiographical section of *A Fable*, Faulkner's runner escapes the battlefields of Northern France to make a sentimental journey to Paris, traveling with "the ghost of his lost youth dead fifteen years now"; he retraces the "perimeter of his dead life when he had not only hoped but believed, concentric about the once-sylvan vale where squatted the gray and simple stone of Saint Sulpice, saving for the last the narrow crooked passageway in which he had lived for three years, passing the Sorbonne but only slowing, not turning in, and the other familiar Left Bank places—quai and bridge, gallery and garden cafe—where he had spent his rich leisure and his frugal money; it was not until the second solitary and sentimental morning, after coffee . . . at the Deux Magots, taking the long way, through the Luxembourg Gardens again among the nursemaids and maimed soldiers . . . and the stained effigies of gods and queens, into the rue Vaugirard, already looking ahead to discern the narrow crevice which would be the rue Servandoni and the garret which he had called home (perhaps Monsieur and Madame Gargne, *patron* and *patronne*, would still be there to greet him)" (802–3).

It's a lovingly passionate and tender passage in this dark and brooding novel of over twenty years later: Faulkner's character haunts the haunts, walks the streets, that Faulkner himself had haunted and walked as a young man, when he, too, had hoped and believed. Faulkner lived in the rue Servandoni during his time in Paris, and I'll bet a lunch of *aiguillette de caneton* at the Tour d'Argent that Monsieur and Madame Gargne were also Faulkner's *patron* and *patronne*.

volumes from a very early age. At the University of Virginia he claimed to read "some of Balzac almost every year" (*FU* 50), and we know that he admired Flaubert and read and even stole from Rabelais. He studied French as a student at the University of Mississippi; among his earliest publications there were translations of Verlaine and Mallarmé. His early works are drenched in self-conscious references to and borrowings from other French writers, especially the *Symbolistes* and the *fin-de-siècle* group (Polk "Introduction"). Clearly, he was very interested in French literature long before he ever got to France, and his immersion in French literature and his love of the French language was doubtless largely responsible for the impact that Paris had on him in 1925: he had primed himself for it, and none of it seemed to have been lost on him.

Images of France give structural and thematic logic to the novel's conclusion in the Luxembourg Gardens. The novel's crucial setting, of course, is the Old Frenchman place, the abandoned farmhouse in rural Mississippi whose weed-choked grounds stand opposed to the formality of the Luxembourg Gardens and whose rustic dilapidation stands equally opposed to the ancient monumental formality of the Palais du Luxembourg, the Gardens' principal building. *Sanctuary* deliberately refuses to hint at the Palais's presence in the scene but it is an inescapable part of the Gardens. The French Senate sits in the Palais; it is thus the home of law and order and rational discourse, precisely the seat of the "civilization" that Horace calls upon so futilely as a stay against the onslaught of modernity. Everybody in *Sanctuary* who thinks "There ought to be a law" might feel at home in this setting, though to be sure the "law and order" that it represents has been severely compromised by World War I.

The setting in the Luxembourg Gardens thus provides *Sanctuary* its only historical dimension. *Sanctuary* is quite remarkable for its almost complete lack of the history of the South that is otherwise integral to Faulkner's œuvre. To be sure, the Benbows and the Sartorises are old established Mississippi families, but Faulkner notes their family histories mostly by suggestion; perhaps the most striking characteristic of Faulkner's revision of *Sanctuary* is his almost complete removal of history. When Horace tells Lee to have faith in justice, in civilization, he doesn't even know that those words are more a mantra than a tool, more wishful thinking than an effective strategy against the world's chaos. Temple desperately appeals to the order that history presumes to impose on the present when she intones "My father's a judge. My father's a judge" (214). Her well-known cry at the moment of her rape—"Something is happening to me. . . . I told you it was" (250)—is a primal articulation of what happens when history refuses to, or cannot, provide a structure in which we can operate. But history is practically inoperative in *Sanctuary*. The fact that her father is a judge does her no good in the immediate crisis. The Palais's marble solidity, its invocation of European history of the previous centuries, stands in sharp contrast to the Old Frenchman place, which in this context stands for all the psychic, social, and cultural discontinuity that is the American world of *Sanctuary*. Temple and her father go to the Gardens precisely for its predictable and solid marbled permanence. Surrounded by "tranquil," even if "stained marble queens" (398), it is an "Old Frenchman place" of a quite different order. But *Sanctuary*'s modern world has lost its claim on order; World War I has loosed chaos upon the world and the center can not, or does not, hold: part of what privilege does is to impose order on history; part of what order does is to impose immobility on living human beings.

In the Luxembourg Gardens converge a number of other specific and evocative references to France. In *Flags in the Dust* Horace returns from serving in France in the YMCA and in *Sanctuary* Lee Goodwin is a veteran of the fighting. Horace's wife and his stepdaughter are Belle and Little Belle, names that evoke both France and the Old South. Ruby's baby lies "in a sort of drugged immobility, like the children which beggars on Paris streets carry" (259). At her gathering following Red's funeral, Miss Reba tells her lady friends about discovering what Popeye and Red were doing in the room with Temple: "I says 'I been running a house for twenty years, but this is the first time I ever had anything like this going on in it. If you want to turn a stud in to your girl' I says 'go somewhere else to do it. I aint going to have my house turned into no French joint'" (358). Temple's room at Miss Reba's whorehouse has a dressing table "cluttered with, toilet things—brushes and mirrors . . . with flasks and jars of delicate and bizarre shapes, bearing French labels" (335). Finally, Temple invokes the French queens directly, in their specific relationship to French kings, when at Miss Reba's she describes to Horace her terror during the night she spent at the Old Frenchman place: "Then I thought about fastening myself up some way. There was a girl went abroad one summer that told me about a kind of iron belt in a museum a king or something used to lock the queen up in when he had to go away, and I thought if I just had that. . . . I was thinking if I just had that French thing. I was thinking maybe it would have long sharp spikes on it and he wouldn't know it until too late . . ." (329).

In one way or another, then, France informs *Sanctuary* from beginning to end, in an extended series of major and minor references, humorous, vulgar, and deadly serious. The most significant invocation of France, however, is, of course, that of *Madame Bovary*. If only for reasons of the French connection, it is appropriate that Horace frames his reaction to Popeye in terms of *Madame Bovary* instead, say, of more modern works by D. H. Lawrence or James Joyce; *Bovary's* sculpted prose contains and controls the chaos that is Emma Bovary's body, as the statues of the French queens become the working metaphors for the cultural forces that control female bodies generally, even while idolizing them and placing them on pedestals. It's difficult to imagine Molly Bloom on a pedestal or as a statue.

I think there can be no doubt that the book in Horace's pocket when he encounters Popeye is *Madame Bovary*. André Bleikasten's sense of the pervasive presence of *Madame Bovary* in *Sanctuary's* system of meanings seems indisputable and essential to understanding *Sanctuary*. He particularly notes the two novels' shared theme of the "morselization" of Temple's and Madame Bovary's bodies, whose parts Flaubert itemizes, names, and depicts in isolation from the body whole. Bodies throughout both novels are in a constant state of rupture, of explosion, of transition from one place or condition to another: they turn inside out, they vomit, they bleed, they spit, they disgorge, they decay, they dissipate. Throughout *Sanctuary* Temple constantly watches her own body in various motions over which she seems to have no control: in several places she watches herself run out of her body and in one scene at Miss Reba's she watches it disappear in a twilight like that in the Luxembourg Gardens: "Holding the towel about her she stole toward the door . . .

her eyes a little blind with the strain of listening. It was twilight; in a dim mirror, a pellucid oblong of dusk set on end, she had a glimpse of herself like a thin ghost, a pale shadow moving in the uttermost profundity of shadow" (281).[3] Her body simply disappears. Throughout the novel she has resisted containment and disappearance by marking herself in the bright bold lipstick scarlets that will perhaps magically at least mark the place where her body was, even if it disappears; on the one hand she dresses in clothes that attract the male eyes that make her visible and on the other hand covers her body with blankets and raincoats that both hide and contain it, protect it from dismemberment and penetration. Bodies in *Sanctuary* and *Madame Bovary* are caught in a constant diffusion of identity that mark the disappearance of boundaries in both novels. As Bleikasten says of *Madame Bovary*, "Even the novel's landscapes are constantly melting away, with fogs, mists, or vapors blurring contours and suffusing all space with their moisture" (38). He could also have been writing about the final scene of *Sanctuary*.

Temple resists precisely this blurring of boundaries—of place, of gender, of identity. She wants most a solid body that will not melt or disappear, a body covering, a visible sanctuary that will protect her from penetration: at the Old Frenchman place, in her underwear, she curiously grabs a flimsy raincoat for cover: curiously, that is, until we remember that the French word for raincoat is *imperméable*: impenetrable. At one and the same time and then at alternate moments, she wants a body that is both sexually powerful and impermeable, a body simultaneously desirable and impenetrable.

Temple needs to be viewed, not as a narcissist might but as a condition of her very existence. Horace thinks that being seen is the condition of selfhood: "he thought how darkness is that agent which destroys the edifice with which light shapes people to a certain predictable behavior, as though by the impact of eyes" (*SO* 145).[4] Thus Temple, like Emma Bovary, postures and primps for the eyes of others and, when she checks her mirror, for herself; the condition of being seen, of being shaped

---

3. See Bleikasten, "Cet affreux" and "Terror and Nausea," and Trouard, "X Marks the Spot," for extended discussions of *Madame Bovary* in *Sanctuary*.

4. See Michel Gresset's essential discussion of the gaze in Faulkner in his *Fascination*.

by the eyes of others, is precisely the condition whereby she confirms her own existence. One condition of being seen is being immobile; no body is more visible than a statue. Temple's motionless solidity among the marbled queens stands in marked contrast to her flitting, terrified running at the Old Frenchman place and to her nervous flitting "in speeding silhouette against the lighted windows" of her dormitory (198), when she refuses to be immobilized by the windows' frames.

It is quite to the point, then, that both *Sanctuary* and *Madame Bovary* are replete with images of statuary and engravings. Indeed, Horace comes back to Jefferson specifically seeking the "imperviousness" of his sister Narcissa, whom Faulkner describes as dressed in white and whom throughout Horace thinks of as partaking of a quality like "heroic statuary" (253). Temple, as noted, imagines herself as one of those French queens with a chastity belt that will protect her bodily integrity by protecting her from violation. In an even more provocative moment at the Old Frenchman place, however, she assumes a position on the mattress, "her hands crossed on her breast and her legs straight and close and decorous, like an effigy on an ancient tomb" (228). She thus makes of herself a stained—or about to be—queen, dead and impervious, marble and safe from violation.

Faulkner was fascinated with the statue, the sculpted idol. His first published book was a long poem, *The Marble Faun* (1924), in which a marble statue of Pan meditates upon a changing natural world that he cannot participate in because the marble binds his sexual nature; in *Mosquitoes* (1927), a sculptor works on a statue of a woman's torso, a body without head to think, without arms to hold him, without legs to leave him; the statue is thus primarily a genital with its necessary organ support system, something that the sculptor can both make and control. The statue invokes Gustave Courbet's grim painting, *L'Origine du Monde*, which is even more specific in its isolation of the vulva from the rest of the body, its combination of fascination with and loathing of the female body. Thirty years later, in *The Town* (1957), Gavin Stevens helps his enemy Flem Snopes design and erect in the Jefferson cemetery a marble monument to Eula Varner Snopes. She has lived her adult life as an adulteress because she is a passionate woman married to an impotent man and because while she lives no respectable community can deal straightforwardly with her unashamed sexuality: disapprove it must, but it must also watch, fascinated, titillated. In her death Jefferson makes of her a marble monument to its own virtue and condemns her to stand, in her death, eternally looking out over a graveyard of people no more dead than those still living in Jefferson who could not accept her, or their own, sexual bodies (Trouard, "Eula's Plot" 295).

Temple and the stained queens of the Luxembourg Gardens are thus best understood as part of Faulkner's pantheon of marbleized women. Though the stained women were queens, they were women first whose potential sexual capacities so concerned their kings and consorts that they had to wear chastity belts when their husbands left town. Temple, though a young woman, a barely post-adolescent Mississippi would-be flapper, also significantly identifies herself with them when at the Old Frenchman place she wishes for a chastity belt to protect her. Thus perhaps we have not asked the right questions about Temple. Indeed, in some ways we haven't asked questions at all but rather have imposed answers and assumptions on her. For all kinds of reasons, when Temple sits among them, she is very much at home with the French queens, and becomes increasingly marbleized throughout the novel.[5]

It little matters, then, whether she is a virgin or not at the time of her rape, whether Doc got his "step-in" from Temple in a sexual encounter or from a whore (199), or whether whoever wrote her name on the lavatory wall did so in celebration of conquest or in repudiation of defeat. It little matters whether her "cool, predatory and discreet" eyes (198) make her an ice maiden or voluptuary or walking vagina-dentata. What does matter is that she is seventeen, experimenting with her sexual urges, trying to come to terms with her sexuality and with the powerful conflicting demands her body and her culture give her. She finds her body being stared at and lusted after by the men of *Sanctuary* who, perhaps too much like the novel's critics, are both fascinated and appalled by what they see and she, doubtless, both fascinated and appalled by

---

5. See Trouard, "X Marks the Spot" for an extended discussion of and description of the statues in the Luxembourg Gardens.

their looking. At the same time that they stare, however, they tell her that she can't do with her body what she wants to do, disparage and punish her when she tries to. To make herself visible she tries out postures and attitudes she has perhaps learned from the males who run the magazines and movies to believe will give her purchase on sexual power in modern America. The novel posits no opposition at all between the college boys at Ole Miss and the underground men at the Old Frenchman place, as Ruby would have it. All the males in the novel, college boys and bootlegging men and father and brothers, give her exactly the same message: be beautiful, be popular, but be sexual only when we say to and only with whom we say, or we'll beat you, we'll humiliate you, we'll even kill you if necessary. Thus Ruby is indeed wrong. She and Temple, as women even from different classes and backgrounds, are no less alike than Temple and the queens, more nearly sisters than antagonists.

At Ole Miss, at the Old Frenchman place, Temple gets initiated not just in to sexuality but into the violence attendant upon her presumption that her body is her own. Popeye's death, so carefully choreographed a part of the Original Text's scene in the Luxembourg Gardens, represents the death of her desire as she comes to terms with the subjugation of female sexuality by a male culture impotent to be its equal except by violence. Temple's culture will not permit her to be sexual on her own terms, anymore than kings would permit their queens to be, and it punishes her violently, grotesquely, for pretending that she can, punishes her no less by whoever has written her name on the lavatory wall than by Popeye in the crib. One central continuity from history to modernity, from queens to Bovary to Temple, is that female sexuality cannot exist on its own terms. It must be controlled, whether in the palaces of the French court, the commercialized bedrooms of Miss Reba's brothel, or the Old Frenchman's place's shuck-filled mattresses.

At the same time that Temple has been "morselized," then, she has also become marbleized: in our first vision of her, she moves among her college boyfriends at the dance, her eyes "blankly right and left looking"; the onlookers are themselves statues, a "row of hatted and muffled busts cut from black tin and nailed to the window-sills" (198); Popeye too, so famously having the "vicious depthless quality of stamped tin" (181) is a statue. At the Old Frenchman place Tommy, like the queens, has a "pale, empty gaze" (206) and even poor Ruby constantly dresses in neat gray clothes that identify her with the queens too. When Temple dances with Popeye at the Grotto, she does so just as she sits in the Luxembourg Gardens, "stiffly and languidly, her eyes open but unseeing; her body following the music without hearing the tune for a time" (343). Finally, in a climactic scene at the Grotto, she leans provocatively against a table to seduce Red and becomes a statue, one with the queens: "She did not move. Her eyes began to grow darker and darker, lifting into her skull above a half moon of white, without focus, *with the blank rigidity of a statue's eyes*" (344, my emphasis). She sits with her kinglike father, who in the courtroom fits her with a chastity belt of brothers; he is also a statue, or becoming one, as "the rigid bar of his moustache bead[s] with moisture like frosted silver" (398). Faulkner could not have been more specific and still have been Faulkner.

In Paris, in the Luxembourg Gardens, Temple surrenders her body, her mind and her corporeal self, to the culture. It's a perfect setting for Faulkner's finale, its large anywhere of women gathered in such profound mute testimony to what happens to women, queen or peasant, slattern or movie star. The queens gaze blankly; they do not see her, for very shame at their mutual abjection. They are "dead" and "tranquil"; Temple, perhaps for the first time in her life, certainly for the first time in the novel, is tranquil and dead or dying because tranquil. Like Bovary on her deathbed, she consults her mirror a final time, a goodbye, perhaps, to her corporeal self, which is not just "sullen and discontented and sad" but also "miniature": her disappearance has already begun. She then yields to the grayness of the day, the summer, the year, the twilight. She yields, finally, to the dissolution that has threatened her bodily integrity, its autonomy, throughout the novel: she "dissolve[s] into the dying brasses" while following the waves of the music across the pool toward the queens opposite, and on into the sky itself, it too, like her, "prone and vanquished." As a female who would be sexual, she has found her destiny at last, among her French sisters.

Testing Masculinity in the
Snopes Trilogy

I've argued elsewhere that race in Faulkner's fiction often serves as a mask for gender. In fact, race occupied him in only four of his nineteen novels and in only one or two of nearly 140 short stories, so that race, statistically at any rate, is a very minor part of his concerns. Sexual and sexualized relationships, on the other hand, are everywhere, on nearly every page. Indeed, in *Absalom* race provides a narrative "out" for Quentin and Shreve's otherwise failed attempts to explain why Henry Sutpen kills Charles Bon. After hundreds of pages of speculation, of convoluted and complex attempts to move their story to its narrative climax they finally, near the end of chapter 8, in a mutual wordless dream-vision, have Sutpen demand that Henry stop Bon from marrying his sister because Bon is his part-Negro son from his marriage in Haiti. From this point it takes just three pages to get Charles killed—no questions, no convoluted meditations: the race card settles it.

This conclusion to the nineteenth-century portions of *Absalom* says much less about the Sutpen family's dilemma than it does about the overwhelming power of the Grand Narrative about race in our culture, operative even in Faulkner criticism, which has taken it for granted for lo these seven decades since *Absalom*'s publication that Bon is unquestionably Sutpen's part-black son and that that is unquestionably why

Sutpen refuses to allow Judith to marry Bon, despite the fact that the novel provides no evidence that this is true while providing plenty to the contrary, and despite the fact that generations of critics have also taken it as gospel that the novel's structural thematic is precisely its narrative indeterminacy—its guesswork, suppositions, postulations, assertions, and retractions—that renders highly suspect any claim on truth or even fact. For though the race card provides a neat solution to Quentin's and Shreve's narrative dilemma, it—more importantly in my judgment—allows the Harvard narrators, and the critics, to sidestep certain questions of more immediate, more intimate concern, questions having particularly to do with gender's expectations of young men (Polk "Artist as Cuckold").

First, in their rush to conclusion the narrators never ask why Sutpen should require his son to stop Bon from marrying his own sister—why, especially if he is the powerful father the narrators depict him as, he should not just take care of it himself. Second, none of the narrators seems at all interested in Judith's feelings in the matter of her own heart. Third, it has hardly occurred to anybody in or out of the novel to wonder whether perhaps Henry kills Bon for the same reason that Quentin in *The Sound and the Fury* wants to murder Dalton Ames: to save—i.e., control—his sister's virginity. Finally, the two half- or completely-naked young men for some reason or other fail to pursue the possible homoerotic relationship between Henry and Bon that Mr. Compson so lasciviously points to as he describes the fey bon vivant from New Orleans who descends upon that provincial college in backwoods North Mississippi and changes Henry's life. Perhaps the ruckus in the library on Christmas Eve, which servants hear through closed doors, is not at all about Bon and Judith but rather about Bon and Henry; perhaps Bon and Sutpen fail to come to terms over Judith's dowry; perhaps Judith has herself rejected Bon and her father supports her wishes, to the dismay of both Bon and Henry who can, they believe, maintain a homoerotic relationship, what Mr. Compson calls "the perfect incest," through Judith, only under the cover of a respectable heterosexual marriage.

Race supplies Quentin and Shreve a way out of having to ask any of these questions which the narrative allows, even encourages, us to ask. Answers to these questions would take them directly in to murky areas of gender and sex roles, perhaps of their own relationship, that they are happy not to have to consider; they might indeed lead the boys to confront directly certain issues about the meaning of masculinity and to admit their own inability to perform masculinity in any of the terms that would be acceptable to their families and their cultures. Quentin cannot be a "man" in *The Sound and the Fury* because he cannot control his sister's sexual life, because he cannot shoot a gun or hold a knife, because he cannot live up to a "tradition" that insists that males behave in certain ways, and not least perhaps because he is struggling with his own homosexuality.[1] He is fascinated with Henry Sutpen, then, because Henry does to Charles Bon, the presumptive ravisher of Judith's virginity, precisely what he, Quentin, fails to do to Dalton Ames. In important ways, then, *Absalom* is Quentin's narrative performance of the masculinity that eludes him in his real life back home, even if he completely sidesteps that parallel by making the issue racial instead of sexual.

I begin with this discursus on *Absalom* to illustrate the degree to which the problematics of masculine enactment and empowerment undergird Faulkner's work, the extent to which his characters feel bound, thwarted, and driven by cultural definitions of masculinity and femininity, definitions which prescribe certain performative features of each and which proscribe numerous other acts which would in effect cancel out the performances of the prescribed. We now know, thanks to two or three generations of excellent feminist scholarship, that "gender" is a cultural construct, a charade that masks its performative nature even from the performers. Without engaging Judith Butler, whose argument is much more complex than my needs here demand, I nevertheless want to note briefly her discussion of gender identity as part of an "epistemological inheritance of contemporary political discourses of identity," of which binary oppositions between male and female, between "I" and "Other," are a significant part. Butler argues the necessity of locating these polarities "within practices of signification" rather than accepting epistemological accounts of identity. The "substantive 'I,'" she says, "only

---

1. See "How Shreve Gets in to Quentin's Pants" in this volume.

appears as such through a signifying practice that seeks to conceal its own workings and to naturalize its effects." "To understand identity as a *practice*," she continues,

> and as a *signifying* practice, is to understand culturally intelligible subjects as the resulting effects of a rule-bound discourse that inserts itself in the pervasive and mundane signifying acts of linguistic life. . . . Indeed, when the subject is said to be constituted, that means simply that the subject is a consequence of certain rule-governed discourses that govern the intelligible invocation of identity. The subject is not *determined* by the rules through which it is generated because signification is *not a founding act*, but rather a regulated process of repetition that both conceals itself and enforces its rules precisely through the production of substantializing effects. In a sense, all signification takes place within the orbit of the compulsion to repeat. . . .
> (144–45)

These compulsively repeated signifying practices help define the performative nature of gender in Faulkner, with this exception: though they cannot completely understand the origins and the workings of the traditional discourses of masculinity which control their needs and their dreams, Faulkner's men are intensely aware of the gestural "significations" of this discourse and that they calibrate them daily, in every aspect of their lives. The "rules" do not conceal themselves at all but enforce themselves upon them with a vengeance, in thousands of economic and social indignities to their sense of self. Arguably, they understand completely how constructed their gender roles are, even if only through their callous- and blister-marked knowledge of the cultural and historical deck that has been stacked against them, and of how difficult it is for them, and how desperately they need, to participate in those "rule-bound discourses" by which alone they can claim some portion of "manhood" in any sense they would recognize or accept. Butler would have it that "agency," self-constructed identity, can be "located within the possibility of a variation" in the "regulated process of repetition" (145). But Faulkner's men seek identity within their communal discourse, where, of course, they have little or no agency. They are thus mystified by and in awe of Flem Snopes, who operates numerous profitable variations on the performance of masculinity and can do so because he instinctively understands manhood as a performance that he can perform to his own advantage; he uses the variations to reify himself within, even directly at the center of, that discourse, by affirming in his "success" the cultural values of heterosexual union and of material success. He thus affirms their dreams even as he eventually discovers that dream's emptiness.

William Faulkner taught himself a lot, in and through his fiction, about the performative, public, nature of gender, and about men's need to have their performances approved by other men—in Faulkner women never approve or need approval—and so construct a public self out of and for the eyes of their audience. He profoundly understood how our culture works to rob men and women both of an instinctual sexual life by forcing them to conform to performative sexual roles.

Most of the criticism on gender in Faulkner has focussed upon the ways culture also works to shape and control the sexual lives of women. I want to focus here upon the ways that same culture works to control the sexual lives of men. I want to think particularly of Eula Varner Snopes, especially in *The Hamlet* (1940) and *The Town* (1957). But his path from *Absalom* in 1936 and *The Hamlet* in 1940 is very much worth noting first. In *The Unvanquished* (1938), for example, most of which he wrote in between stints on *Absalom* and *Pylon* (1935), Bayard Sartoris performs his *rite du passage* into manhood by rejecting the traditionally masculine role of avenger of his father's violent death and by his concurrent rejection of the oedipal sexuality that his stepmother Drusilla offers him in exchange for his (her) revenge, which she offers as a ticket of admission into his manhood: by killing his father's killer he will make himself as worthy of his surrogate mother as if he had killed his father himself. But Bayard refuses to continue his father's tradition of violence, and does so in terms of the tradition of Southern Honor, by facing his father's killer unarmed (see Wyatt-Brown).

In his next two novels, *If I Forget Thee, Jerusalem* (1939) and *The Hamlet*, Faulkner reverses his usual narrative device, so prominent in *The Sound and the Fury*, *Absalom*, and *As I Lay Dying*, by which males construct an ideal woman or, rather, more precisely, bemoan the failure of a particular woman to live up to some ideal of womanhood that they first impose on her and then judge her by how far short of it she falls. One thinks obviously of Caddy Compson, the "absent center" of *The Sound and the Fury*, and of Addie Bundren who though given a central monologue in *As I Lay Dying* is nevertheless like Caddy in being also an "absent center," a construct of her men's narration. She of course specifically rejects her untenable position as central absence and exacts a revenge upon her family that forces males—her husband, sons, and daughter—to be aware of her as a literal corporeal presence: a rotting corpse. In *If I Forget Thee, Jerusalem* and *The Hamlet*, however, Faulkner plunks the ideal woman down in their midst to see what they can do with corporeal embodiments of their collective and individual desire. In these novels, Faulkner examines masculinity by testing it against its own constructedness.

Charlotte Rittenmeyer and Eula Varner are mirror images of each other, differing but related apotheoses of the male imagination's ultimate female. In these two novels, Faulkner tests the ideal female against the actual not by contrasting the ideal with a debased form but by giving to men what they have always thought and, in the Hollywood-ized language of sexual satisfaction, loudly proclaimed they wanted, and by watching what they do with it.

Charlotte Rittenmeyer is *If I Forget Thee, Jerusalem*'s *femme de trouble*, on whose will Harry Wilbourne is borne—and "born" too. She manufactures for him a moveable sexual paradise outside of conventional morality in which literally all he has to do is *keep it up*, to be constantly ready, like women in pornography, to get on with what she euphemistically calls "bitching." She becomes the aggressor, the "masculine" in their makeshift, ramshackle life, he the stay-at-home "wife"; she feeds him, makes the money, does the cooking. With Harry helpless in her wake, she flees her husband and two children, inspiring herself and Harry with the idea that their love will not get bogged down in bourgeois domesticity: their love will be "all honeymoon," she insists, thus freeing him and herself from the domesticity that married men in Faulkner see as both the ultimate trap and the ultimate form of security. When they get too domesticated in one place, Charlotte forces a move. Harry proclaims his feminization by writing stories for less-than-reputable magazines on the theme of "female sex troubles," stories beginning "I had the body and desires of a woman yet in knowledge and experience of the world I was but a child" (577), stories, the point of view of which suggests the degree to which his experiences with Charlotte have demasculinized and even infantalized him: during a sojourn in the woods of Northern Michigan, Harry's passivity reduces him to a "drowsy and foetuslike state, passive and almost unsentient in the womb of solitude and peace" (570). Nature refuses them their continual honeymoon when in a mining camp in the Utah mountains Charlotte's douchebag freezes and she gets pregnant. Harry kills her when he botches an abortion, which he can't perform on her (though he has successfully performed one on their friend), almost certainly because he cannot destroy the child of his own loins, the child which would have made them a family instead of a honeymoon and would have dragged them into the very domesticity they have been running from.

Thus at some simplistic level, *If I Forget Thee, Jerusalem* is a tragic cautionary tale that warns men in particular to be careful what they wish for, because they just might get it. That cliché, however, is much too reductive of *If I Forget Thee, Jerusalem*'s complexities to stand scrutiny. For *If I Forget Thee, Jerusalem* is Faulkner's shrillest and most intense examination of the relationship between passion and domestic love. The hapless Harry tries to explain this relationship to McCord, a Hemingway-like newspaperman in the Chicago train station as they await the train that will take Harry and Charlotte to Utah. Though the words are from Harry's mouth and though the sentiments are usually associated with a male view of domesticity, in this case the discourse is Charlotte's: bourgeois domestic life, he tells McCord, is "worse than death or division even: it was the mausoleum of love, it was the stinking catafalque of the dead corpse borne between the olfactoryless walking shapes of the immortal unsentient demanding ancient meat" (590). Love in the twentieth century has become commercialized and debased not so much by Hollywood's crass glamorization of women and sex as by respectability. As he tells McCord, "it is one of what we call the prime virtues—thrift, industry, independence—that breeds all the vices—fanatacism, smugness, meddling, fear, and worst of all, respectability" (585).

Harry and Charlotte—or rather perhaps Charlotte through Harry—act on the principle that love is debased by the accumulation of baggage that bourgeois ownership, respectability, brings with it: the car, the garage, the mortgage and, especially, the children. They constantly flee that baggage, which would force a deadening regularity and security upon their lives, only to find death when Charlotte's pregnancy disrupts the regularity of her menstrual cycle. In *The Hamlet*, Faulkner takes his inquisition into the domestic several remarkable steps further. Though set in the backwoods of late nineteenth-century North Mississippi, and though its characters are mostly sharecroppers with precious little of this world's goods, *The Hamlet* likewise takes as its thematic *parti-pris* the complicated and paradoxical premise that men perceive domesticity as a trap which at the same time provides them with the house, the mortgage, children, horses, mules, wagons, furniture, children, a wife—in general, ownership: all those trappings of bourgeois domesticity that Harry and Charlotte seek to escape, but which are the very signs to which the males of Frenchman's Bend so desperately cling for their identities as males. Thomas Sutpen tells General Compson that to accomplish his design, he would need "money, a house, a plantation, slaves, a family—incidentally of course, a wife" (*AA* 218). For Sutpen the wife is secondary, necessary only to insure the legality of his progeny and to promote the desired image of heterosexual domesticity: sexuality doesn't seem to be any more a part of his needs, except perhaps "incidentally, of course" than of Flem Snopes's. The males of Frenchman's Bend might not make a wife so sharply "incidental" as Sutpen does, but they would certainly agree with the sentiment and with certain of his reasons, but not with all of them. Both they and Sutpen want the virgin wife their traditions have taught them they have a right to, but Sutpen wants one merely to insure the sons he passes his design to are indeed his own. This may well be why he so unhappily and problematically yokes with the daughter of the most upright Methodist in North Mississippi: if anybody could insure virginity in a daughter, he apparently thinks, Coldfield could. So far as we know anything about it, however, he neither takes sexual pleasure nor worries about sexual inadequacy.

Not so with the males of Frenchman's Bend, who have nothing to leave their progeny but the same grinding poverty, the same bleak, backbreaking labor they and their fathers and grandfathers had been heir to in their time, and who must bear the added effrontery of the fear that Will Varner, their boss, the man who holds their lives in fee, is screwing their wives every chance he gets. Thus the males of Frenchman's Bend associate social and sexual power with money, with ownership; questions about their sexual potency aside, all they have to trade and bargain with and even work for are the signs of potency, needs among which a wife and children are by no means "incidental," but absolutely central. Faulkner litters Frenchman's Bend with a riot of sexual jokes and phallic symbols, sexual icons in distress: the diminutive spotted ponies, traditional symbols of masculinity, that the males of Frenchman's Bend buy at auction but then cannot catch, even with the help of their neighbors; Ab Snopes's horse that Pat Stamper inflates artificially with a bicycle pump and trades back to poor Ab, who of course doesn't recognize it in its more erect state; the teacher and football hero Labove whom Eula Varner's thirteen-year-old presence in his classroom renders incompetent. Even the studliest of the young local studs, Hoake McCarron, is phallically challenged: when his courting competitors find him and Eula stopped in their buggy, they attack; though Hoake has a loaded gun with him, he nevertheless cannot, or does not, use it, not even to fire it up in the air as a warning or threat. In the struggle *Eula* fights his competitors off, using the butt of the buggy's horsewhip. Hoake gets his arm broken in the struggle and, after Eula has changed clothes and her father has set Hoake's limp and flaccid arm, she trots him right back to the very site of the fight and insists upon giving him her virginity; but she, alas, has to hold him up, support him, so that he can perform (*H* 860).

But I get a bit ahead of myself. Into this phallus-impaired Mississippi backwoods, Faulkner drops the wonder of creation, Eula Varner. Charlotte Rittenmeyer is a tightly-packaged and self-contained combination of male and female: the real estate agent who describes her to the doctor that rents her and Harry the house on the beach says she is wearing pants that are "too little for her in just exactly the right places any man would want to see them too little but no woman would unless she had them on herself" (*Jer* 497). Eula, by contrast, is unbounded and uncontainable female plenitude itself: she is a "girl of whom, even at nine and ten and eleven, there was too much—too much of leg, too much of breast, too much of buttock; too much of mammalian female meat" (*H* 822). She had "overtaken and passed her mother in height in her tenth year. Now, though not yet thirteen years old, she was already bigger than most grown women and even her breasts were no longer the little, hard, fiercely-pointed cones of puberty or even maidenhood." More: she is practically supernatural, classical in her dimensions and in her origins: "her entire appearance suggested some symbology out of the old Dionysic times—honey in sunlight and bursting grapes, the writhen bleeding of the crushed fecundated vine beneath the hard rapacious trampling goat-hoof" (817). She is an extravagance of the feminine, "too much" to be contained by any of the containers her family tries to keep her in. She quickly outgrows the perambulator her father makes for her. Her legs depend longly out from under her skirt as she straddles her brother Jody's horse on the way to and from school twice each way every school day, to the consternation of the good old boys who regularly gather at Varner's store in order to be consternated. Jody constantly rubs his hands all over her to discover whether she has extruded from or carelessly forgot or merely burned away her binding undergarments. To him, as they ride to school on that horse, her body "even motionless in a chair seemed to postulate an invincible abhorrence of straight lines, jigging its component boneless curves against his back. He had a vision of himself transporting not only across the village's horizon but across the embracing proscenium of the entire inhabited world like the sun itself, a kaleidoscopic convolution of mammalian ellipses" (822). Some years later, an adult and by common knowledge an adulterer, Eula walks across the Square "always alone; not, as far as we knew, going anywhere: just moving, walking in that aura of decorum and modesty and solitariness ten times more immodest and a hundred times more disturbing than one of the bathing suits young women would begin to wear about 1920 or so, as if in the second just before you looked, her garments had managed in one last frantic pell mell scurry to overtake and cover her. Though only for a moment because in the next one, if only you followed long enough, they would wilt and fail from that mere plain and simple striding which would shred them away like the wheel of a constellation through a wisp and cling of trivial scud" (*T* 9).

She is an Olympian in Frenchman's Bend, which hamlet, V. K. Ratliff thinks, is no more than "a little lost village, nameless, without grace, forsaken, yet which wombed once by chance and accident one blind seed of the spendthrift Olympian ejaculation and did not even know it, without tumescence conceived, and bore" her (867). She is far more than sexual, however; indeed, she is in most ways a parody of the merely sexual, as the opening paragraph of the "Eula" section makes clear. For Faulkner and the good old boys of Frenchman's Bend she is clearly symbol, but also more than symbol: she is the signified and the signifier wrapped into one sprawling package whose containers keep falling away from her "plain and simple striding." Charlotte Rittenmeyer is the apotheosized and very modern attainable imaginary, the word made flesh with a vengeance, the always already ready porn queen who promises orgasm without complications or baggage; Eula Varner is the apotheosized and very traditional unattainable imaginary, the word made flesh with spirit-sapping abundance, her "rich mind- and will-sapping fluid softness" (*H* 823). If *If I Forget Thee, Jerusalem* is a sustained meditation upon having the woman of your dreams, *The Hamlet*, indeed the entire Snopes Trilogy, is a sustained meditation, more lyrical and infinitely more complex, mostly articulated by V. K. Ratliff and then by Gavin Stevens, on what it means to attain or not attain that dream in the flesh, on how to have it by not having it and not have it by having it.

It's precisely their investment in phallic heterosexuality that renders the men of Frenchman's Bend vulnerable to Flem Snopes and to the cultural forces that Flem represents, those forces that value appearance over reality: that is, the forces of respectability. But it's more than public appearance. It's private appearance, too: not just what they believe other men see when they look but also what they can see or fail to see of themselves when they look inside. Eula is thus the supreme threat to their innermost places; she is Allwoman, All Women; she is the "supreme primal uterus" (*H* 835) as Labove thinks, to which men in fear and worship prostrate themselves.

Eula sets the men of Frenchman's Bend and Jefferson not just against each other but against their own self-definitions: she flushes them out from where they are hiding. Her visceral presence, as an openly, unashamedly vital and sexual human being, nearly a pagan at the Christmas cotillion in *The Town*, renders all masculine expectation, all systems of knowledge and of order, completely moot. In *The Hamlet* she creates a "priapic hullabaloo" (842) in Labove's classroom and in his equanimity, by disrupting hierarchy. She was "neither at the head nor at the foot of her class . . . because the class she was in ceased to have either head or foot twenty-four hours after she entered it. Within the year there even ceased to be any lower class for her to be promoted from, for the reason that she would never be at either end of anything in which blood ran. It would have but one point . . . and she would be that point, the center . . . tranquilly abrogating the whole long sum of human thinking and suffering which is called knowledge, education, wisdom . . ." (836–37).

In Jefferson, as an adult, as Mrs. Flem Snopes, Eula does much the same thing to the hierarchies. The town's knowledge of her eighteen-year-long affair with Mayor de Spain and her unashamed sexual presence titillates the very proper good citizens of Jefferson; they confederate in silent watching and imagining to sustain their communal titillation. She has the same effect on Jefferson, then, as on Frenchman's Bend. In *The Town* Charles Mallison describes the central episode of the town's Christmas cotillion, in which Eula dances in public with her lover, flaunting not so much the affair as her open sexuality. Her dancing has a devastating effect on the town:

> Then all of a sudden . . . everybody else stopped dancing and kind of fell back and . . . saw Mrs Snopes and Mr de Spain dancing together alone in a kind of aghast circle of people . . . [who saw her] . . . dancing that way in public, simply because she was alive and not ashamed of it . . . was what she was and looked the way she looked and wasn't ashamed of it and not afraid or ashamed of being glad of it, nor even of doing this to prove it since this appeared to be the only way of proving it, not being afraid or ashamed, that the little puny people fallen back speechless and aghast in a shocked circle around them, could understand; all the other little doomed mean cowardly married and unmarried husbands looking aghast and outraged in order to keep one another from seeing that what they

really wanted to do was cry, weep because they were not that brave,
each one knowing that even if there was no other man on earth,
let alone in that ball room, they still could not have survived, let
alone matched or coped with, that splendor, that splendid unshame.
(65–66)

The city men respond with infinite sadness for their own finitude,
the country men with a profound anxiety, perhaps because the city men
will leave the cotillion and go back to their respectable bourgeois homes,
the façades of respectability, the signs of heterosexual domesticity, the
things, including their wives, that they own so visibly, even ostenta-
tiously, for all the world to see and which therefore confirm them in
their masculinity, no matter the frequency of sexual activity or degree
of impotence behind the façade. In town, respectability and masculinity
become cultural performances, ritualized and rigidly traditional dramas
of appearances with, males imagine, an audience of observers as tough
and unforgiving as a Kabuki or opera critic, performances in which getting the difficult gestures right, singing the difficult aria right, is crucial
not just to the performance of the individual act but crucial also to
the tradition which both validates and is validated by the individual
gesture. Gavin Stevens's pathetic "defense" of Eula after her dancing
with Manfred de Spain is precisely such a gesture, quixotic; as Faulkner
said of Andrew Jackson's defense of his wife's honor, he fights for the
"principle that honor must be defended whether it was or not because
defended it was whether or not" (Appendix 1127). Faulkner's parody
turns the chivalric tradition inside out, but with a point. Stevens's assumption that Eula needs or wants him or anybody else to defend her
behavior likewise turns on him with a vengeance because Manfred beats
him bloody and because Eula, the putative maiden whose honor he has
defended, denies him the honor by offering him, as unashamedly as she
had danced, that "honor" he thinks he has defended. Like every other
man in Yoknapatawpha, he cannot cope with Eula's open sexuality, so
he deflects his repressed sexual response to her into an avowedly avun-
cular friendship with Linda, Eula's daughter, and remains hilariously
conscious of how ludicrous he must appear to the townsfolk as he tries
to "improve Linda's mind" and save her from Snopes. Finally, in *The*

Mansion, he marries an old family friend, a woman middleaging and beyond, the widow of a New Orleans gangster whose childbearing years and, he apparently presumes, her sexual needs are long since past.

The men of Frenchman's Bend have no such Sears Roebuck dens to retreat to, no collocation of the artifacts of respectability to hide behind, no house full of furniture or signifying gestures. They don't have things in abundance, the men of Frenchman's Bend, but they have public gestures aplenty—their skills at trading, hunting, or fighting, for examples—that demonstrate their masculinity and bond them with other males. In most cases, they do not want or even need to perform these things themselves but to appreciate and admire those that do, which is why they can and do admire Flem Snopes, one of their own, for the trading skills that give him victories over Ratliff, Will Varner, themselves, and, especially, over Mrs. Armstid when she tries to get back from him the five dollars that her husband Henry has so foolishly spent to buy one of those spotted ponies.

What the countrymen have in common with their city brethren are their families, the children and incidentally of course a wife: public signs of their sexual potency. But their incidentally of course wives are anxiety-producing potential bombs that can destroy that potency privately and publicly. As wives, they bring to them the very vulnerability that family, respectability, proposes to protect men from. Simply, they inspire males' centuries-old fears of being cuckolded: Chaucer's Miller was doubtless not the first to suggest that "Who hath no wyf, he is no cokewold." Unlike Sutpen, they insist on female chastity not as a function of any patriarchal desire to pass on an estate to a blooded son, since they have no such estate, real or otherwise, but rather as a function of their need to own, to claim, at least one virginity—their natural right as men, they believe, which right, they fear, Will Varner, or his ilk wherever the sharecropping system renders them vassals to a feudal lord, may have abrogated through the *droit de seigneur* that his control over all of their lives gives him. The fear of cuckoldry, of course, may not always be a fear of impotence but it is always a fear of insuffiency, a fear of not being able to satisfy the sexual machine that is woman. Men fear, finally, the Charlotte Rittenmeyer in their wives. Then, when their wives are inevitably unfaithful, they fear the public intelligence of their insufficiency, since men, like women, will kiss and tell.

Hence their inevitable retreat into the homosocial (Polk "Ratliff's Buggies"), perhaps, their daily gathering on the front porch of Varner's store to ogle Eula, to regale each other with raunchy stories, but mostly, one suspects, to keep an eye on each other and to escape from the actual site of their domestic lives, the sharecropper shacks where they must constantly face both their economic and their sexual inadequacies. Simpler to abandon the proper site for the practice of masculinity in the private sphere of their cabins for a more public stage on which they can perform it for their similarly-anxious peers. They would rather, in effect, watch Isaac Snopes diddle a cow, speak bawdily of Eula's emerging legs, and perhaps slap each other on the butt or give each other high fives than be home making love to their wives and being responsible husbands and fathers. They have thus replaced not just masculinity but also the act of sex with its signs, divesting themselves of the fear of insufficiency by replacing their penises with what they think are more dependable symbols of it. The respectability they court in each others' company is the novel's cultural phallus—erect, rigid, solid, traditional.

Yoknapatawpha thus defines masculinity as a claim upon one or more of the following: 1. economic viability—ownership; mobility: hence the premium upon horses and wagons, even while the good old boys cannot shake their tethers; 2. mastery at home, which they can perform publicly even if not privately: hence Henry Armstid publicly beats and humiliates his wife when she tries to keep him from buying that diminutive pony; and, finally, 3. actual phallic power and prowess. In an economic and social sense, Yoknapatawpha's men's insufficiency is historically determined by the circumstances into which they are born. In so far as their history, their economic circumstances, keep them from possessing any or all of these marks of masculinity, history renders them impotent.

Thus in the Snopes Trilogy Faulkner tests masculinity not to count the number of erections, since he knew too, as Ratliff puts it, though in another context, that for all her magnificence, Eula is still, in the economic sense, "just galmeat . . . and God knows there was a plenty of that" (*H* 869). Phallic sexuality and its possible failure to satisfy insatiable woman are thus at the core of Yoknapatawpha males' collective and individual lives, the abyss from the edge of which they cannot retreat no matter how many high fives or slaps on the butt. But Eula does not cause their impotence; rather, she provides a backdrop against which their performances of masculinity play themselves out.

How do the men of Yoknapatawpha do on their test? The group on Varner's front porch don't do very well, of course, but they are not, like those city men in Jefferson, really in the race, except in fantasy. But several males in Frenchman's Bend add dimensions to the composite portrait of masculinity in Yoknapatawpha. Hoake McCarron's competitors, the young bucks who also court Eula, simply leave town when they learn that Eula is pregnant—not so much because they fear Varner's wrath, though they do, as because they hope that their fleeing will prove that they indeed are the guilty—i.e., victorious—party and that their fleeing is the sign of their success; the schoolteacher Labove, who, after his humiliatingly abortive attempt to rape Eula in his classroom, wants to believe that his beating or even murder by Jody Varner will prove that he has done that which he did not do. Will Varner, Eula's father, witnesses the hullabaloo his family makes over her pregnancy, and remarks sardonically, in what may be the healthiest and most upbeat statement about female sexuality in the whole trilogy, maybe in the whole Faulkner canon: "What did you expect—that she would spend the rest of her life just running water through it?" (864).

Mink Snopes and Jack Houston, whose confrontation provides one of the novel's, and the trilogy's, important moments, have no connection with Eula at all. Mink is so sexually powerful that when he is summoned to her bed he persuades an insatiable and openly sexual woman to leave her incredible position as the "confident lord of a harem" (953) at the logging camp her father runs, whose workers she summons, at her will, to service her. Faulkner treats their courtship in a series of comic extravagances: the heavy bed she sleeps and loves in nevertheless, when she makes love with Mink, "would advance in short steady skidding jerks across the floor like a light and ill-balanced rocking chair." She marries Mink, leaving the relative affluence of her position at the sawmill for a life as a sharecropper; she even refeminizes herself, letting her hair grow out. She says "I've had a hundred men, but I never had a wasp before. That stuff comes out of you is rank poison. It's too hot. It burns itself and my seed both up. It'll never make a kid" (954), but they have two children. And even the hyper-potent Mink, like the other men of Yoknapatawpha, constantly frets over his wife's fidelity: "By God, they better be mine" (955). But he seems to realize, as they do not, that "even if they were not, it was the same thing. They [the children] served to shackle her too, more irrevocably than he himself was shackled" (955). Like the others, he is jealous of her previous sexual experience: "he was resigned to the jealousy and cognizant of his fate. He had been bred by generations to believe invincibly that to every man, whatever his past actions, whatever depths he might have reached, there was reserved one virgin, at least for him to marry; one maidenhead, if only for him to deflower and destroy. Yet he not only saw that he must compete for mere notice with men among whom he saw himself not only as a child but . . . that when he did approach her at last he would have to tear aside not garments alone but the ghostly embraces of thirty or forty men; and this not only once but each time and hence . . . forever: no room, no darkness, no desert even ever large enough to contain the two of them and the constant stallion-ramp of those inexpugnable shades" (953). Mink's story thus provides Faulkner an occasion to articulate what the other men in Yoknapatawpha seem to feel, though he is not, like them, rendered sexually impotent by what seems to make the others inadequate.

Neither is Jack Houston, Mink's nemesis and murder victim, concerned with Eula, but his story too is instructive. At the opposite end of the economic spectrum from Mink, Jack also flees domesticity, the ever-present Lucy Pate, into a domestic liaison with a prostitute in San Antonio. Like Mink he lives with his paramour's previous sexual experience, not knowing "how much time, just what span of chastity, would constitute purgatorium and absolution, but he would imagine it—some instant, mystical still, when the blight of those nameless and faceless men, the scorched scars of merchandised lust, would be effaced and healed from the organs which she had prostituted" (929). Unlike Mink, however, he cannot conquer those previous lovers, so he allows himself to be drawn back to the almost certainly virginal Lucy, however reluctantly. For a wedding present he gives her a stallion, a symbol of "polygamous and bitless masculinity" (931), as a symbol of his now "bit-ted" masculinity. The horse kills her in a stall; Houston kills the horse in a rage and then buys another stallion which he rides up and down the roads of Yoknapatawpha County, in arrogant and roughshod grief. Mink, of course, can't beat him in an economic confrontation (as he learns when he tries to winter his calf at Jack's expense) but he wins their phallic confrontation by shooting Jack off of that horse with his miserable old uncertain gun.

Only Ratliff and Flem in *The Hamlet* deal successfully with Eula: Ratliff, the perennial bachelor, the constantly mobile sewing-machine salesman, does so by abjuring domesticity, Flem by embracing the signs of domesticity without seeming to worry one way or the other about the sexual.

Ratliff's take on Eula constitutes the bulk of the novel's "meditation" on masculinity and femininity; Gavin Stevens continues it in *The Town* and *The Mansion*. In an important scene, Ratliff thinks about the courting buggies the now-fled young men used to visit Eula in; they evoke in him all of youth's dangerous passion. He is fixated on those buggies. He imagines he sees them still tied to the fence around Varner's yard: "those buggies were still there. He could see them, sense them. Something was [there]; it was too much to have vanished that quickly and completely." The air is "polluted and rich and fine which had flowed over and shaped that abundance and munificence. . . ." "Polluted" is the operative word here, evoking the connection between sexuality and corruption that is so common in Faulkner's work. But the buggies, Ratliff finally understands, are "merely a part of the whole, a minor and trivial adjunct, like the buttons on her clothing," compared to Eula herself: "so why," he wonders, in his most intimate and self-revelatory passage: "so why should not that body at the last have been the unscalable sierra, the rosy virginal mother of barricades for no man to conquer scot-free or even to conquer at all, but on the contrary to be hurled back and down, leaving no scar, no mark of himself." Ratliff almost reproaches himself for not having made his own desperate and futile attempt on that height, even one time, at no matter what cost. But that—the passionate and injurious assault on such an "unscalable sierra"—that, he concludes, "would never have been for him, not even at the prime summer peak of what he and Varner both would have called his tom-catting's heyday." The phrase—"what he and Varner both *would have called*"—argues that Ratliff's "tomcatting heyday" wasn't, as he might put it, no great shakes of a heyday. "He knew," Faulkner tells us, "that without regret or grief, he would not have wanted it to be" for him to assail that height (877).

Ratliff, then, has simply opted out of sexual life. He tries to explain to himself his inadequacy before the likes of Eula—before Woman: "It would have been like giving me a pipe organ, that never had and never would know any more than how to wind up the second-hand music-box I had just swapped a mail-box for," he thinks. He is not jealous of Flem, though, he thinks, because he knows that "regardless of whatever Snopes had expected or would have called what it was he now had, it would not be victory" (877). He is wrong, of course, because he thinks that Flem's relationship to Eula is based in the same sexual anxieties that plague him and the other Frenchman's Bend men. Ratliff thinks that Flem wants the same thing out of marriage that the men of the Bend do, but Flem clearly doesn't. From all we can tell from *The Hamlet* and *The Town*, Flem accepts his cuckolding as a part of Eula's exchange value: what he must pay to possess her, to have her long enough to trade her, as he trades the Old Frenchman place, for whatever he wants to own next.

Ratliff believes that even Eula will grow old and, growing old, fail to measure up to his and every other man's dream of her. At best Flem's marriage will, like all others, succumb to the ordinary; at worst, marriage will be for Flem the same domestic trap it is for every other man. And which best, Ratliff wonders: "to have that word, that dream and hope for future, or to have had need to flee that word and dream, for past" (868). He wants to know whether it is better to have and hold the physical Eula from now on, to live with her in the sorry, imperfect, unbeautiful, mundane give and take of domestic life, to watch her fade and grow old, and to believe, to know that you will not be enough for her sexual needs, that she therefore will be unfaithful? Or to have had her once, as Labove wants her, to have had the passion and the grand release but not the problematics of possession, then to be free of her except as the grandest of perfect and unchanging memories. Labove, of course, does not want her as a wife. He just wants her one time, even knowing that that one time will emasculate him: he wants her "one time as a man with a gangrened hand or foot thirsts after the axe-stroke which will leave him comparatively whole again" (839). That is, like Quentin Compson, he wants the castration that will free him of sexual desire. Ratliff doesn't want her at all; we learn in *The Mansion* that he prefers her perfection: he dedicates one of the rooms of his house to Eula, making it a shrine to her. In *The Hamlet* he believes that Eula has been wasted on Yoknapatawpha County: "What he felt was outrage at the waste, the useless squandering; at a situation intrinsically and inherently wrong by any economy . . . : as though the gods themselves had funnelled all the concentrated bright wet-slanted unparadised June onto a dung-heap, breeding pismires" (877–78).

Like nearly all the other men in Yoknapatawpha County, then, Ratliff measures Eula against his own fear of insufficiency; he is not even courageous enough to try Eula or any other woman, because sexuality is for him, as for Quentin Compson, something "polluted," bestial perhaps, and fraught with peril.[2] Eula is beautiful, he thinks, but behind that beautiful face lurks "only another mortal natural enemy of the masculine race. And beautiful: but then, so did the highwayman's daggers and pistols make a pretty shine on him" (869). Women are the enemy: they steal your life and your soul.

Only Flem Snopes can have Eula Varner in any sense because only he of all the Yoknapatawpha males understands sex as a negotiable, not as an absolute value. Sexual satisfaction itself is no more a part of his agenda than of Sutpen's and he seems to fear neither impotence nor the public knowledge of his cuckolding. Because he is not personally invested in her—or his own—sexual nature, Flem can convert what she represents into currency: he can, that is, commodify her. Indeed, in *The Town* he commodifies his own cuckolding too, making that part of the currency he uses to buy his way into the topmost realms of Jefferson's power structure, becoming both banker and Baptist deacon. Money,

---

2. In *The Hamlet*, Ratliff shuts down the barnyard peep-show that features Ike Snopes and his paramour cow, but not before he watches, long enough to identify with Isaac: "He did look, leaning his face in between two other heads; and it was as though it were himself inside the stall with the cow, himself looking out of the blasted tongueless face at the row of faces watching him who had been given the wordless passions but not the specious words" (913).

respectability, thus contains Eula in ways the men of Frenchman's Bend cannot. She returns from her Texas honeymoon not as Eula, nor even as Eula Varner, but as "Flem Snopes' wife" (*H* 1016).

Faulkner ends the first paragraph of Book II of *The Hamlet*, the book devoted to Eula's disruption of the community, by noting that she "seemed to be not a living integer of her contemporary scene, but rather to exist in a teeming vacuum in which her days followed one another as though behind sound-proof glass, where she seemed to listen in sullen bemusement, with a weary wisdom heired of all mammalian maturity, to the enlarging of her own organs" (817). Near the end of Book II, Ratliff watches her and Flem leave for their honeymoon on the train from the Jefferson station; he observes her as a "calm beautiful mask seen once more beyond a moving pane of glass, then gone" (869); here, indeed, pregnant, her organs are enlarging. The image of her face behind the pane of glass takes us in two directions: first to the back of his buggy where sits a house-shaped box in which he keeps the demonstrator sewing machine model that he sells around the county; painted on all four sides of this house is a window out of which stares a female face. The package suggests the proper place for women, as Ratliff prefers it: contained inside, silent: barefoot and pregnant.

The image also takes us to an especially poignant moment after Flem and Mrs. Snopes return from Texas not just with a baby but with a herd of those wild miniature spotted diminutive symbols of masculinity that the Texan, Buck Hipps, manages to sell at auction to the poor saps of Frenchman's Bend. After the sale, of course, Hipps leaves it to the purchasers to catch and contain the horses they have bought, and during the rest of the evening the pathetic sounds of the chase ring throughout the countryside. When Henry Armstid breaks a leg in the chase, Ratliff and a couple of others bring him to Mrs. Littlejohn's boarding house. She sends them to get Will Varner, who is only a veterinarian, but, she says, he will do for a mule like Armstid. The men walk through the spring moonlight, through the "silver air" which holds all the shouting of the chase:

> They went up the road in a body, treading the moon-blanched dust
> in the tremulous April night murmurous with the moving of sap

and the wet bursting of burgeoning leaf and bud and constant with the thin and urgent cries and the brief and fading bursts of galloping hooves. Varner's house was dark, blank and without depth in the moonlight. They stood, clumped darkly in the silver yard and called up at the blank windows until suddenly someone was standing in one of them. It was Flem Snopes' wife. She was in a white garment; the heavy braided club of her hair looked almost black against it. She did not lean out, she merely stood there, full in the moon, apparently blank-eyed or certainly not looking downward at them—the heavy gold hair, the mask not tragic and perhaps not even doomed: just damned, the strong faint lift of breasts beneath the marblelike fall of the garment; to those below what Brunhilde, what Rhinemaiden on what spurious river-rock of papier-mache, what Helen returned to what topless and shoddy Argos, waiting for no one. (1016–17)

Thus the magnificent Eula: not just finally trimmed of her excess femininity: not just *owned* by Flem Snopes but completely domesticated now, contained as a picture in that window frame. And not merely a painting: the "marblelike fall" of her garment makes her a statue. Brunhilde, Rhinemaiden, even Helen: *waiting for no one*. Goddess turned human turned commodity turned to stone, standing there, a monument to the hegemonic order she had once so completely disrupted. And waiting for no one: how sad no one is worthy of her.

But the dead are not worthy of the living anyhow, and it remains now to note how *The Town* literalizes the metaphor which turns Eula to marble. In the closing pages of that novel, Eula dies from a gunshot through the first beauty parlor coif she has ever had. A good deal of the rest of the novel involves Gavin Stevens's efforts to get her buried properly as the completely respectable wife of a banker and a Baptist deacon. He conspires with Flem Snopes to get an Italian marble mason to create a statue of her out of photographs he sends to Italy; when the statue arrives, he plants it, literally putting Eula on a pedestal, in the Jefferson cemetery. The hard stone cold marble standing over and replacing the vital warm fluid and disruptive body now so lost to the living world becomes a firm hard monument to the masculine culture that has finally shaped her to its own needs: literally, she has become the culture's erection. As Dawn Trouard puts it, Eula arrives at the cemetery,

> where she has always been heading. By the time of *The Town*, Faulkner's sympathies and understanding of what male-female relationships have done to women allow him to get the image right, and in putting a marble nymph in the Jefferson cemetery, he may be offering us his profoundest and most moving rendering of what it must be like to be a sexual female in such as Yoknapatawpha. The marble faun [of Faulkner's first book, of poetry, in 1924, thirty-five years earlier] looks out over a fructive garden whose vital life he cannot participate in; the marble nymph [of *The Town*]—perhaps a more tragically apt symbol of the twentieth century's wasteland than a marble male faun—looks out over a dead dead world of men, and women too, who cannot either accept what she has to offer, sexual or otherwise, or reconcile themselves to their failure of her, and so must force her to join them in the cemetery. ("Eula's Plot" 295)

In one sense, of course, masculinity does *not* fail the tests Faulkner and Eula administer, since so clearly it wins at least this particular skirmish by overriding and banishing and replacing the teacher. It finally sets her, immovable, fixed, and visible, on the pedestal of its admiration of itself, forcing her to tell and retell its own narrative of sexual and communal order and control. Eula thus *becomes* the community's phallus. Masculinity finally does fail, however, hoist on the very petard by which it defines itself, the erect phallus, the totem structure and the totem spirit of patriarchy. Soft and malleable, men cannot be men, so they erect marble monuments to hardness. If we are only soft, we are not men; but only erect, only rigid and inflexible, we preside over a cemetery.

Pity the poor penis, then, defunctive ever, since though to be sure tumescence is blood and pride, it is need most of all: an emptiness, a begging not a boast, a prostration not a victory, and obeisance is its end. Was ever such an abyss between a signifier and all its attendant signifieds as that between penis and phallus? It's more than any six inches, or twelve either, can or should be asked to bear. Erect or not, it signifies *too much*, because we think only in the mutually exclusive binary terms of hard or soft, up or down, in or out, success or failure. We cannot think of the penis's corporeal existence as simple meat, as an appendage to the body, but rather make the body the appendage that always fears the contemptuous dismissal in the dread word *impotence*, as though the penis were the source of power rather than its crude and inefficient symbol.

Masculine identity in Faulkner, then, defines and destroys itself at one end or the other of the continuum between hard and soft, because it cannot locate for itself a safeplace somewhere between hard and soft that would allow masculinity the more fluid life that women have and which men fear.[3] In Faulkner, sex is almost never joyful and pleasure is seldom the operative issue in sexual relationships. For his men sex is mostly a duty, a heavy responsibility to convention and tradition (and, for sharecroppers at any rate, a necessary economic activity: marriages must produce additional laborers for the cottonfields). Focussed on the rigid, the singular, the simple, the powerful, the successful—the hard—, men in Faulkner cannot experience the jouissance, the frictive multiplicities and complexities that women, even those who are not Eula Varner, not even those of our dreams but those at our sides, offer: who also too often wait for no one.

---

3. See Trouard's use of Luce Irigaray to explicate the Snopes Trilogy.

Reading Blood and History in
Go Down, Moses

I saac McCaslin's renunciation of his birthright is an iconic moment in American literature. Early critics accepted the renunciation as a heroic act—and therefore accepted Isaac as Faulkner's hero—because the language of his renunciation fit the high idealism of the time that believed that Jim Crow racism was a plague on the land and that Isaac's sacrifice was Faulkner's answer to it. Later critics, noting how little effect Isaac's act had on the condition he sought to cure, concluded that he was a failed hero whose noble intentions and high sentence failed to alter the stark realities of racism. But though re-assessing the practical effects of Isaac's act, no one seriously questioned the sincerity or the nobility of his intentions; and nobody in the fifty or sixty years of serious Faulkner criticism has suggested that Isaac's reading of the ledgers or his accusations against his grandfather are anything but Gospel Truth.

In the spring of 2002 Richard Godden and I published a longish essay in which we argued that Isaac's reading of those family ledgers is rather a deliberate if not completely conscious misreading of a document that provides him the excuse he needs to renounce. It's a misreading not completely conscious because of a crucial fact about his father that he tries to but cannot suppress from his reading, a fact both hidden and revealed in the ledgers.

Perhaps the single most curious entries in the ledgers are those that report on Percival Brownlee, the only slave either of the twins, Isaac's father and uncle, ever bought, and an "anomaly," as Faulkner calls him, in more ways than one. He is, we infer from Buddy's naming him "Spintrius" at the conclusion of the episode, a flagrant, even flaming, homosexual, and the ledgers make it pretty clear that that is why Buck, Isaac's father-to-be, buys him in the first place and tries to keep him even after he understands that Brownlee doesn't justify the $265 he paid for him. Further, the ledgers and "Was," the novel's opening chapter, permit us to infer that Buck and Buddy are themselves incestuous homosexual lovers and that Brownlee's advent causes what amounts to a lover's quarrel between them, a quarrel conducted in the ledgers and suggested by the periods of sometimes up to several weeks between entries in the ledgers that seem to indicate that they dont otherwise communicate with each other at all. Faulkner leads into the Brownlee materials through Isaac's consciousness by noting that by this time the twins write in the ledgers because they were "past all oral intercourse," a phrase that to be sure might be completely innocent, but which, in the context of Brownlee and several other circumstances, simply refuses to be erased.

Isaac, of course, claims to renounce his patrimony because he adduces from the ledgers what he claims is incontrovertible proof that his patriarch grandfather L.Q.C. McCaslin committed incest upon his own daughter by a slave woman. The ledgers, however, provide no such proof, nor does family lore. Isaac instead ekes out this interpretation from bits of information that his father and uncle have inscribed in the ledgers in their almost identical hands, pieces of information that may or may not be related. The first entry is in his father's handwriting: *"Eunice Bought by Father in new Orleans 1807 $650. dollars. Marrid to Thucydus 1809 Drownd in Crick Cristmas Day 1832."* Six months later Buddy enters a sharply laconic note that calls Eunice a suicide: *"Drowned herself,"* he writes, and we are left to wonder what in the six months following her death has led Buddy to conclude that she was a suicide and, if he had thought so at any earlier point, why he waited six months to write it down and why he wrote it down at all. Is he for some reason absolving or accusing somebody on the plantation of murdering Eunice? is he protecting their father? himself? his brother? Thucydus, her husband? We simply cannot tell from the ledgers. Two days later Buck forcefully, perhaps angrily, asserts that she could not have been a suicide by appealing to what he would have considered Negro nature: "*Who in hell ever heard of a niger drownding himself,*" a question whose premise is contradicted by the evidence of Negro suicide, or contemplation of it, in "Pantaloon in Black" and "The Fire and the Hearth." Buck waits nearly two months before responding, then repeats himself categorically in a tone that brooks no argument: "*Drownd herself*" (197). We and Isaac are left to wonder what minimal portion of anguish, recrimination, or even simple grief the brothers record here, but we cannot know from the ledgers how Eunice drowned or why Buck is as adamant that it was not suicide as Buddy is that it was, or why it seems to matter one way or the other. We can't even know from the ledgers whether the twins talk about that or about anything else during these days as they go about the business of running the plantation. They are, remember, "past all oral intercourse." Nor do we know whether Isaac gives us everything that passes between them in the ledgers: if he does not, we may well wonder why he isolates this data from whatever else he chooses to suppress.

Isaac seems not to worry overmuch about this apparent friction between his father and uncle but jumps straight to two other entries which satisfy him that Eunice was a suicide and, moreover, which supply her a motive. The text treats his discovery of this motive as a foregone conclusion: "He knew what he was going to find before he found it" (198): "*Tomasina,*" he reads, "*called Tomy Daughter of Thucydus & Eunice Born 1810 dide in Child bed June 1833 and Burd. Yr stars fell*" (198). The other entry records the birth of Turl, the son born to Tomy's fatal childbed. Isaac links the two entries in a cause-effect relationship and makes his case against L.Q.C. If Tomy gave birth at full term in June 1833, then on Christmas day 1832 she would have been around three months pregnant and showing sufficiently for the truth of her condition to be known. Though the ledgers give no indication who fathered Turl, Isaac reads the words "*Fathers will*" as the legal document whereby his grandfather leaves Turl $1000 and concludes that his grandfather had sired Turl on his own daughter Tomy.

The ledgers, thus interpreted, answer all of Isaac's questions but raise numerous others for us. How does Isaac know what's he's going to find before he finds it? Why does he *need* to find what he knows he's going to find? Put simply, he knows that it will not be easy to renounce the land, because by doing so he will simultaneously renounce the patrimony his by right as the direct blood descendant of his grandfather and he knows all the powers of reason and tradition that will be leagued against him to keep him from renouncing. He needs, and finds, a compelling reason situated in the loftiest moral ground he can locate. To justify what he wants to do he must paint his family's patriarch in the worst possible terms, to make him as morally reprehensible as the worse excesses of the slave system allow, so that he can renounce from the highest possible moral ground. He takes on himself the mantel of Jesus by becoming a carpenter; he takes on Moses, too, telling himself and Cass that by renouncing he can set the Negroes free. He does more as well: he renounces his own history, believing that he can simply sidestep both those historical forces represented by what he accuses his grandfather of doing, which he can face and think about, and those more sinister, more powerful and more immediate forces, represented by his father, which he can't face or think about, but must repress. Curiously, in his argument with Cass he fails to mention his grandfather's sin even once. We have to wonder why. Perhaps it's simply that he fears that Cass, who lived with Buck and Buddy, knows more about his father and Percival Brownlee than the ledgers tell and so might give him the lie and thereby invalidate the reason to renounce he creates for himself out of his reading. Except for the ledgers, Cass is Isaac's primary source for his family history and he may fear that invoking his grandfather here will prompt Cass to invoke his father. Those forces represented by his father work on him more powerfully than those of his grandfather: they represent what he is really renouncing, no matter what he tells Cass or himself.

Given the number and kinds of erotic attachments between his heterosexual siblings it should not surprise us to find Faulkner pushing his male twins toward incestuous homoerotics, especially when we understand incestuous twins as the last logical, perhaps inevitable, step, the reduction ad absurdum, for those who fear blood contamination and the impurity—southerners, and others, called it amalgamation and mongrelization—that blood mixing implies. A family that insists upon pure blood, whatever that means, in effect insists on its own extinction, closing itself off through endogamy first (cousins and nieces and nephews) then through sibling incest, then twins of the opposite sex, as in Poe, then twins of the same sex, and finally the sterile isolation of masturbation.

That's the dilemma faced by landowners in the western patriarchal tradition. It may be the fundamental flaw in Thomas Sutpen's failed attempt at dynasty: it's at least among the cultural principles assumed by *Absalom*'s several narrators and generations of critics. That principle assumes a direct and proper connection between blood and property; the lineal co-transmission of blood and patrimony is one of the several markers of regional history in the West, so twinned in the cultural mind are property and blood. Such considerations have appeared in Faulkner long before *Go Down, Moses*, though *Go Down, Moses* presents them in a context which foregrounds them and by doing so provides a larger context for understanding incest in the earlier Faulkner: the vague eroticization of the relationship between the young Bayard Sartoris and his twin brother John in *Flags in the Dust*; the lugubrious incestuous feelings between Horace and his sister Narcissa Benbow in *Flags* and *Sanctuary*; the equally lugubrious and apparently incestuous longings[1] of Quentin Compson for his sister and perhaps even of Mrs. Compson and her brother Maury in *The Sound and the Fury*. *Absalom* addresses the issue in Mr. Compson's narration when he describes the triangular relationship between Henry, Judith, and Charles Bon as "the perfect incest," since Henry, he believes, thinks he can take his sister's "virginity in the person of the brother-in-law, the man whom he would be if he could become, metamorphose into, the lover, the husband; by whom he would be despoiled, choose for despoiler, if he could become, metamorphose into the sister, the mistress, the bride" (80). There's a serious component of homoeroticism in this triangle, of course, as there is in the Quentin-Caddy-Dalton Ames triangle in *The Sound and the*

---

1. But see "How Shreve Gets in to Quentin's Pants" in this volume.

Fury. But *Absalom* addresses the connection between incest and patriarchy more particularly when Quentin and Shreve have Henry justify his longing for Judith by specific reference to that tradition: "But kings have done it! Even dukes! There was that Lorraine duke named John something that married his sister. The Pope excommunicated him but it didn't hurt! It didn't hurt! They were still husband and wife. They were still alive. They still loved!" (281).

Which is better—pure blood or extinction of the line? In some ways the question is moot, of course, since according to Cass there is no such thing as pure blood, as he tells Isaac in "The Old People" when he's explaining Sam Father's origins as the son of an Indian chief and a quadroon slave, a combination that gives him mathematically one-eighth white blood, if we assume that's all that's in the mix. The white blood, Cass tells Isaac, renders white people aliens in the Big Woods, while Sam's predominant "blood on both sides . . . knew things that had been tamed out of our own [white] blood so long ago that we have not only forgotten them, we have to live together in herds to protect ourselves from our own sources" (124). Cass doesn't seem bothered by his own blood's impurity, but his statement claims the civilizing and therefore superior influence of white blood and admits that "civilization" is essentially a white gathering in cities to deny and escape the influence of that part of white people's makeup which is not white because it got bleached out over the centuries of transmission.

Cass's argument is a somewhat less terrifying version of what Shreve says near the end of *Absalom*, when he makes the inflammatory prediction that causes Quentin's famous response that ends the novel. When Shreve asks, "Why do you hate the South?" he throws the reality of miscegenation in Quentin's face, not from the past, as Cass does, but from the future, where the mixing of bloods becomes not a temporary fear of white southerners but a fact of genetic life: he says "I think that in time the Jim Bonds are going to conquer the western hemisphere. Of course it wont quite be in our time and of course as they spread toward the poles they will bleach out again like the rabbits and the birds do, so they wont show up sharp against the snow. But it will still be Jim Bond; and so in a few thousand years, I who regard you will also have sprung from the loins of African kings" (311).

I have tried for years to understand what Shreve and Faulkner mean and why Quentin's response to the question is so haunting to white southerners: "*I dont hate it,*" Quentin thinks: "*I dont. I dont! I dont hate it! I dont hate it!*" (311). I've failed to understand it because I've approached the question rationally, while Shreve's prediction and question and Quentin's response speak directly to the irrational terror with which white southerners have regarded the specter of amalgamation. I could think only that in Shreve's future, blackness would constantly diminish and then finally extinguish itself with whitening, and that difference itself would disappear. But the fear is precisely the loss of difference. What southerners, doubtless not just southerners, fear is tied up in Cass's description of our mixed beginnings; no matter how white we are, no matter how white the ancestors, whites fear that some residual drop of black blood, perpetuated through some inextinguishable half-life of blackness that will never be obliterated, no matter how many times halved or quartered or eighthed or sixteenthed, will lie there always, recessive but waiting like a bomb to explode at some inconvenient reproductive moment: difference obliterated finally by that very one-drop rule that whites invented to describe and maintain difference. At this remove from slavery and Jim Crow we can more easily see what arbitrary and malicious categories "black" and "white" are and we know what woe they have worked and continue to work.

Racism is thus in *Go Down, Moses* tied to whites' deep repressed knowledge that no matter how white our skin we share ancestors with the slaves and their descendants whom we have patronized exploited and murdered. Even poor Isaac, our Moses, finally admits, in "Delta Autumn," that this is at the bottom of his rejection of the nearly white woman, Roth Edmond's kin and lover and the mother of his child, a rejection that specifically repudiates his repudiation of the land by denying the high idealism by which, he tells himself, he has led his life. When he discovers, not through her skin color but through her ancestry, that the woman is part black he tells her that it is not yet the right time for blacks to be free: go to Chicago and "marry a black man," he says, and leave the South and white southerners alone. She repudiates him with a stinging rebuke that evokes a love, a passion, that cuts across all racial divides and which is singularly missing from Isaac's life. Roth's example might even allow us to read backward in to old Carothers' case and conclude that perhaps there was love there too, not just exploitation.

The woman leaves Isaac lying on his bunk meditating, retreating first to his innermost self to admit and then immediately deny how accurately she has hit home, and through a logic we can now understand connect the rapidly shrinking big woods directly to the issue of blood and race mixing:

> "This Delta, he thought: "This Delta. *This land which man has deswamped and denuded and derivered in two generations so that white men can own plantations and commute every night to Memphis and black men own plantations and ride in jim crow cars to Chicago to live in millionaires' mansions on Lakeshore Drive, where white men rent farms and live like niggers and niggers crop on shares and live like animals, where cotton is planted and grows man-tall in the very cracks of the sidewalks, and usury and mortgage and bankruptcy and measureless wealth,* Chinese and African and Aryan and Jew, all breed and spawn together until no man has time to say which one is which nor cares. . . ."* (269, my underlined emphasis)

Even Isaac, self-deluded champion of black humanity, self-appointed to set them free, cannot free himself of that all-important difference.

Isaac's quarrel with his grandfather is a quarrel with many of the elements of his own personal history that render him uncomfortable, to put it mildly, in his own skin. When he argues with Cass, trying to convince him that he is right to renounce, he argues from a lofty construction of history that is far indeed from his quarrel with Old Carothers. He creates a cockamamie teleology about God's intentions with regard to the subjugated race, a teleology that begins with the "old world's corrupt and worthless twilight" and works its way inexorably through America's promise corrupted by slavery and land ownership, through the debacle of the Civil War, God's design for raising the "white man's curse" from the land, then on through the end of the War and in to Reconstruction: God's purpose, Isaac claims, is an unstoppable juggernaut headed directly at him:

—and no hope for the land anywhere so long as Ikkemotubbe and Ikkemotubbe's descendants held it in unbroken succession. Maybe He saw that only by voiding the land for a time of Ikkemotubbe's blood and substituting it for another blood, could He accomplish his purpose. Maybe He knew already what that other blood would be, maybe it was more than justice that only the white man's blood was available and capable to raise the white man's curse, more than vengeance . . . when He used the blood which had brought in the evil to destroy the evil as doctors use fever to burn up fever, poison to slay poison. Maybe he chose Grandfather out of all of them He might have picked. Maybe He knew that Grandfather himself would not serve His purpose because Grandfather was born too soon too, but that Grandfather would have descendants, the right descendants; maybe He had foreseen already the descendants Grandfather would have, maybe He saw already in Grandfather the seed progenitive of the three generations He saw it would take to set at least some of His lowly people free— (191–92)

Maybe, he says, God saw *me*.

Cass counters that history is not determined by God or Telos since so much of what happens happens by chance—especially in the Civil War when, for example, Longstreet one night gets accidentally shot out of his saddle by his own men—that it is impossible to find a design and therefore a purpose in history. This is of course an ancient argument and not resolvable. But much in Isaac's own life, his own history, confirms Cass's side of the debate. For example, though he reveres Sam Fathers' lineage as an "old dark man sired on both sides by savage kings" (122), Isaac conveniently forgets that Sam's own father, Ikkemotubbe, became king—the man, Doom—through intimidation and a palace coup, as it were; he forgets that more is at work in history than the simple transmission of blood. But a good deal of Isaac's life is at odds with his teleological views, views he has obviously developed to keep from having to talk about his real reasons for stepping aside. What's in Isaac's blood?

The novel's first chapter, "Was," is a story about the "courtship" of Isaac's and Lucas Beauchamp's parents. It's a comic story, told to him by his cousin Cass, who was sixteen years old and participated in the episode; we dont know how many times or whether Cass ever told it other than as a comic portrait of Isaac's problematic parents-to-be. Cass's tone in the telling must have had a profound effect on Isaac, especially if Cass's tone always included ridicule of Isaac's mother, whom Cass depicts as a Southern belle out of some outlandish parody of *Gone with the Wind*: a foolish roan-toothed old maid playing the coquette out to get married and conniving with Turl to trap Buck. Though there seems to be some communal sense on the plantation and in the surrounding world that Buck and Buddy are a domestic couple, it is hard to know how much of his father's homosexuality Cass imparts to Isaac, but "Was" hints at it in pretty broad strokes. Cass's depiction of the twins allows the possibility of their homosexual relationship that part 4's Percival Brownlee episode more strongly argues. He depicts Buddy as the feminized cook and keeper of the house and kitchen while Buck, since he does sire Isaac, may be bisexual. In "Was," Buck escapes being trapped into marriage with Sophonsiba by Uncle Buddy's bluff and the turn of a card in the poker game. That is, Buck escapes this time, but the title of an early version of this narrative, "Almost," allows us to speculate that at a later date the trap worked, the cards fell against him, and that he did indeed have to marry Sophonsiba. The entire narrative argues the improbability that Isaac should even have been conceived at all, much less that all of Western history had its eye on him. And though Faulkner never gives us any portraits of life in that family (Buck dies when Isaac is seven; Sophonsiba before he turns ten), it seems hardly likely that his experiences of life in his few short years in a problematically heterosexual domestic atmosphere could have promoted in him either tranquility or any healthy sense of either the masculine or the feminine or even of sexuality itself.

The one hint we get of Isaac's life before he began hunting occurs when he and his mother catch Uncle Hubert *in flagrante delicto* with a black woman, catch him committing the same sin, at least the miscegenation part of it, that he accuses his grandfather of and, at least partly thanks to his mother's over-reaction, he first confronts sexuality as something shameful and miscegenous. If this is not strictly a "primal" scene in the Freudian sense, it functions as one to the extent that it provides a partially-repressed memory of a childhood trauma that marks his consciousness forever; it is the only such scene of his family life that Faulkner gives us, and it is suggestive. Here, already, is the miscegenation that Isaac repudiates in his grandfather, accompanied by his mother's shrieks of condemnation and shame, shrieks which, arguably, Isaac takes into himself, absorbs, and never forgets, as he never forgets the "exciting and evocative" (225) black mistress. The scene may thus suggest a pathology for Isaac. Part of his revulsion from a compounding of his family's miscegenation is precisely his attraction to it: he rejects in his family what he so fears and loathes in himself.

Further, Uncle Hubert gives to him at his birth a silver cup filled with gold coins which he keeps more or less publicly hidden behind a loose brick in the hearth. Perhaps he keeps it there more for its being handy than hidden, however, since he, Hubert, takes from it over the years, leaving Isaac at twenty-one with a tin coffee pot and a handful of IOUs: a fit emblem of the promissory notes from his McCaslin antededents that he thinks he has so gingerly sidestepped. From the McCaslins Isaac receives not even IOUs but merely their blood, since he has repudiated everything else.

About Isaac's blood there may be another skein. Nearly at the close of part 4 of "The Bear" Faulkner introduces a curious new character. Buck and Buddy are dead (226) and Hubert lives "in the almost completely empty house," Warwick, with "Tennie's ancient and quarrelsome great-grandfather" (226). We do not know where the great-grandfather comes from, but given his connection to Tennie we may assume that he is a Beauchamp too. Faulkner seems clearly to be suggesting some sort of intimate family connection. His brief appearance complicates Isaac's ancestry: Isaac is, we learn from Hubert's IOU, "Isaac Beauchamp McCaslin" (227), so that he already shares a name and lineage with the black Beauchamps long before he "discovers" how his McCaslin ancestors have supplied him with a black McCaslin family. That Hubert and the old man "lived, cooked and slept in one single room" may seem to hint at a relationship like that of Buck and Buddy, though the difference in their ages probably argues against a homosexual relationship (he is old enough to "claim to have seen La Fayette" [226]); and, indeed, perhaps they merely live together so that the old man can care for Hubert if he is black, or vice-versa if he is not; Faulkner does not tell us the old man's race, though their living together might argue that he is white.

Is the old man Hubert's great-grandfather too? At the very least, their living together supposes a very close relationship, perhaps a blood connection, which would therefore imply a blood connection between himself, Sophonsiba, and Tennie, and also, therefore, between Isaac and Tennie. As Tennie's great-grandfather, the old man is of the generation of L.Q.C.'s father. The possible blood connection makes it reasonable to speculate that at least part of Sophonsiba's horrified reaction to Hubert's dalliance with his black lover is that her brother repeats his own ancestor's acts of miscegenation. It may also permit speculation about the genetic mix of Isaac's blood. I can discover no other reason for Tennie's great-grandfather to be introduced here than to suggest something of this sort to us or to Isaac. Perhaps Isaac fears that one drop or more in his own allotment which will one day out him or his children; as a child he's likely to be confused about his parents, since it is almost certainly Tennie, the object of Tomey's Turl's amatory visits to the Beauchamp plantation, his nursemaid and nanny, who represents mother to him: she presides over his waking consciousness from the moment he is born and almost until he dies; and finally re-appears, presiding over Isaac's final humiliation, in the person of Tennie's granddaughter, the young woman Isaac shuns in "Delta Autumn." Likewise, he may also fear that in his blood is his father's homosexuality: when he begins to add to the ledgers he notes how his own handwriting resembles his grandfather's "queerly" (202), a word that in context simply refuses to be erased, as Isaac's sense that by the time his father and uncle were writing in the ledgers they were "past all oral intercourse." If we accept the possibility of their homosexual relationship, we may have a better sense of the historical baggage Isaac doesn't want to inherit. Depending on which side of the color line his one drop falls, he may be black and queer: no wonder he is terrified of history and wants out.

Of course blood is but a metaphor for genetics, a hope that claims, and hopes to impose, a direct and undeviating connection with the most ancient of our antecedents. I like Jay Watson's argument that in *Light in August* Faulkner *de-figures* blood by separating its literal from its figural functions, forces its literal meaning on us through a variety of bloods: bleeding genitals, male and female, Joanna's cut throat, Joe's castration, and Joe's sacrificed lamb. The hunting portions of *Go Down, Moses* begin with a splash of literal blood, that that Sam Fathers wipes across Isaac's ten-year-old face after he has shot his first buck. Faulkner thus notes, right up front, that history is made by spilled blood as well as by that contained and transmitted biologically. It is also significant that the blood Sam splashes on him is from a "buck"—symbolically the blood of his own father, also a "Buck."

Blood courses fiercely through Isaac's thoughts as he renounces and then lives with the results. I've already noted that though he reveres Sam Fathers as "an old dark man sired on both sides by savage kings," he forgets that Sam's father, Ikkemotubbe, became king through intimidation and murder of his own kin: another blood, another history, appropriated violently, which he of course hopes to pass on to his own descendants. Nor does Isaac seem to understand that the characters in his world who have mixed blood—Lucas Beauchamp, Tennie Beauchamp, Sam Fathers, Boon Hogganbeck, and even the mongrel dog Lion—are the strongest and most able, even the most admirable and the most worthy of his love and discipleship. But his admiration of these figures comes at an exorbitant price, as Roth's beloved tots up the cost when she responds to Isaac's feeble offer of Roth's money: "Old man," she excoriates him, "have you lived so long and forgotten so much that you dont remember anything you ever knew or felt or even heard about love?" (268).

Closing his discussion with Cass, his final shot, as it were, Isaac invokes his wilderness heritage by claiming that "Sam Fathers set me free"—set him free, that is, from history: a problematic claim if only because the last thing Fathers in Faulkner ever do is set their sons free.

Isaac's case occurs in a disconnect between blood and history: he can halt the transmission of his blood but not of his history. In passing on Roth's blood money and the hunting horn to Roth's lover, he becomes history's slave, not its master. No matter his good intentions, he fears the loss of his difference. In renouncing, he tries to protect himself from his sources.

It seems clear, then, that Isaac doesn't want to free the Negro; he wants to free himself of the poker hand that history has given to him and to save his children from a tainted heritage. Yet how can Negroes ever be free of us or we of them, he might think darkly, when we are so inextricably linked? But that link to otherness is precisely what he wants to escape, a link that could well supply the salvation for himself and his beloved South that renunciation never could. But the only salvation from blood or history is never to be born at all. Though Isaac claims to want a son, it's easy to feel that he'd really rather not: that he'd really rather be *Uncle* Ike, not *daddy*: Uncle Ike to half the county—and father to no one.

Faulkner and the Commies

I begin by noting three scenes in *The Unvanquished*. The first occurs a couple of pages into the second part of "Retreat," the second of *The Unvanquished*'s chapter-stories. Bayard and Ringo, in Jefferson for supplies for their trip to Memphis, encounter Uncle Buck McCaslin. Buck, whom we know far better from *Go Down, Moses*, had served under Bayard's father, John Sartoris, in the regiment Sartoris and Thomas Sutpen had raised and taken to fight in Virginia. Because Buck will play a significant part in the boys' lives over the course of this narrative, Bayard takes a couple of pages to introduce him and his twin brother Buddy as practitioners of a new social philosophy: "Father said" that they

> were ahead of their time; he said they not only possessed, but put into practice, ideas about social relationships that maybe fifty years after they were both dead people would have a name for. These ideas were about land. They believed that land did not belong to people but that people belonged to land and that the earth would permit them to live on and out of it and use it only so long as they behaved and that if they did not behave right, it would shake them off just like a dog getting rid of fleas. They had some kind of a system of book-keeping which must have been even more involved than their

betting score against one another, by which all their niggers were to be freed, not given freedom, but earning it, buying it not in money from Uncle Buck and Buddy, but in work from the plantation. Only there were others besides niggers. . . .

These "others" are

dirt farmers, the people whom the niggers called 'white trash'—men who had owned no slaves and some of whom even lived worse than the slaves on big plantations. It was another side of Uncle Buck's and Buddy's ideas about men and land, which Father said people didn't have a name for yet, by which Uncle Buck and Buddy had persuaded the white men to pool their little patches of poor hill land along with the niggers and the McCaslin plantation, promising them in return nobody knew exactly what, except that their women and children did have shoes, which not all of them had had before, and a lot of them even went to school. (351–52)

The second scene occurs close to the end of part 2 of "Riposte in Tertio." Granny returns to Brother Fortinbride's church to share with the church members, and any others, her profits from her project of "requisitioning" mules from and then selling them back to the Yankees. Her method of "sharing" is curious, to say the least: "Bring the book," she says:

It was a big blank account book; it weighed almost fifteen pounds; they opened it on the reading desk, Granny and Ringo side by side, while Granny drew the tin can out of her dress and spread the money on the book. But nobody moved until she began to call out the names. Then they came up one at a time, while Ringo read the names off the book, and the date, and the amount they had received before. Each time Granny would make them tell what they intended to do with the money; and now she would make them tell her how they had spent it, and she would look at the book to see whether they had lied or not. And the ones that she had loaned the brand blotted mules that Ab Snopes was afraid to try to sell would have to tell her how the mule was getting along and how much work it had done; and now and then she would take the mule away from one man or woman and give it to another, tearing up the old receipt and making the man or the woman sign the new one, telling them on what day to go and get the mule. (413)

The "reading table" seems clearly the church's pulpit, so that "the book" becomes "the Bible," the word of "God" and the source of His—and Granny's—authority on earth.

These two seemingly disparate scenes have in common three characters' mutual but apparently uncoordinated presumption to organize working people obviously disenfranchised by the War into units dependent on their bounty to supply them with necessities for living. Granny's charity, if we may call it that, is particularly patronizing and offensive because it requires the dispossessed working folks publicly to accept her bounty and publicly to endure her contumely if for some reason they do not fulfill their part of the contract implied in their acceptance of the bounty. The language of her distribution of these goods is weighty with her power over them: she would "*make* them tell," they "would *have* to tell her," she would "*take*," "*give* it," "*making* the man or woman," "*telling* them." At best it's an officious and moralistic form of charity. To be sure, sharing these ill-gotten goods may be her penance for lying and stealing and for involving Bayard and Ringo in those activities too: even if it is part of the War effort, it is still immoral to lie and steal, as she argues, even from Yankees.

What Granny gets out of her "sharing," then, is a somewhat cleaner conscience and, not incidentally, a restoration to what she would consider her rightful place in a class structure that the War threatens to turn upside down: the Yankees have burned the plantation and left the white Sartorises to share Loosh and Philadelphy's slave cabin and so in effect become slaves in the new social order. The McCaslin twins, for their part, use the males of the families they have helped shoe and feed and educate as a mediæval lord used his serfs: as cannon fodder, soldiers expendable to their own larger purposes. Though nobody knows "exactly" what Uncle Buck and Buddy have promised them, Buck seems certain that he can form them into a company to oppose the one that Bayard's father, John Sartoris, is forming if Sartoris doesn't let them join his regiment: "They told Father that if he did not let them go, the solid bloc of private soldier white trash votes which they controlled would not only force Father to call a special election of officers before the regiment left the pasture, it would also demote Father from colonel to major or maybe only a company commander" (352). Clearly, Buck and Buddy have a political and military interest in the worker-serfs no less patronizing and perhaps even more exploitative than Granny's (since they expect their workers to die in battle) and have no compunction about extorting loyalty from them and then using it to their own ends. Father says that Buck and Buddy are "ahead of their time" and have "put into practice, ideas about social relationship that maybe fifty years after they were both dead people would have a name for," ideas which "people didn't have a name for yet." Maybe so, but Karl Marx and Frederich Engels had published their most important book in 1848 and did in fact give a name to what Buck and Buddy, and Granny in her own way, were practicing: Communism.

The third scene has a slightly more complex relationship to these scenes and to the rest of *The Unvanquished*. In "An Odor of Verbena," Drusilla tells Bayard's about his father's dream of an ideal world, to explain his propensity for using violence to settle political and economic matters. His father, she tells Bayard, "is thinking of this whole country which he is trying to raise by its bootstraps, so that all the people in it, not just his kind nor his old regiment, but all the people, black and white, the women and children back in the hills who dont even own shoes—Dont you see?" Bayard is confused: "But how can they get any good from what he wants to do for them if they are—after he has—" he says. Drusilla responds: "Killed some of them? I suppose you include those two carpet baggers he had to kill to hold that first election, dont you?" When he argues that "They were men. Human beings," Drusilla responds coldbloodedly:

> They were northerners, foreigners who had no business here. They were pirates. . . . A dream is not a very safe thing to be near, Bayard. I know; I had one once. It's like a loaded pistol with a hair trigger: if it stays alive long enough, somebody is going to be hurt. But if

it's a good dream, it's worth it. There are not many dreams in the
world, but there are a lot of human lives. And one human life or two
dozen—"

"Are not worth anything?" [Bayard asks].

Drusilla concludes, laconically: "No. Not anything . . ." (471).

All four self-proclaimed "reformers"—Buck, Buddy, Granny, and
John Sartoris—speak a common language, the language of their dream
of community among the poor, the displaced and dispossessed workers
of the South, black and white. If the new ideas about land ownership
and social relations that John Sartoris doesn't have a name for yet is
Communism, Faulkner has written in to *The Unvanquished* a current
political dimension that we haven't quite noticed yet if only because
we haven't quite yet taken this book seriously enough. It could be that
John Sartoris actually does know the name but for some reason doesn't
want to use it. Marx and Engels published *The Communist Manifesto* in
1848 in German; its first English translation appeared in London two
years later, and it would not have been the oddest of the volumes in
John Sartoris's library, which include, among other oddities, a "thousand and ninety-eight page treatise on astrology" and a "History of
Werewolf Men in England, Ireland and Scotland and Including Wales
by the Reverend Ptolemy Thorndyke, M.A. (Edinburgh)" (330)—a list
which proves only that he did have books from England and could have
had others. But it's to no purpose to demonstrate whether Father, or
Faulkner, had in fact read Marx and Engels; perhaps Faulkner finessed
the problem and saved himself some research by claiming that the ideas
did not yet have a name. What is to the purpose is to argue that in these
three scenes and in Father's description of those new ideas Faulkner
writes in to *The Unvanquished* a reaction to American intellectuals' dalliance with the Communist Party in the twenties and thirties in order
to explore the social and political consequences of a singleminded commitment to ideological purity.

He does so by proposing certain rough, inexact parallels between the
social and economic convulsions of the American Civil War and those
of the Russian Revolution, both of which threatened to overthrow the
ruling classes and to replace them with a classless, landless, and property-

less world in which everybody would be equal, would have all they needed, and would always work for the common good. In *The Unvanquished*, to that same inexact extent, Faulkner's re-writes Reconstruction, placing it in a worldwide historical context: the language of both revolutions was the language of freedom and equality; leaders of both revolutions used that language to rally and mold the masses. But, revolution accomplished, even the highest-minded leaders in the South and in Russia discovered that power, like nature, abhors a vacuum and that since power is the only stay against chaos, even a classless society must have leaders to provide cohesion; leaders become privileged because of their increased responsibilities. In Russia the revolution finally devolved not into a change of system so much as a change of the language used to describe the system. Under the leadership of Lenin and then Stalin Russia quickly turned back into a system like the Tsarist one they had been rescued from, except that it was a decades-long nightmare more terrifying and bloodier by millions of corpses than the tsar could have ever imagined, even if the language was nicer. Likewise, no revolution took place in the United States. Almost nothing changed but the language used to describe the world: slavery became sharecropping, a draconian form of economic peonage.

In the South of *The Unvanquished*, Faulkner's revolutionaries are the slaves, of course, inspired by the language of freedom, and typified by the firebreathing Loosh, who destroys Bayard and Ringo's mockup of the battle of Vicksburg in order to celebrate its final capitulation to Grant on July 4, 1863. In an often-quoted passage, Loosh articulates to Granny his own sense of who owns what and whom when Granny remonstrates with him as he tries to take some Sartoris silver with him as he leaves:

> "I going. I done been freed; God's own angel proclaimed me free and gonter general me to Jordan. I dont belong to John Sartoris now; I belongs to me and God."
>
> "But the silver belongs to John Sartoris," Granny said. "Who are you to give it away?"
>
> "You ax me that?" Loosh said. "Where John Sartoris? Whyn't he come and ax me that? Let God ax John Sartoris who the man

name that give me to him. Let the man that buried me in the black
dark ax that of the man what dug me free." (369–70)

These are issues, a point of view, that obviously Granny has never con-
sidered. So she drops the conversation and appeals unsuccessfully to
Philadelphy, Loosh's wife, not to go with him, but to stay with her.

Loosh heads toward Jordan, a metaphor made literal in "Raid,"
when untold hundreds or thousands of ex-slaves heading toward the
freedom they believe awaits them just across that river find themselves
a congealed mass of humanity, a flood of people moving inexorably toward Jordan; the ones in front pause at the river by force of the Yankee
soldiers in front who plan to blow up the bridge that they want to cross
but get pushed forward by the stronger force of those behind, who do
not know that those in front have stopped. Granny, Bayard, and Ringo
are in the middle of this mass in the wagon, Granny singlemindedly
trying to get back the silver and mules that the Yankees had taken from
them: John Sartoris's silver is the most important thing in the world
to her, since she risks life and limb for it, far more important than the
lives of the hungry suffering masses around them. As a river might, the
crowd of slaves lifts up the wagon as it surges, turns it sideways, and
takes it over the edge into the river with them just as the Yankees blow
the bridge. James Hinkle and Robert McCoy inform us that in fact it
was the Confederates who blew up the bridge that this incident is based
upon, not the Yankees (107–8). It may be that Faulkner simply didn't
want to face that fact. But for my purposes here I'd rather believe that
he changed it so that the black masses get destroyed by the devices of
the very people who brought them the language of freedom and whom
they thought they were following into it.

Granny wants that silver. The invading Yankee army has burned
Sartoris and other plantation houses to the ground, forcing the white
owners to move into and share with them the cabins of their former
slaves. Thus, as noted, they have themselves become slaves of the revolution. That John Sartoris intends to rebuild Sartoris right on the very
spot where the house formerly stood, where that way of life vanished,
is Faulkner's pretty clear statement of what's at stake for Father and the
Sartoris family. In one sense, then, *The Unvanquished* looks at revolu-

tion from the point of view of the ones who stand to lose most, the ones being revolted against. Revolution is not in their best interests.

Father's relationship with his men and with his son, who narrates his story some time after he is dead, is at best precarious. Bayard is conflicted too, because he understands, as he writes, that violence as a way of dealing with political issues is not viable for his generation and that that old way of life is dead no matter how many times they rebuild Sartoris. In the opening chapter/story, "Ambuscade," Bayard emphasizes over and over how big Father *seemed*, on his horse, in his imagination, offering "the illusion of height and size which he wore for us" (326). But he repeatedly undercuts his repeated claims about Father's "bigness" by also drawing our attention to how small he actually was: he is so short that when he stands on the steps to the house his sword will not clear the step. At some level Bayard wants us to believe that his father was a war hero, a gallant fighter, but he gives us plenty of evidence, for example, that he is, like Ab Snopes and Granny, a horse thief and some considerable evidence that he was really no great shakes as a Colonel: he was in fact demoted by his company (354). Bayard gives no reason for the demotion but we may easily understand that they did so because he, Father, led his men to retreat at Manassas; Bayard doesn't say which battle of Manassas but it doesn't matter, since the Confederates won both of them: Father's retreat from a victory may or may not tell us anything about his leadership abilities and his courage. And, finally, there's some convincing evidence that most of what he did after being demoted was steal horses (361). Even as he tries to write nice convincing things about his father, then, Bayard quietly deconstructs him and the cavalier myth that he has represented to so many readers.

Much of the relatively small amount of commentary about *The Unvanquished* has centered around the figure of John Sartoris. Most critics, convinced of Faulkner's political and historical naiveté, especially about the South, have taken it for granted that he is one of Faulkner's heroes and that, as Myra Jehlen puts it, the book suffers from "the uncritical way in which Faulkner depicts the cavalier legend" (50). Far from deconstructing Father, she argues, Bayard's language creates "a Napoleonic Sartoris [who] is the bigger man for Bayard's disclaimer, having gained spiritual stature at the cost of mere physical inches. In fact and in a manner which might at first seem paradoxical, with each of these realistic qualifications, Bayard only propels his father's legendary character a little farther from reality" (40).

But far from approving of John Sartoris, Faulkner shows him acting just as a man in his position of power would act if he needed to. John Sartoris is in fact a powerfully realistic dictator-in-the-making. He sets out without any uncertainty to restore the lost kingdom, to rebuild the castle in the same place, to re-establish an order amenable to him and his kind, and before he finally has had enough of killing he is well on his way to becoming the same kind of tyrant that Faulkner knew ruled Germany and Russia, who believed that one or two or a million and more lives were nothing compared to the beauty of the dream. Sartoris does restore an order amenable to his class and kind, even though, ever an opportunist, he steps down from his position as planter/aristocrat and joins the bourgeoisie by building and operating a railroad. He joins Granny and Buck and Buddy in the capitalist enterprise to control the distribution of goods. In "Retreat," when Bayard tries to explain Uncle Buck's threat to use his serfs to demote John Sartoris from "colonel to mayor or maybe only a company commander," he concludes with a statement perhaps even he doesn't completely understand the truth of: "Father didn't mind what they called him; colonel or corporal, it would have been all the same to him, as long as they let him tell them what to do" (352). Bourgeoisie, aristocrat, colonel—he doesn't care what he's called, so long as he can give the orders.

Drusilla tries to convince Bayard that her husband's "dream" is more important than a few lives, especially lives of carpetbaggers and foreigners. Though his father does the killing, Bayard never records that his father actually talks about that dream and there is plenty of reason to believe, as some have noted, that Drusilla's dream animates John Sartoris after the war, not his own. There may be reasons: in a curious speech to Bayard in "Raid," she compares her life before and now during the War, describing what the War has accomplished:

> Living used to be dull, you see. Stupid. You lived in the same house
> your father was born in and your father's sons and daughters had

the sons and daughters of the same negro slaves to nurse and coddle, and then you grew up and you fell in love with your acceptable young man and in time you would marry him, in your mother's wedding gown perhaps and with the same silver for presents she had received, and then you settled down forever more while your husband got children on your body for you to feed and bathe and dress until they grew up too; and then you and your husband died quietly and were buried together maybe on a summer afternoon just before suppertime. Stupid, you see. But now you can see for yourself how it is, it's fine now; you dont have to worry now about the house and the silver because they get burned up and carried away, and you dont have to worry about the negroes because they tramp the roads all night waiting for a chance to drown in homemade Jordan, and you dont have to worry about getting children on your body to bathe and feed and change because the young men can ride away and get killed in the fine battles and you dont even have to sleep alone, you dont even have to sleep at all and so all you have to do is show the stick to the dog now and then and say Thank God for nothing. (387)

War has rescued Drusilla from the bourgeois life of endless, stultifying repetition of routine from generation to generation, which is precisely the bourgeois life to which her post-war husband now aspires, and it seems obvious from this point of view that what makes her the "Greek amphora priestess of a succinct and formal violence" (468) is her prospect as a post-war wife of having to return to the monotony of that middle-class existence and having to endure a husband who might get "children on [her] body." After a wartime of chaos and violence she cannot live with the monotony of peace, a condition a lot of Faulkner's male warriors also have. Behind the scenes she clearly pushes John Sartoris into more and more violent confrontations with more and more people, a Lady Macbeth to her husband's faltering king-in-the-making; she of course pushes Bayard toward the same confrontations.

"Skirmish at Sartoris" juxtaposes two "skirmishes" that restore order and middle-class respectability to Jefferson or, rather, restore their forms. The comic skirmish involves the ladies' conspiracy to get Drusilla and John married, to make her "respectable" again after she has spent the war among men, dressed like them, fighting with them, and God knows what else. The more serious skirmish concerns John's murder of two carpetbaggers and his contravention of the law of the land by literally stealing and stuffing the ballot boxes which would have elected a Negro as marshal—all done, he claims, in the name of "working for peace through law and order" (460): yes, but peace and law and order as people of his own class define them. Again, there's been no revolution, only a change in the language used to describe the resultant order. Jefferson culture can no more tolerate a Negro as marshal than it can tolerate a woman who dresses like a man, behaves like a man, and hangs out with men. John Sartoris understands the one as well as he understands the other.

The thirties in America were not just the Depression. It was, as Eugene Lyons called it, *The Red Decade*. As Daniel Aaron has shown in his classic study, *Writers on the Left*, American intellectuals enthusiastically embraced the promise and the dream of the Russian revolution, adopted Communism as the only acceptable alternative to capitalism and the mess it had made—of which, of course, the Depression stood as Exhibit A. Communist ideology, which insisted that literature take more interest in the working masses, came to control or greatly influence literature, especially literary criticism. American intellectual commitment to Communism got several shocks to its system as it strained to ingest and make sense of Stalin's murderous crackdown first, in the early thirties, on the counterrevolutionary enemies of the soviet state, and then, beginning in the middle of the decade, his equally murderous crackdown on many of his revolutionary compatriots and compadres and even his closest friends, in the show trials, during which his henchmen tortured and otherwise persuaded completely innocent Party officials to admit publicly that they were guilty of heinous crimes against the soviet state, against the people; many of these went to their executions singing the praises of the Communist Party and their love of Comrade Stalin. That is, Stalin, or his minions, persuaded them to testify publicly how much more important the Party's ideas—its dreams, if you will—were than their own lives, than any individual life. Arthur Koestler described the process of this persuasion in his compelling novel *Darkness at Noon*, published in English in 1941. Many American intellectuals continued their ideological commitment to communism despite the emerging evidence that Stalin held it in place by murdering those whose commitment he saw flagging.

The show trials lasted for a little over three years, ending in 1938. Faulkner wrote most of the stories that became *The Unvanquished* in relief from stints on *Absalom, Absalom!* from 1934 to 1936, and began work to revise them into a book in the fall of 1937. Among the significant additions to these stories is the episode involving Buck and Buddy McCaslin's experimentation with new ideas about land and social relationships that they didn't have a name for yet, and the entire concluding story, "An Odor of Verbena." It's difficult not to think of at least these additions as being Faulkner's response to the ideological monologue the Party required of its members, to the purges themselves, and to the Party's belief in the individual as a minor, disposable function of the commune. He would no doubt have agreed with Koestler's analysis: "In the social equation, the value of a single life is nil; in the cosmic equation, it is infinite. . . . Not only communism, but any political movement which implicitly relies on purely utilitarian ethics, must become a victim to the same fatal error. It is a fallacy as naïve as a mathematical teaser, and yet its consequences lead straight to Goya's Disasters, to the reign of the guillotine, the torture chambers of the Inquisition, or the cellars of the Lubianka" (*The Invisible Writing*). Faulkner knew this, John and Bayard Sartoris know it, but apparently Drusilla does not.

The Unvanquished in some ways looks forward to the dark later fiction, especially to *A Fable*, most noticeably in that wonderful crowd scene but more importantly in its understanding of what was at stake in the ideological wars of the twentieth century. Though in his public life in the fifties he became a Cold War warrior, traveling for the US State Department and representing American values throughout the world, he never in his fiction misunderstood who, where, and what the enemy was. The conflict between East and West, communism and capitalism, was the conflict easy for the masses to understand; this was the conflict that made it easy for world leaders to mobilize patriotism and nationalism to their own political and military ends. The real conflict, as Faulkner understood it, was not that horizontal east-west one, but the vertical one, a problem of class, which pitted the workers and the have-nots of all nations and regions against their own leaders, the haves, who control their own people by offering them ideological assurance—the ideological assurance that drives patriots to sacrifice themselves in the name of and for the sake of the greater good that that ideological assurance provides, who have been carefully taught to believe that the individual's life is less important than the country's.

In *The Unvanquished*, Faulkner expresses his deep suspicion of saviors with a hand full of take this and a mouth full not even of much obliged but of think this do that shoot these gas those and then Don't you feel better now with the Jews taken care of and a chicken in every pot (I do not forget the looming dark imminence of Hitler or of the example of the late Huey P. Long) and his utter disdain for the mindless, hopeful, and all-too-trusting masses who chew that pasty pabulum as the Eucharistic bread and take salvation as they swallow it, only to find it poison. Whatever they called it, it was neither nourishment nor freedom.

War and Modernism in
A Fable

M odern European sculpture and painting appear promi-
nently in two scenes in *A Fable*. The sculpture appears
in an intricately staged setting for the old general's interview with the three women, his son the corporal's sisters and wife, who
have come to Allied Headquarters at Chaulnesmont to ask him to spare
their kinsman's life. The interview takes place in a sparsely-furnished
ante-room in which sit a table, a chair behind it, and a bench against the
opposite wall. On the ends of the table perch two bronzes, "a delicate
and furious horse poised weightless and epicene on one leg, and a savage
and slumbrous head not cast, molded but cut by hand out of the amal-
gam by Gaudier-Brzeska" (928). The old general has just come from
a roundtable discussion with other Allied generals about the Christ-
corporal who has masterminded the mutiny whereby an entire battalion of French soldiers has refused to charge the enemy as ordered. The
mutiny has caused the Allied officers to confer with a German general about how to get the war re-started with a minimum of damage to
civilization—that is, of course, to the civilization of the wealthy and
powerful upper classes of the nations at war with each other. As the runner
says, with perhaps a nod toward Jean Renoir's great 1937 film, *La Grande
Illusion*, all of the generals "speak the same language, no matter what

clumsy isolated national tongues they were compelled by circumstance to do it in" (961): some things are more important than war. Prior to the German general's entrance, the lesser Allied generals offer personal testimony as to the several forms and names under which the corporal has appeared on and around the battlefields, the various miraculous acts he has performed, the ways in which he has died and been buried, and the legends his activities have created throughout the trenches; the discussion the old general is about to have with the corporal's three kinswomen will cover more mundane but equally important facts about the corporal's actual birth, life, and participation in the war.

The painting appears during the "horsethief" episode, before the New Orleans lawyer begins a long-planned speech defending the old Negro handler and the cockney groomsman against the crowd that wants to free the thieves and squirrel them safely out of town to where they will be safe from prosecution for stealing the astonishing, legend-making race-winning three-legged horse. The lawyer, pausing a moment before speaking to reflect on his position in the world, remembers a picture he owns,

> a painting, no copy but proved genuine and coveted, for which he
> had paid more than he liked to remember even though it had been
> validated by experts before he bought it and revalidated twice since
> and for which he had been twice offered half again what he had paid
> for it, and which he had not liked then and still didn't and was not
> even certain he knew what it meant, but which was his own now
> and so he didn't even have to pretend that he liked it, which—so he
> believed then, with more truth than any save himself knew—he
> affirmed to have bought for the sole purpose of not having to pre-
> tend that he liked it; one evening, alone in his study . . . suddenly he
> found himself looking at no static rectangle of disturbing Mediter-
> ranean blues and saffrons and ochres, nor even at the signboard
> affirming like a trumpet-blast the inevictable establishment in coeval
> space of the sum of his past. . . . (835–36)

The lawyer would seem to have bought himself a Cézanne, perhaps a Braque or a Derain, but almost certainly a Fauviste painting or one of the Vorticist school. Thomas L. McHaney thinks there's reason to believe that the lawyer miraculously owns one of Cézanne's *Chateau Noir* canvases.[1] Indeed, all five in the *Chateau Noir* series fit Faulkner's description of the lawyer's infuriating and disconcerting possession. *Chateau Noir* also has other intriguing resonances with Faulkner's work: one reasonable translation of the French is "Dark House," a working title for two of his most famous novels, which each time he rejected in favor of *Light in August* and then *Absalom, Absalom!* He might have seen one of the *Chateau Noir* paintings in the Louvre, but I am less concerned to prove that the lawyer owns a Cézanne or to demonstrate that Faulkner had seen one than to note these paintings' and Cézanne's stature as precursors of modernism and to suggest the significance of the fact that at two dramatic moments in *A Fable* Faulkner introduces the modern in twentieth century European art, almost incidentally, casually, as interpellations in the larger narrative, as the horsethief episode in America intervenes in the novel's larger European theatre.

These modernist works of art form part of a multitude of references to European art and politics and history throughout the novel, so thickly woven into the novel's various narratives that they become part of its fictional texture. For example, the original mutinous regiment "had been raised in this district, raised in person, in fact, by one of the glorious blackguards who later became Napoleon's marshals, who delivered the regiment into the Emperor's own hand, and along with it became one of the fiercest stars in that constellation which filled half the sky with its portent and blasted half the earth with its lightning" (669). Faulkner elevates one minor character out of his very minor-ness by his slender connections with that history. He is a "staff officer already four years a captain even though only five years out of St Cyr, descendant of a Napoleonic duchy whose founder or recipient had been a butcher then a republican then an imperialist then a duke, and his son a royalist then a republican again and—still alive and still a duke—then a royalist again . . . who should have been the idol pattern and hope not merely for all career officers but for all golden youth everywhere, as was Bonaparte

1. I would like to thank Professor McHaney and Professor Benjamin Harvey for their advice and counsel on all matters pertaining to art in this essay.

not merely for all soldiers but for every ancestorless Frenchman quali-
fied first in poverty, who was willing to hold life and conscience cheap
enough. . ." (902–3).

Dozens of such references fugue throughout the text—*Gaston de la
Tour*, Clovis and Charlemagne, Dickens and Hugo, Flemish painters,
Antipas and Tiberius, Desmoulin and Robespierre, Hannibal, Caesar,
Gauguin, Byron, Tiberius, Agincourt and Crecy—alongside similar
references to the Levant, for obvious reasons, given the geographical
sources there for the story of Christ and its relationship to Europe and
the rest of the West. Not incidentally, he interweaves that rich past with
what the Christian world at any rate has accepted as the central event
in world history: Christ's direct intervention in that history. We may
easily enough argue that Faulkner included such references in *A Fable*
to give ponderable historical weight to the setting of his novel at such a
crucial moment in European and world history, but I think much more
is at stake in his depiction of the simultaneous advent of the new Christ
and Modernism.

Faulkner binds these two scenes together in a number of ways beyond the sculptures and the painting, by his usual method of carefully-
sculpted comparisons and contrasts, here based in European and, to a
lesser extent, American history. He describes the New Orleans lawyer
as a man of some "bulk: . . . not only tall but big" (824), the general as
very small: he looks like "a masquerading child beneath the illusion of
crushing and glittering weight of his blue-and-scarlet and gold and brass
and leather" (925). He sits "motionless in the chair whose high carven
back topped him like the back of a throne, his hands hidden below the
rich tremendous table which concealed most of the rest of him too"; he
sits "not only immobile but immobilised beneath the mass and glitter
of his braid and stars and buttons, he resembled a boy, a child" (884–85)
too small for all the "crushing and glittering weight" of the "braids and
stars and buttons" of that history, which "immobilize" him. But the
braids and stars and buttons, which create merely the "*illusion* of crushing and glittering weight" (925, my emphasis), suggest that the weight
of command is a charade enacted by commanders to manipulate the
commanded. Even at his advanced age, he is an infant relative to the
long history of the civilization he has inherited, whose weight he bears

and defends. To be sure, he claims that he defends order, which he opposes to the corporal's presumptive gift to humanity of individual freedom—which, unfettered, would lead to the chaos that the old general and his class abhor as antithetical to everybody's best interests. Thus his commitment to the "crushing" weight of the illusion may smack of the self-serving longsuffering of the king's sleepless complaint that "Uneasy lies the head that wears a crown" (2 *Henry IV*, III.i.31).

Likewise, the New Orleans lawyer, in Missouri, before his romanticized confrontation with the crowd, wanting to make himself part of European and American history, one among the Greats, looks "across the flimsy barrier" that separates him from the crowd "into no brick-and-plaster barn built yesterday by the God-fearing grandfathers of other orderly and decorous and God-fearing Missouri farmers, but back a hundred years into the stone hall older than Orleans or Capet or Charlemagne, filled with the wooden sabots until yesterday reeking with plowed land and manure" (826). He begins to play the hero, imagining himself among the great manipulators of the human masses as he stands in the courtroom "solitary," "but anything but alone amid, against, as a frieze or tapestry, that titanic congeries, invincible and judgmatical, of the long heroic roster who were the milestones of the rise of man—the giants who coerced compelled directed and, on occasion, actually led his myriad moil: Caesar and Christ, Bonaparte and Peter and Mazarin, Marlborough and Alexander, Genghis and Talleyrand and Warwick, Marlborough and Bryan, Bill Sunday, General Booth and Prester John, prince and bishop, Norman, dervish, plotter and khan, not for the power and glory nor even the aggrandisement; these were merely secondarily concomitant and even accidental; but for man" (833–34). The lawyer's one among the giants, here in the Missouri backwoods, playing Caesar with a ragtag bunch of country folks and failing spectacularly. Like the general, he lives under the illusion that he and all his predecessors want what's best for humanity; but we may well doubt the intentions of both.

Both the lawyer and the old general deal with crowds; they stand for long periods looking out of upper-storey windows down on the crowds whom they feel it is their destiny—and duty—to influence and control. The old general disdains them: "They want only to suffer," he tells his aide, who wants to close the shutters on their noisy moiling (884). The crowd that has gathered to await word of the fate of the mutineers and the thirteen ring-leaders are bound by their common history; they are helpless to thwart it and rendered incompetent by it: an officer in the streets with the crowd, trying to keep them from stampeding themselves, thinks contemptuously of the "stupidly complicating ineptitude of civilians at all times" (672). They crowd into the *Place de Ville*, "filling it again, right up to the spear-tipped iron fence beyond which the three sentries flanked the blank door," they stumble clumsily against each other, "until even if they had wished to stream, stumble, pant back to the compound and at least be where they could hear the volley [from the executioners' rifles] which would bereave them, there would have been no room to turn around in and begin to run; immobilised and fixed by their own density in that stone sink whose walls were older than Clovis and Charlemagne" (789). The French masses are bound by that long history that goes back past even Clovis, the founder of modern France, who inherited his kingdom from the finally defunctive Romans. As Keen Butterworth long ago pointed out, the huge walls of the ancient fortified city of Chaulnesmont, like that history, work to contain and control the masses; inside the walls the crowd "bunch[es] onto itself like a blind worm thrust suddenly into sunlight, recoiling into arrestment." Outside those city walls, where their history cannot shape them, they "spread out fanwise across the plain, so that already they no longer resembled a worm, but rather again that wave of water which had swept at dawn across the *Place de Ville* . . ." (786).

The American crowd is quite different, not having that history or those walls. The doors to the courtroom, even barred, are no match for their right to, their ownership of, the courtroom they want to enter; only a slight wooden fence and an easily-breached gate keep them on the audience side of the courtroom, flimsily separated from the lawyers' tables and the prisoners' dock and the jury's pen and the judge's bench. The lawyer tries to contain them on the viewers' side of the fence with his speech, but they will have none of it, flinging the gate open and simply lifting the lawyer out of their way toward the justice—freedom— they claim for the three-legged horse and the Negro and the cockney groom.

Standing there, thinking of the rhetorical opportunity to sway the crowd, the lawyer imagines the crowd confused, stumbling into and against each other, much as the crowd in France at the *Place de Ville* behaves. For him it is as if they "had walked full tilt, as into an invisible wall, into the room's massed and waiting cynosure; and on through the swing gate into the enclosure, to stop facing the massed room in almost the same prints he had stood in ten minutes ago" and he believes that he is still in control, that he can control his destiny and theirs, "by putting some of him in one motion in one direction, by him of him and for him, to disjam the earth, get him for a little while at least out of his own way;—standing there a moment . . . still holding in his palm like putty, the massed anonymity and the waiting as the sculptor holds for another moment yet the malleable obedient unimpatient clay, or the conductor across his balanced untensile hands the wand containing within its weightless pencil-gleam all the loud fury and love and anguish" (833–34).

Before he begins this speech, however, he thinks of that Cézanne. Looking at its Mediterannean blues and saffron and ochres, he sees not a revolutionary modernist masterpiece but rather a flag heralding himself centuries backward in to a castle where like the Norman earl he can contemplate the usable poverty of his serfs: the painting is the "cognizance," that is, a banner "of his destiny like the wind-hard banner of the old Norman earl beneath whose vast shadow not just bankers and politicians clicked and sprang nor governors and lieutenants blenched and trembled but at the groaning tables in whose kitchens and sculleries or even open courtyards and kennels daily sixty thousand who wore no swords and spurs and owned no surnames made the one last supreme sacrifice: the free gift of their pauperism" (836). He's completely wrong about the Cézanne: he buys it so that he doesn't have to like it (835); he doesn't like it because it is the precursor of the modern, not a testament of the history he wants to be part of. Like the orators and military leaders of the European and American history that he identifies with, he thinks that he holds the crowd "in his palm like putty, the massed anonymity and the waiting as the sculptor holds for another moment yet the malleable obedient unimpatient clay" (834). It's no accident that he thinks of himself as a sculptor, but unlike Gaudier-Brzeska, he is clearly thinking of molding the crowd into traditional, even representational sculptures based in the traditional history that the orators and military leaders he invokes represent.

He does well to dislike the Cézanne and would no doubt dislike the Gaudier-Brzeska too, if he could, if only because they augur an intervention in history that would make him, the would-be Norman earl, obsolescent. His speech, which the American crowd ignores, demonstrates his assumption, like the old general's, that history will always operate as it has always operated, in his own interests: his language, predicting a millennium of peace, parodies the political rhetoric that keeps his class in power, that assures the world that his class alone can maintain order and security. Speaking in the summer of 1914, literally on the precipice of the yawning abyss, the lawyer assures his constituency that the election of Woodrow Wilson on "the fourth of November two years ago" has inaugurated "the sun of a thousand years of peace and prosperity such as the world has never seen" (836). Even Europe, he claims, has "already entered into its own millennium of peace and reason, freed at last after two thousand years of war and the fear of war" (837).

Unlike the French hordes who patiently await the word from on high, the American crowd will have none of his speechifying, and they simply move him out of their way as they go about their business of freeing the Negro and the groom whom the turnkey has already spirited out of town. Americans can move without the great man to lead them—for a while yet, at any rate.

At the center of the novel's themes is the interview between the old general and corporal, during which the old general tempts his son to save his life by joining with him to rule the world rather than forcing him, the old general, to make him a martyr to the tradition that the old general upholds. The corporal represents no tradition except himself: he "seemed to have [no] history at all beyond the day when [he] had appeared, materialised seemingly out of nowhere and nothingness in the quartermaster's store-room" (784). The interview articulates the competing claims of the history and tradition that the old general represents and the corporal's revolution against that tradition, the competing claims of the mass need to be shaped by the ideological ordering forces of history and of the burgeoning individual's need to speak, act, and create individually: the old alliances and systems versus the new. The corporal-son argues that European history fears the voice of the individual; the general-father finesses him by arguing that he alone, the scion of that history, can create value out of the son's act of self-sacrifice: by executing him, he can make his son the martyr he wants to become and then interpret that martyrdom to the masses as he finds necessary and useful to his own interests. He argues his tradition, of course, as "an alternat[ive] to chaos" (972).

Their interview takes place at the "old Roman citadel" that sits above the city of Chaulnesmont, whose "stone weight . . . seemed to lean down and rest upon them like a ponderable shadow" (983). The citadel does not "loom" above them but "squat[s], not Gothic but Roman: not soaring to the stars out of the aspiration of man's past but a gesture against them of his mortality like a clenched fist or a shield" (983). Faulkner's choice of such a setting for this climactic confrontation between father and son, between the generations, places that confrontation directly in the compromised shadow of the European history in which the general and the lawyer base their traditions and values, and, of course, their sense of privilege: imperial Rome's, Ozymandius's, hybristic "gesture . . . of . . . immortality."

At a climactic moment in their dialogue the old general claims that the two of them are articulations of "the two inimical conditions [freedom and order] which . . . must contend and—one of them—perish." He begins with a curious image: "we are not two Greek or Armenian or Jewish—or for that matter, Norman—peasants swapping a horse . . ." (988). But they are swapping a horse, not one horse for another horse, but two symbolical ones, Faulkner's own prized symbol of masculinity and personal empowerment for a bronze sculpture of one, one historical tradition for a new way of thinking about humanity's relationship to that history. The old general, sitting between the bronze horse and the bronze Gaudier-Brzeska head, then, is poised between the old and the new, the one which is changing into the other which he despises. Richard Godden has suggested that the bronze horse, surging upward on one leg, supplies the fourth leg for the three-legged horse in the Horsethief narrative (82–83); if Godden is right, and I think he is, the crippled "epicene," effeminized representational horse stands in contrast to both the three-legged American horse and the Gaudier-Brzeska sculpture. The American horse is not at all fey or feminized or epicene, though it is crippled: indeed, the cockney groom kills him precisely to prevent the owner's economic interests in the horse's bankable sperm from putting him out to stud for the rest of his life. Even so, on both sides of the Atlantic the horse is a crippled and doomed creature, increasingly useless under the onslaught of the modernizing forces that Gaudier-Brzeska represents. Faulkner, writing on our side of World War II and, as I think, actually thinking of World War II though writing about World War I, would have understood the obsolescence of the horses that he loved, especially as a defense against the German panzers. Paul Fussell cites Robert Wernick's *Blitzkrieg*: "Witness the behavior of the Polish cavalry in September, 1939, setting out with impressive élan to repel the invading panzers: In a few minutes . . . the cavalry lay in a smoking, screaming mass of dismembered and disemboweled men and horses" (5). The old general staunchly opposes the new, as his long tirade against tanks, probably based, in Faulkner's mind, on the ferocious battle of Kursk that comes near the end of his dialogue with the corporal, suggests. The creatures of modernism, of mechanical mobility, he fears, will be a "frankenstein" which "roasts [man] alive with heat, asphyxiates him with speed, wrenches loose his still living-entrails in the ferocity of its prey-seeking stoop" (994). Henri Gaudier-Brzeska was also, along with Ezra Pound and others, a proponent of Vorticism, a modern theory of art and life that specifically embraced the energy of the new, the personal, the vital, especially as they expressed themselves in the mechanical. If the "Savage and slumbrous head" on the general's desk alludes to Gaudier-Brzeska's well-known head of Pound, Faulkner has added a literary dimension to the range of revolutionary art in *A Fable.*

Like Pound and Eliot in language, Picasso and Braque in art, Schoenberg and Stravinsky in music, Cézanne and Gaudier-Brzeska propounded a new language for a new time. Modernism addressed directly the traditions of language, history, and convention that made European crowds into worms within the high constricting walls of their histories and mere water on the plain when they are outside those walls. They wanted to intervene into and revise that history so that it would stop endlessly repeating itself for the benefit of the ruling classes. Jesus too: Faulkner's corporal. It is no coincidence that the only two names the Allied generals have known the corporal by are Brzonyi and Brzewski, both of which connect him directly to Gaudier-Brzeska, who was killed in the trenches of northern France in 1915: this, too, no coincidence: both of them, working against the traditional, killed precisely by the forces of that tradition that was struggling to keep itself alive.

Scar

A nation is a community organized for war.
—League of Nations
Huxley (76)

The least bloody battle of the Civil War occurred at Harrykin Creek, on the Sartoris farm just outside Jefferson, Mississippi, on 28 April 1862, just after the fall of Memphis. According to Bedford Forrest's official written report of this battle, the only victim was Lieutenant P. S. Backhouse.

Perhaps "battle" is too grandiose a name for what actually happened. "Skirmish" might be more apt. Some days earlier, a band of a half dozen Yankee scavengers had shown up to steal the family silver. With all the skill and discipline of a general herself, Granny Rosa Millard, every night almost for the duration of the war, had made the family practice burying the silver in a spot in back of the house, to protect it against such scavenging. All her plans, however, depend on her having sufficient warning of the Yankees' advent to have time to get the heavy chest from its hiding place behind her bed upstairs, to drag it down the stairs and out to the burying spot, and finally put into the ground and covered over. Of course the crisis comes without sufficient warning, as crises always do, and the best they can manage is to get the chest to the outhouse and to have Cousin Melisandre sit on it, draping her large skirt over it. The Yankees, however, on to this trick, have brought with them a huge log pole, carried on braces between their paired and yoked horses. They dismount and, carrying the log, ram the flimsy backhouse, which "explode[s]" (*CS* 677), and exposes Cousin Melisandre sitting there, screaming. She is of course not doing anything we should not be privy to but she is humiliated nevertheless—guilt by association, one might say—so that even though Lieutenant Backhouse falls instantly in love with her, she steadfastly refuses to have anything to do with him because of his name: more guilt by association.

The dejected Lieutenant Backhouse takes out his frustrations on Yankees, adopting Bedford Forrest's guerilla tactics to disrupt Yankee plans throughout the region. He becomes such a loose cannon that even Forrest knows he must be reined in, if only so that he himself can become once again the sole author of chaos for the Yankees. But he can't harness Backhouse's energy until he gets the lieutenant's raging libido under control. Melisandre, however, is adamant: she will not become Mrs. "Backhouse." So Forrest and Granny Millard conspire to have Backhouse killed off and to replace him with a very similar Lieutenant named Backus. Granny writes out and Forrest signs a citation that notes simultaneously the death in battle of Lieutenant Philip St.-Just Backhouse and the appointment of Philip St.-Just Backus to the rank of Lieutenant. Forrest then tells Granny to get another sheet of paper because he's "got to have a battle." "A battle?" Granny asks. "To give Johnston," he replies. "Confound it, Miss Rosie, can't you understand either that I'm just a fallible mortal man trying to run a military command according to certain fixed and inviolable rules, no matter how foolish the business looks to superior outside folks?" He proposes to call it the "Battle of Sartoris," but Granny refuses, primly: "Not at my house," she says, perhaps for the same reasons Melisandre refuses to be Mrs. Backhouse. The narrator, the young Bayard Sartoris, pipes up to remind them that the only shots during the battle had been fired "down at the creek" (*CS* 696).

The Battle of Harrykin Creek, then, is not purely of whole cloth, but almost. Forrest's insistence on having something written to perpetrate his well-intended and bureaucratically essential fraud, on having a paper to show his general, a bureaucratic paper for the bureaucratic files, reminds me irresistibly of the passage in *A Fable* which describes how the "bizarre convulsion of that military metabolism . . . does everything to a man but lose him, [it] learns nothing and forgets nothing and loses nothing at all whatever and forever—no scrap of paper, no unfinished record or uncompleted memorandum no matter how inconsequential or trivial" (888) .

I'm completely charmed with the notion of Bedford Forrest as bureaucrat, a soldier best-known for his disregard of traditional rules of warfare, his brilliant and resourceful and usually spontaneous battle tactics that caught his opponents off guard and rendered them vulnerable precisely because they, the Yankees, continued to expect their enemies to play by traditional rules of combat. That even Nathan Bedford Forrest should be so concerned with rules and regulations of any kind takes us several steps toward what I want to discuss. My epigraph holds that the very definition of "nation" is based in its degree of "organization for war," that is, its arrangement of systems for recruiting and distributing soldiers and supplies, of the means to control information, and of hierarchies of authority; each rank, as it exists on the next rung up, positions itself farther and farther from the actual fighting, the eminent danger, so that those at the top are, of course, completely exempt from the grime and sweat and danger of the battlefield.

That system, as Faulkner depicts it, requires the expendability of a certain number of those at the bottom. I want to focus on those at the bottom, mostly from the point of view of those at the top who are not expendable, who thrive upon the others' expendability. I am not here concerned with the pathologies of martyrdom or the ideological certitude of the super-patriot, both of which make citizens willing, even eager, to die for a cause: willing to lead the charge across the open field directly into enemy fire, to be the first over the wall, the first up the high bluff, the first out of the landing craft. I am more interested in the workings of the political and cultural apparatuses that create and nurture a national state of mind that will insure that enough young people will be willing to die to promote a nation's purposes, whatever they may be, however they may be redefined from generation to generation, from administration to administration. In so using its expendables, a nation is neither moral nor immoral, not even amoral, no more than digestion or breathing are, but like digestion and breathing simply necessary, and it is sentimental to think otherwise.

In fact, I want to caution against sentimentality in thinking about such matters, against anger and indignation about the condition of our own fathers and brothers and sisters and children, who are and have ever been the expendables, the mud- and blood-fouled grunts who shoot the rifles, man the barricades, stop the bullet or the shrapnel and bear the scar that writes the word "grunt" on their bodies. It is easy enough to weep over the body counts, over the coldly, perfectly-aligned rows of crosses and the crisply green manicured lawns of cemeteries at Normandy, Vicksburg, and Arlington, and ossuaries all over Europe where lie the bones, the shattered and fragmented chaotically-jumbled and desiccated remains, of nameless millions who gave their lives for reasons patriotic and religious and personal, for reasons heroic and trivial, virtually since time began; easy enough to weep reading accounts of Civil War battles which ended with the bodies of the dead and the wounded so thick and so entangled that observers could not see the ground for acres around, battles which had to be recessed because bodies, rotting and stinking in the July sun, were piled so high where they fell that the attacking armies could not step over them to advance.

I also want to caution against patriotism, a peculiarly virulent form of sentimentality, the more virulent because it cannot recognize itself as sentimentality. To put it very unsentimentally, a nation—a community organized for war—very unsentimentally requires such "ultimate sacrifices" of its young people, traditionally men, of course, but of women too now, as a condition of its existence as a nation, whether the sacrifice is for a nation's aggression or its defense. Whether its cause is just or unjust, no nation can live unless it plans for the slaughter of some of its young. To think sentimentally about this condition of nationality would blunt our edges and so thwart my purposes here, by exciting our anger and cynicism, which would lead to quick and easy condemnations of war and of governments; to think patriotically is to excite us to an equally mindless defense of war and governments, and to be patriotic is in fact to perform our parts in the national script of war, to do what we are told and expected to do. To understand the real monstrousness of war, we must not even think of it as monstrous, if only because that is too damned easy: we must instead focus on the cool bloodless dispassionate and completely unillusioned bureaucratic maneuvers a nation must make to sacrifice its young to whatever ends its leaders discover to be the national interest. Nations use patriotism to blunt our anger and our rage over our losses; they find the bones and bodies of their dead, bring home what remains, reassemble the shattered parts if possible, build huge cemeteries and monuments to the gallant dead, and grant us our grief in an orgasm of patriotic weeping. Thus we become a Grateful Nation. We put names on the crosses if we know the names, if enough parts are left to own a name. We even designate one grander monument to honor the unknown soldier, the body which stands for all bodies, the unnamed apotheosis of all the named and unnamed lost. So please: we cannot afford to be sentimental here, for sentimentality is the grease that oils the wheels of war. And besides, Steven Spielberg is sentimental enough for us all. *Saving Private Ryan* is a sop to the heroic dead, which never questions, apparently never even notices, the economy of sacrificing a whole platoon of soldiers to save one soldier's life: it's the heroism that counts, the death for something noble: several deaths to save a mother's heart. Saving mama's baby is a good thing: but what of the mothers of those who die that he might live?

Part of any nation's necessary business, then, is to prepare its young to be willing to offer their individual bodies for the common good and, not less necessary, to prepare those who are *not* called upon to die to be willing to offer their fathers and mothers and children and grandchildren and brothers and sisters and cousins to the good of the nation. Nations do this by creating and sustaining by infinite repetition a national narrative, a history that glorifies the sacrifices others have made for us, the unselfish sacrifices of our ancestors, whom we celebrate through daily pledges to flags and the singing of national anthems at sporting and other public events.[1] When such rituals fail to produce the

---

1. In a 1955 piece on a hockey match he wrote for *Sports Illustrated*, Faulkner wondered what "a professional hockey-match, whose purpose is to make a decent and reasonable profit for its owners, had to do with our National Anthem. What are we afraid of? Is it our national character of which we are so in doubt, so fearful that it might not hold up in the clutch, that we not only dare not open a professional athletic contest or a beauty-pageant or a real-estate auction, but we must even use a Chamber of Commerce race for Miss Sewage Disposal or a wildcat land-sale, to remind us that liberty gained without honor

necessary sheep for slaughter, nations resort to conscription, for sheep for slaughter they must have. I do not forget that a nation also demands that its expendables kill and maim the expendables of other nations and trains them to do so, and that the promise of adventure or aggression may motivate considerable numbers to join any military. War is legal murder: we not only give our children a license to kill, we insist that they will be heroic in proportion to the numbers they do kill. I am not, however, concerned with the aggressives or the martyrs, but with those good-hearted, patriotic, even gentle apples of their mothers' eyes, who go to battle knowing that there is a very fine chance they will not return at all or, if they do, will return dismembered. They leave in groups, amid the gaiety and swirl of civic panoply; they return alone, no matter how many they return with.

Few things are more chilling than the willingness of a nation's young to pledge their lives to the führer, no matter which country he leads, which country he invades, which peoples he defeats, no matter what reasons he gives. Tens of thousands, North and South, eagerly enlisted during the Civil War and marched off to their deaths; many returned minus a limb or an eye, or sporting a scar; and thousands of others during the World Wars, like Faulkner himself, longed for war so intensely that they lied about their ages or went to Canada to enlist, and even when they did not fight returned with lies, canes, and stories about metal plates in their heads. Mr. Compson describes the north Mississippi young marching off to the Civil War:

> fathers and mothers and sisters and kin and sweethearts of those
> young men—were coming to Oxford from further away than
> Jefferson—families with food and bedding and servants, to bivouac
> among the families, the houses, of Oxford itself, to watch the gallant
> mimic marching and countermarching of the sons and the brothers,

---

and sacrifice and held without constant vigilance and undiminished honor and complete willingness to sacrifice again at need, was not worth having to begin with? Or, by blaring or chanting it at ourselves every time ten or twelve or eighteen or twenty-two young men engage formally for the possession of a puck or a ball, or just one young woman walks across a lighted platform in a bathing-suit, do we hope to so dull and eviscerate the words and tune with repetition, that when we do hear it we will not be disturbed from that dream-like state in which 'honor' is a break and 'truth' an angle?" ("Innocent at Rinkside").

drawn all of them, rich and poor, aristocrat and redneck, by what is probably the most moving mass-sight of all human mass-experience, far more so than the spectacle of so many virgins going to be sacrificed to some heathen Principle, some Priapus—the sight of young men, the light quick bones, the bright gallant deluded blood and flesh dressed in a martial glitter of brass and plumes, marching away to a battle. . . . (*AA* 101)

Why Mr. Compson finds the sacrifice of soldiers more moving than the sacrifice of virgins is a question perhaps for another occasion, but the implied comparison is apt because the connection suggests the atavistic nature of the blood sacrifice of war, a practice held over from ancient worlds long after the sacrifice of virgins had been abandoned by most civilizations. *A nation is a community organized for war.*

The Battle of Harrykin Creek, as Forrest and Granny Millard write it, is thus fought by one for the benefit of another; one dies that another might live. The battle report, the history of that battle, is written by a third party for his own purposes—that is, to benefit his nation. That the sacrificer and the sacrificee are one and the same is also to the point, since the cause of the willingness to die in battle is the complete identification of the one with the other, of the dead with the living and the living with the dead. To put it another, more relevant way, the nation's need, the group's, subsumes those of the individual. Though bullets or grenades from another nation do the maiming and the killing, our own people put us in front of the wall, blindfolded and ready for the executioner's bullet (and, until recently, gave us free cigarettes to smoke while we waited, at least hoping we would live long enough to smoke enough to repay the tobacco companies' investments). We die for those we love, who watch us leave with lumps in their throats if not actual tears in their eyes, who love us even more when we die for them, who are to be sure grieved that we die but happy enough to accept our sacrifice so that they can live and continue to grieve and be grateful and, the nation would say, free. If these words sound vaguely religious, that is by design: little wonder that Faulkner embodied, then dis-embodied, the full meaning of his *Fable* in the person of a Christ figure in World War I, a figure named Stefan, for Steven the Martyr, but nearly always called "the corporal" to emphasize his body, his flesh-bound corpo-reality, which yields itself passively to and who dies literally for his Father's land, for its and his purposes, for in him father and land unite.

A death is one thing, a scar is another, but closely related. The scar, the stump, are the visible signs of a soldier's brush with annihilation: not so much a badge of courage, as Stephen Crane's Henry Fleming would have it, but rather a marker of chaos, a site where death has tapped him on the shoulder in grim reminder. A scar symbolizes a rupture and the rupture's necessity. If it marks a healing in the smooth surface of the skin it also marks the rupture too and thus marks the violence which caused the rupture and is thus a sign of the reasons for the violence which caused the rupture which left the scar. A scar is a constant, inescapable memento mori, a reminder of flesh's vulnerability, of its all too feeble hold on its own cohesion. War, in this way, literally writes itself on the bodies of a nation's most expendable citizens. Human scars have counterparts in the body of the nation: graves and monuments are scars, too: graves are the essence of the trench: monuments heal them over, anneal the national rupture. A scar is a carapace, tougher and uglier and deader than the flesh it has replaced; monuments, too, no matter how magnificently marbled, are invariably uglier and deader than the flesh they replace and stand for: they signify national resiliency and steadfastness of purpose while proclaiming the nation's vulnerability. A scar is the sign of the death each nation claims as its due, the Damocles sword hanging over each citizens' head, a sword to which each citizen pledges allegiance.

Faulkner's fiction is littered with scars and stumps, the residue of wars. At the metaphorical center of *Soldiers' Pay* sits Donald Mahon's vividly undescribed scar across his brow. His scar is the mirror into which all the characters look, seeing themselves in pity and revulsion and even pride; it is a text in which they read their own narratives. The very young Cadet Lowe, like Faulkner—they "stopped the war on him" (3)—with no experience of war, sees it as "dreadful" (21), but longs for it: "To have been him!" he moans. "Just to be him. Let him take this sound body of mine! Let him take it. To have got wings on my breast, to have got wings; and to have got his scar, too, I would take death tomorrow. . . . To be him, to have gotten wings, but to have got his scar too!" (33–34). Cecily's younger brother Robert makes a peep show of sorts out of the scar, bringing his buddies by to show off his personal access to the war-scarred hero; but they come and "go away fretted because he [Donald] wouldn't tell any war stories" (118). Neighbors of Donald's father, the rector, chat about Donald's "scarred oblivious brow"; former girlfriends come "to look once upon his face and then quickly aside in hushed nausea, not coming anymore unless his face happened to be hidden on the first visit (upon which they finally found opportunity to see it)" (117–18). Mrs. Powers, herself a war widow, believes that the man "that was wounded is dead and this is another one: a grown child. Its his apathy, his detachment from everything that's so terrible. He doesn't seem to care where he is nor what he does. He must have been passed from hand to hand, like a child" (92). Cecily Saunders, Mahon's fiancée, is frantic, torn between her engagement and her simple revulsion: "How can I [marry him], with that scar? How can I?" (103). "Donald, Donald!" she cries. "I will try to get used to it, I will try! Oh, Donald, Donald! Your poor face! But I will, I will" (108). Donald's father believes that Cecily "is the best medicine he can have," that she can "make a new man of him in a short time" (89). Januarius Jones sees "death in his face" (51), and the doctor believes he is "practically a dead man now. More than that, he should have been dead these three months were it not for the fact that he seems to be waiting for something. Something he has begun but has not completed, something he has carried from his former life that he does not remember consciously. That is his only hold on life that I can see" (122).

Other scars and stumps, bodies and dis-embodiments: Ab Snopes limps, apparently from a Civil War wound. The German prisoner in "Ad Astra" has a bandage around his head (*CS* 411) and under it a "high, sick face" (423); a French officer has a "gaunt, tragic face," highlighted by one glass eye, "motionless, rigid in a face that looked even deader than the spurious eye" (422); even the whole characters feel their flesh separated from their bones (427). In "Crevasse" two of a party of soldiers carry a third whose "head is bound in a bloody rag," who "stumbles his aimless legs along" (465). They pass through a wasteland of "old healed scars of trees" whose leaves are "neither green nor dead" (469). "Pallid grass bayonets saber at their legs" (468) until the grass bayonets become real ones and the land becomes filled with "chalky knobs thrusting up through the soil" (469–70) which when turned over reveal themselves to be skulls, turning upward their "earth-stained eyesockets and . . . un-bottomed grin[s]" (470). This soil opens up and they smell an upward explosion of "rotted flesh," then drop into the darkness where other skeletons of soldiers killed by gas await them. Faulkner may have had in mind the famous Trench of Bayonets at Verdun, a memorial marking the spot where the earth did in fact cave in on several soldiers, enclosing them in dirt, while leaving their bayonets sticking up straight out of the ground. The narrator of "All the Dead Pilots" has a mechanical leg (512), as the narrator of "The Leg" has a wooden one. Weddel Saucier in "Mountain Victory" is missing an arm. This list speaks nothing of the corpses, broken, decayed, and stinking, among which the drunken detail finds a complete corpse to offer the French nation as the Unknown Soldier in *A Fable*; nor do I forget the fabulous scar that envelopes half of the runner's body, of which more shortly.

Monuments write war, too, as I say, but do so on the home front. The problem with the nation's necessary and ongoing sacrifice of its young to the maw of war is that each missing body or body part leaves a gap, a wound—a grief, a terror—back home, creates a fissure in, a disruption of, local lives, local histories, local emotional economies, fissures that can be healed over only by the ideological soundness, the prevailing moral "rightness" that public monuments to dead soldiers so massively represent: the monumental cultural scar that both conceals the bloody wound and reveals it in bright glaring marble effigy: the promise that the sacrificial lambs have died in the service of something larger, more magnificent, than any local need, something larger and more important than any mere local grief. A grieving parent or spouse or sibling or child becomes, through the scar, part of the Grateful Nation. *And a nation is a community organized for war.*

Thus division commander Gragnon, in *A Fable*, believes himself to be the "perfect soldier: pastless, unhampered, and complete." He is an orphan, raised in a "Pyrenean orphanage run by a Catholic sisterhood, where there was no record of his parentage whatever, even to be concealed" (684). Though he longs for mother, for family, he has none to grieve him if he dies or is maimed; that's why he is the perfect soldier:

with no mother, he gives himself to Fatherland. In the same manner, the nameless, faceless, sergeant who feeds the hungry woman in the crowd in the novel's opening scene, thinks of the military as the "vocation and livelihood to which twenty years ago he had not merely dedicated but relinquished too, not just his life but his bones and flesh . . . relinquishing volition and the fear of hunger and decision to the extent of even being paid a few sure sous a day for the privilege and right, at no other cost than obedience and the exposure and risk of his tender and brittle bones and flesh, of immunity forever for his natural appetites" (674–75). By resigning themselves to their own expendability, Gragnon and this sergeant have absolved themselves of what the runner calls "that sort of masturbation about the human race people call hoping" (722).

Those who hope—that is, those grunts for whom hope is the only defense against their expendability—become vulnerable to prophets and visionaries such as the runner, who leads them to their deaths. They are also vulnerable to the financial dealings of the foulmouthed cockney groom, who advances the members of his society, the masons, 10 bob, or 120 pence, which they repay at a usurious rate of 6 pence a day or 180 pence a month before they can get another advance. The groom thus gets a 150 percent return on his money if his clients live long enough to repay. Perhaps he is the ultimate cynic, exploiting their need to make the most of each day they have left; but since he is gambling that they will live and they are gambling that they won't he may be instilling in them that hope the runner despises them for. The groom is thus the only one in the novel who gambles that more soldiers will live than will die; at worst his clients get to enjoy their last few days alive with whatever pleasures and satisfactions money can bring.

The farther removed from the citizens and the grunts a soldier is, the higher up the ranking ladder, the more contempt he has for the grunts. The supervising sergeant in the novel's opening pages feels that his dedication to his "vocation and livelihood" places an "insuperable barrier" between him and the masses (674); he gives the hungry woman bread: "Here," he says, "harshly, with that roughness which was not unkindness but just impatience" (673). He helps her to her feet "not roughly, just impatient at the stupidly complicating ineptitude of civilians at all times" (672). The runner, made an officer by virtue of his valor in battle, tries to resign his commission because he hates the grunts for being so helpless: "When I, knowing what I have been, and am now, and will continue to be . . . can, by the simple coincidence of wearing this little badge on my coat, have not only the power, with a whole militarised government to back me up, to tell vast herds of man what to do, but the impunitive right to shoot him with my own hand when he doesn't do it, then I realise how worthy of any fear and abhorrence and hatred he is" (721–22).

He claims to despise humanity because it hopes, but he despises their odor too: "the stench too, the smell, the soilure, the stink of simple usage: not the dead bones and flesh rotting in the mud, but because the live bones and flesh had used the same mud so long to sleep and eat in" (721). Even so, he wants to return to the ranks because he does not want official power, the power of life and death over them. When he won't shoot himself in the foot to inflict the crippling wound that will get him decommissioned, he arranges to flout the military's rules so flagrantly that the higher-ups bust him back to the ranks. When his commanding officer persuades him not to return to the trenches he asks to become a runner, a position fluid and mobile and therefore de-hierarchized that gives him freedom to move horizontally from trench to trench, from battleground to Paris, and vertically up and down the chain of command, from grunt to officer to general. He thus refuses to be part of the system that takes the lives of its own young—refuses with impunity, he thinks. It's only the more savagely ironic, then, that he pursues his idealistic goal of peace by murdering three, perhaps five or six, guards, including the cockney groom, and causes the deaths of thousands who follow him, unarmed, into that No Man's Land where they are greeted by barrages from both sides, from both nations—enemies, who have teamed together, as they have throughout the novel, to keep the war going.

Division Commander Gragnon, whose division's mutiny initiates the action of *A Fable*, is a Company Man if ever there was one. Unlike the runner, Gragnon actually *insists* on his right, as commander, to pull the trigger on his disobedient troops. He is frustrated by his own superiors' refusal to allow him to, and will himself be murdered by three newly-arrived American privates, at the behest and in the pay of his own nation, precisely because he insists that the system's rules must be obeyed. He has not learned, apparently, that a nation is bound by its "rules" only when the rules are useful and that expedience may well dictate an abrogation or at least a re-interpretation of the rules. All organizations are conservative and the first thing any organization must conserve is itself, even if it has to break its own rules to do so. Gragnon's conversation with the notorious general, his group commander, known as Mama Bidet, to whom he goes to request permission to shoot his mutinying troops, is instructive about the system's attitude toward the masses.

Mama Bidet has no use for humanity except its military uses. For him, for all the officers to some extent, "human being" and "individual" are value-laden terms completely useless, even antithetical, to a community organized for war; individuals have value only when their individual fingers can pull individual triggers, stop individual bullets. Mama Bidet is very clinical about "humanity": he has a

> pitiless preoccupation with man, not as an imperial implement, least of all as that gallant and puny creature bearing undismayed on his frail bones and flesh the vast burden of his long inexplicable incomprehensible tradition and journey, not even in fact as a functioning animal but as a functioning machine in the same sense that the earthworm is: alive purely and simply for the purpose of transporting, without itself actually moving, for the distance of its corporeal length, the medium in which it lives, which, given time, would shift the whole earth that infinitesimal inch, leaving at last its own blind insatiate jaws chewing nothing above the spinning abyss: that cold, scathing, contemptuous preoccupation with body vents and orifices and mucous membrane as though he himself owned neither, who declared that no army was any better than its anus, since even without feet it could still crawl forward and fight. (713)

Bidet sets fire to Gragnon's resignation and drops it into his own waste-filled chamberpot, to show his contempt for Gragnon's inability to recognize military reality. Gragnon insists that "there are rules. . . . Our rules" (715); we must enforce them, he argues, or we—the officers, the military—will die. But Bidet disagrees; we, officers, didn't invent war, war created us, at mankind's need and behest, its simple inability to behave itself: "From the loins of man's furious ineradicable greed sprang the captains and colonels to his necessity. We are his responsibility," he concludes; "he shall not shirk it." That is, officers, the entire military establishment, emerged as an orderly, systemic response to the chaos which the masses both cause and fear, their "furious ineradicable greed." They thus created us, Mama Bidet argues, and we shall hold them responsible, even though they inevitably let us down on occasion: "They may even stop the wars, as they have done before and will again; ours merely to guard them from the knowledge that it was actually they who accomplished that act. Let the whole vast moil and seethe of man confederate in stopping wars if they wish, so long as we can prevent them learning that they have done so." Breaking the rules won't destroy the system. What *will* destroy it is the "simple effacement from man's memory of a single word." When Gragnon doesn't know which word, Bidet supplies it: "Fatherland." He then concludes, "let them believe that they can stop it, so long as they dont suspect that they have. . . . Let them believe that tomorrow they will end it; then they wont begin to ponder if perhaps today they can. Tomorrow. And still tomorrow. And again tomorrow. That's the hope you will vest them in" (715–16). He knows that that masturbation called hoping is what keeps the war going.

At a later point in the novel, the old general himself undertakes a deeper, more comprehensive meditation on the hierarchy at the summit of which he sits; though measurably more humane than Mama Bidet's sense of human beings as good for little more than to supply fingers to pull triggers with, the old general is no less certain of the implacability of the national hierarchy, no less certain that the structure is in the nature of things and not constructed, and that it is the only alternative to chaos.

On Wednesday evening at sunset, he takes a moment standing at the open window of his quarters to contemplate the two different crowds below. The first is the crowd of civilians gathered in the *Place de Ville*, awaiting the verdict to be given about their relatives in the mutinous regiment. They hate the corporal because he has led their soldier-kin to forsake their lives in advance of victory or defeat in order to stop the war; they do not realize that their own nationalism, their commitment to Fatherland, has already pledged those deaths. Being nationalistic, of course, being a community organized for war, they can think only in the binary terms of victory and defeat, submission and dominance, of being Number One or the national humiliation of being anything less than Number One. They dare not think of compromise or of peaceful coexistence with enemies or inferiors or just plain Otherness. Their hatred and fear of the corporal is all the more bitter because he is an alien, a foreigner, and so unknown, an other, and necessarily antagonistic to the national good. As Keen Butterworth long ago showed, these folks are constrained by those structures of civilization symbolized by the walls of the ancient city of Chaulnesmont, which give them shape, even if only the constantly malleable shape of water, to which they are frequently compared. That is, the city's shape—in walls, in history, in law—gives the crowd what shape and coherence it has; when once they follow the lorries carrying the prisoners out of the city, they lose their coherence and dissipate out into the plain (22).

The other crowd the old general contemplates is that one formed by the jailed mutineers, the three thousand. Like the civilians, they too seek coherence in the old forms: released into the open yard of the abandoned factory where they are being held, they

> coalesce without command into the old sheeplike molds of platoons and companies. . . . [They] shuffle and grope for the old familiar alignments, blinking a little after the dark barracks, in the glare of sunset. Then it began to move. There were no commands from anywhere; the squads and sections simply fell in between the old file-markers and -closers and began to flow, drift as though by some gentle and even unheeded gravitation, into companies in the barracks streets, into battalions onto the parade ground, and stopped. It was not a regiment yet but rather a shapeless mass in which only the squads and platoons had any unity, as the coherence of an evicted city obtains only in the household groups which stick together not because the members are kin in blood but because they have eaten

together and slept together and grieved and hoped and fought
among themselves so long. . . . (873)

As the old general contemplates these two faceless, nameless, voice-
less, shapeless masses of humanity from his second-storey window,
watching the three allied national flags furl and listening to the three
allied national bugles blow colors simultaneously, together but in dis-
cord, he meditates on these people's relationship to the civilization at
whose apex he stands. The meditation is actually, finally, about *their*,
the mass's, capacity to endure, but "endurance" in his thinking is barely
a step or two above vegetating, if that far: the city, the nation, the civilization, is "immune to man's enduring," he thinks. It doesn't have to
care whether any individual survives or not, for there will always be
billions more. His confidence lies in the city itself, one of the central
structures and symbols of his nation. He notes that the city of Chaulnesmont, at evening, is

> already immune to man's enduring, was even now free of his tu-
> mult. Or rather, the evening effaced not man from the *Place de Ville*
> so much as it effaced the *Place de Ville* back into man's enduring
> anguish and his invincible dust, the city itself not really free of either
> [the anguish or the dust] but simply taller than both. Because they
> endured, as only endurance can, firmer than rock, more invincible
> than folly, longer than grief, the darkling and silent city rising out of
> the darkling and empty twilight to lower like a tumescent thunder-
> clap, since it was the effigy and the power, rising tier on inviolate
> tier out of that mazed chiaroscuro like a tremendous beehive whose
> crown challenged by day the sun and stemmed aside by night the
> celestial smore. (887)

"First and topmost," at the apex of civilization's hierarchy, the old
general muses, are such as himself: "the three flags and the three supreme generals who served them: a triumvirate consecrated and anointed,
a constellation remote as planets in their immutability, powerful as
archbishops in their trinity, splendid as cardinals in their retinues and
myriad as Brahmins in their blind followers" (887). First, indeed, are the

three flags, the symbols of the nations, the immutable signs of their immutable ideological values, their national narratives and their national cohesion, standing first, above and apart from the generals themselves but identified with them and, indeed, investing them with their power. The generals are "a triumvirate consecrated and anointed." The old general does not bother to ask by whom he has been consecrated and anointed; we can only wonder whether he even thinks of these terms as problematic—terms usually reserved for popes and kings—or whether he questions his fitness to be where and who he is. Perhaps he does, since we know that for the first several years after his graduation at the top of his class at St. Cyr, the French West Point, he did everything he could to escape his "doom"; he volunteered for a post in the deepest of Saharan Africa then retreated, in escape, to the high Himalayas, where he fathered the corporal, who has returned to him as surely as the repressed and whose life and death he now holds immediately in his hand—has, in effect, held it since the day he, the general, was born, and in more ways than one. It simply may not occur to him to wonder the why of his placement, but he finally accepts it as his birthright, his fate, since he is, as he tells his corporeal corporal son, the scion of one of the wealthiest and most powerful families in Europe: he was "born heir to that power as it stood then, holding that inheritance in escrow to become unchallenged and unchallengeable chief of that confederation" (989). He is, as Faulkner describes Flem Snopes in *The Mansion*, "a pillar, rock-fixed, of things as they are" (*M* 530).

Next in the hierarchy, just under him, are the "three thousand lesser generals" who are the three supreme generals'

> deacons and priests and the hierarchate of their households, their
> acolytes and bearers of monstrance and host and censer: the colonels
> and majors who were in charge of the portfolios and maps and
> memoranda, the captains and subalterns who were in charge of the
> communications and errands which kept the portfolios and maps
> up to date, and the sergeants and corporals who actually carried the
> portfolios and mapcases and protected them with their lives and
> answered the telephone and ran the errands, and the privates who
> sat at the flickering switchboards at two and three and four oclock

in the morning and rode the motorcycles in the rain and snow and
drove the starred and pennoned cars and cooked the food for the
generals and colonels and majors and captains and subalterns and
made their beds and shaved them and cut their hair and polished
their boots and brass. . . . (887–88)

Because of the mutiny, Chaulnesmont is now so crowded with generals
"of high rank" that there develop ranks within the ranks of officers, at the
bottom of which are the wounded, the outcasts and untouchables, the

men who had actually been in, come out of, the battle zone, as
high in rank as majors and even colonels sometimes, strayed into
the glittering and gunless city through nobody knew what bizarre
convulsion of that military metabolism . . . ; a few of them were
always there, not many but enough: platoon or section leaders and
company commanders and battalion seconds stained with the filth
of front lines who amid that thronged pomp and glitter of stars and
crossed batons and braid and brass and scarlet tabs moved diffident
and bewildered and ignored with the lost air of oafish peasants
smelling of field and stable summoned to the castle, the Great
House, for an accounting or a punishment: a wounded man arm-
less legless or eyeless was stared at with the same aghast distasteful
refusive pity and shock and outrage as a man in an epileptic seizure
at high noon on a busy downtown corner. (888)

Not only do civilian structures parallel and support the military's
rigid organization, they march in lockstep with it, share its goals, and,
like the military, always operates in its own best interests:

Antipas his friends and their friends, merchant and prince and
bishop, administrator and clacquer and absolver to ministrate the
attempt and applaud the intention and absolve the failed result,
and all the nephews and godsons of Tiberius in far Rome and their
friends and the friends of the wives and husbands of their friends
come to dine with the generals and sell to the generals' governments
the shells and guns and aircraft and beef and shoes for the generals

to expend against the enemy . . . mayor and burgher, doctor attorney director inspector and judge who held no particular letter from
Tiberius in Rome yet whose contacts were still among generals and
colonels and not captains and subalterns. . . . (888–89)

The list goes on until it reaches the least of these their brethren, the
people of the city, the lowest rung of civilization's people, the bees,
the workers, the teeming class that supplies the soldiers who fight the
wars that keep the structure in place, the point toward which the old
general's powerful meditation has been aiming:

> and last even anonymity's absolute whose nameless faceless mass
> cluttered old Jerusalem and old Rome too while from time to time
> governor and caesar flung them bread or a circus as in the old snowy
> pantomime the fleeing shepherd casts back to the pursuing wolves
> fragments of his lunch, a garment, and as a last resort the lamb
> itself—the laborers who owned today only the spending of what they
> earned yesterday, the beggars and thieves who did not always under-
> stand that what they did was beggary and theft, the lepers beneath city
> gate and temple door who did not even know they were not whole,
> who belonged neither to the military nor to the merchants and princes
> and bishops, who neither derived nor hoped for any benefit from
> army contracts nor battened by simply existing, breathing coeval with
> the prodigality and waste concomitant with a nation's mortal agony,
> that strange and constant few who each time are denied any opportu-
> nity whatever to share in the rich carnival of their country's wasting
> lifeblood, whose luck is out always with no kin nor friends who have
> kin or friends who have powerful kin or friends or patrons. . . .

He thinks of those "who owned nothing in fact save a reversion in endurance without hope of betterment nor any spur of pride—a capacity
for endurance which even after four years of existence as tolerated and
rightless aliens on their own land and in their own city still enabled
them without hope or pride even in the endurance to endure, asking
or expecting no more than permission to exercise it, like a sort of immortality" (889–90).

These "tolerated and rightless aliens . . . in their own city" have, the old general knows, no shape or coherence other than what he gives them, as he will claim in his dialogue and demonstrate when he orders the corporal's execution. Doubtless he is thinking of these "tolerated and rightless aliens" when toward the end of that dialogue with the corporal, he foresees the day when wars will be fought not by people at all but by machines—tanks—in which case a nation, a community organized for war, would have nothing to do with its billions and billions of constantly reproducing individual human beings. The conclusion is thus inescapable that one of the reasons for war is to prevent the burden of overpopulation.

Then, ratcheting his meditation's intensity up a notch or two, the old general articulates a considerably more poetic version, a magnificent version, of Mama Bidet's belief that humanity had created the military, had created the city, had created the church, the inextricably interlocked principal structures of civilization which converge here in the general's powerful imaging: "Out of that enduring and anguished dust [the people, the city] rose, out of the dark Gothic dream, carrying the Gothic dream, arch- and buttress-winged, by knight and bishop, angels and saints and cherubim groined and pilastered upward into soaring spire and pinnacle where goblin and demon, gryphon and gargoyle and hermaphrodite yelped in icy soundless stone against the fading zenith" (890).

Division Commander Gragnon works through a related sort of system, though his is the horizontal one of history, not the old general's vertical one of hierarchy and privilege. But these two systems are intimately related in ways that demonstrate the relationship between history and the structure of a community perpetually organized and organizing for war. Gragnon stands before the three supreme generals to make his case for executing the mutinying regiment, which is simply that the rules demand that he do so. Having been turned down at the lower levels, he knows that his appeal to this ultimate triumvirate will fail, too, and he plans to commit suicide when they refuse him. He understands the system's needs, however, and so knows that they will not permit him a suicide, will not permit him that much control over his own life, especially if his life can be useful; he knows that they will execute him and, for the nation's purposes, advertise his death as a heroic one, a glorious death in battle. He delivers the speech, arguing the necessity, the efficacy of the rules. Faulkner blanks out the actual speech, however, since it is essentially the same one he gave to Mama Bidet, in favor of Gragnon's thinking while he delivers it; his meditation is thus a counter-narrative to the speech. He knows that both the speech and his need to give it are "much older than that moment two days ago in the observation post when he discovered that he was going to have to make it. Its conception"—his acceptance of the principle that orders must be obeyed—"was the moment he found he was to be posted to officers' school, its birth the day he received the commission, so that it had become, along with the pistol and sabre and the sublieutenant's badges, a part of the equipment with which he would follow and serve his destiny with his life as long as life lasted. . . ." The speech, he knows, is deadly and is connected to the bullet with which, out of honor to his profession, he plans to take his life. The bullet is the speech's

> analogous coeval . . . that one of the live cartridges constant through the pistol's revolving cylinder, against the moment when he would discharge the voluntary lien he had given on his honor by expiating what a civilian would call bad luck and only a soldier disgrace, the—any—bad luck in it being merely this moment now, when the need compelled the speech yet at the same time denied the bullet. In fact, it seemed to him now that the two of them, speech and bullet, were analogous and coeval even in more than birth: analogous in the very incongruity of the origins from which they moved, not even shaped yet, toward their mutual end [his death on principle]:—a lump of dross exhumed from the earth and become, under heat, brass, and under fierce and cunning pressure, a cartridge case; from a laboratory, a pinch, a spoonful, a dust, precipitate of earth's and air's primordial motion, the two condensed and combined behind a tiny locked grooved slug and all micrometered to a servant breech and bore not even within its cognizance yet, like a footman engaged from an employment agency over the telephone. (879–80).

The analogy with the bullet connects national history with his personal history: Bullet and speech are both part of a design much grander, larger, more terrifying:

half Europe went to war with the other half and finally succeeded in dragging half the western hemisphere along: a plan, a design vast in scope, exalted in conception, in implication (and hope) terrifying, not even conceived here at Grand Headquarters by the three old generals and their trained experts and advisers in orderly confer- ence, but conceived out of the mutual rage and fear of the three ocean-dividing nations themselves, simultaneously at Washington and London and Paris by some immaculate pollenization like earth's simultaneous leafage, and come to birth at a council not even held at Grand Headquarters but behind locked and guarded doors in the Quai d'Orsay—a council where trained military experts, dedicated as irrevocably to war as nuns are married to God, were outnumbered by those who were not only not trained for war, they were not even braided and panoplied for it—

He means the civilians, the politicians and bankers and merchants who drive the military:

> the Prime Ministers and Premiers and Secretaries, the cabinet members and senators and chancellors; and those who outnumbered even them; the board chairmen of the vast establishments which produced the munitions and shoes and tinned foods, and the mod- est unsung omnipotent ones who were the priests of simple money; and the others still who outnumbered even these: the politicians, the lobbyists, the owners and publishers of newspapers and the or- dained ministers of churches, and all the other accredited travelling representatives of the vast solvent organizations and fraternities and movements which control by coercion or cajolery man's morals and actions and all his mass-value for affirmation. (880–81)

Gragnon's vision of the structure of civilization is far more com- plex and demonic than the old general's. Whereas the old general and Mama Bidet, beneficiaries of the system, believe the human moil, the sheep, the bees, have created the military, Gragnon understands how the powerful establishment figures of church, state, and opinion, have combined in deviously intricate ways to serve themselves at the expense of the grunts and such as he who must die that they might live not just more abundantly but very abundantly indeed. Gragnon thinks of

> all that vast powerful terror-inspiring representation which, running all democracy's affairs in peace, come indeed into their own in war, finding their true apotheosis then, in iron conclave now decreeing for half the earth a design vast in its intention to demolish a frontier, and vaster still in its furious intent to obliterate a people; all in conclave so single that the old gray inscrutable supreme general with the face of one who long ago had won the right to believe in nothing whatever save man's deathless folly, didn't need to vote at all but simply to preside, and so presiding, contemplated the plan's birth and then watched it, not even needing to control it as it took its ordained undeviable course, descending from nations confederated to nations selected, to forces to army groups to armies to corps; all that gigantic long complex chronicle, at the end reduced to a simple regimental attack against a simple elevation of earth too small to show on a map, known only to its own neighborhood and even that by a number and a nickname dating back less than four years to the moment when someone had realised that you could see perhaps a quarter-mile further from its summit than its foot. (881)

The old general envisions civilization as a pyramid that puts him and the other military leaders at the top and the teeming sheeplike masses at the bottom, creating together a structure with the strength and du-rability and majesty of a gothic cathedral. Gragnon sees an inverted pyramid, the old general's turned upside down and depending for its existence on the strength of its smallest unit, the human individual, on whose back the pyramid's downturned point rests, and he believes that the structure therefore is as fragile as an eggshell: its strength depends upon the individuals, alone or in groups, to abide by the laws which keep the fragile structure in place.

They agree on this: a community can not organize itself for war without the willingness of its expendable citizens to die for it or to give up its young: a community organized for war must write its wars with and on the flesh of its young. The individual who refuses to die or at least who refuses to die for culturally-sanctioned reasons thus confounds the system, clogs it up so that it must huff and puff, readjust its methods and its own laws, evict or co-opt the foreign refusive body so that it can function smoothly again, be a community organized for war again. Rejected by the nation whose laws he had faithfully served, Gragnon threatens to become a clog in that smooth functioning. But one has only to consider the chaos that would follow if all human beings refused to play their class-determined role: civilization depends on order, so it must insist that the vast majority obey all the rules, give up their individuality—even that individuality that Faulkner spoke of so often in his public statements in the fifties—so that they, we, can all live reasonably in an orderly world.

The generals co-opt Gragnon by executing him for their own purposes: they plan to have him shot full in the face and then to advertise his death as a glorious heroic one. According to the war they will write, he will have died a hero, in the name and for the glory of France. Gragnon resists his executioners' clumsy methods and twists his head away just as the gun goes off, so that the bullet hits him behind the ear instead of in the face (1019); the executioners repair the damage with wax from a candle they are looking for when the scene ends. He thus fights his own Battle of Harrykin Creek, though this battle is very bloody indeed.

Thus Gragnon becomes my hero in this novel, a fact I didn't realize until the moment I wrote the previous paragraph. Unlike Levine, who commits suicide because his nation betrays his high patriotic idealism, Gragnon, equally betrayed by his country, disengages himself from the nation, refuses to be used as its hero, as the poor corporal is to be used. He, Gragnon, is also more heroic than the idealistic runner if only because his own sacrifice doesn't require the lives of any soldier. He and the runner essentially trade ideological positions as regards the value of the rules, the value of the lives of the grunts. Gragnon begins by insisting upon the rule that says he can execute his disobedient troops; the runner doesn't want that responsibility, so he defaults from his position as officer to his position as runner. But in his eagerness to save humankind from war, the runner is more than willing both to murder three or more guards and to sacrifice the lives almost literally of every soldier who will follow him. All he need do is provide the sign, he thinks—the Masonic sign which he gets from the cockney groom and from Tooleyman—to get all soldiers to embrace in the middle of No Man's Land and just refuse to fight. He would sacrifice them all to that end. Unlike Gragnon, who imagines a single bullet predestined for him alone, the runner constructs a system which will fail precisely because he thinks that there simply aren't enough officers or bullets to execute an entire army of mutineers, envisioning with a sort of grim, sardonic glee, a parody of Gragnon's and the old general's systems, his own a fantastic system which would simply wear itself out trying to execute all the guilty peaceniks:

> it would not matter whether Authority knew about it or not, since even ruthless and all-powerful and unchallengeable Authority would be impotent before that massed unresisting undemanding passivity. He thought: *They could execute only so many of us before they will have worn out the last rifle and pistol and expended the last live shell,* visualising it: first, the anonymous fringe of subalterns and junior clerks to which he had once belonged, relegated to the lathes and wheels to keep them in motion rifling barrels and filling shell-cases; then, the frenzy and the terror mounting, the next layer: the captains and majors and secretaries and attachés with their martial harness and ribbons and striped trousers and brief-cases among the oilcans and the flying shafts; then the field officers: colonels and senators and Members; then, last and ultimate, the ambassadors and ministers and lesser generals themselves frantic and inept among the slowing wheels and melting bearings, while the old men, the last handful of kings and presidents and field marshals and spoiled-beef and shoe-peg barons, their backs to the last crumbling rampart of their real, their credible, their believable world, wearied, spent, not with blood-glut at all but with the eye-strain of aiming and the muscle-tension of pointing and the finger-cramp of squeezing, fired the last puny scattered and markless fusillade as into the face of the sea itself. (728)

There are simply too many such citizens to be controlled if they refuse to obey orders. But their refusal can only be effective against the system if they act as a group. Thus the runner would have them refuse to be one group, subservient to the state, only to become another group, subservient to the high idealism of his own leadership and the sign of authority that he offers them. He leads them into the middle of No Man's Land, where both sides bombard them. We don't know how many of them are killed or injured; we know only that the runner himself receives his own scar, in a "soundless rush of flame which enveloped half his body neatly from heel through navel through chin" (964), creating the "vermilion" scar that is so terrible and so symbolic.

A Fable ends as it began, in a crowd scene. This one occurs in Paris some years after the war's end when the Grateful Nation honors the old general and the unknown soldier with burial at the Arc de Triomphe; we know that the "unknown soldier" is his son, whom he, like other parents in a Grateful Nation, sacrificed to the national good. That is, when he orders his son's execution, he does no more than other fathers and mothers do who think *dulce et decorum est pro patria mori*. Their burial here, together, continues the dialogue begun the evening before the corporal's execution, the always ongoing dialogue between the one and the many, the specific body of the individual and the abstract body of the state; between a system which insists and the body, the corporeality the system insists upon, whose death, whose scars, are essential to the nation's life.

The runner disrupts this solemn occasion. He is now "not a man but a mobile and upright scar, on crutches, he had one arm and one leg, one entire side of his hatless head was one hairless eyeless and earless sear, he wore a filthy dinner jacket from the left breast of which depended on their barber-pole ribbons a British Military Cross and Distinguished Conduct Medal, and a French *Médaille Militaire* . . ." (1070). His medals for bravery, hanging ironically on his tattered coat and body, give him passage through the crowd to the center, where he rips them off his coat and flings them at the caisson on which the old general's body lies, shouting at him the clichés of nationalism, of Fatherland, of patriotism, which had gotten the nation into and then out of the war: "You too helped carry the torch of man into that twilight where he shall be no more; these are his epitaphs: They shall not pass. My country right or wrong. Here is a spot which is forever England—" (1071). The crowd, the police, finally grab him to shut him up. The walking scar, the ugly national wound and symbol of all their pain and anguish, which they all want to forget, is thus cast off out of sight, thrown literally into the gutter, its bearer untouchable because he reminds them that wars are dirty, ugly affairs fought not by generals in their safe clean headquarters or by führers in Berchtesgadens or presidents in oval offices, but by the corporealities of their own individual families, the vulnerable issue of their own flesh, and they cannot afford to let themselves think of that now that this war is over, now that this pain is gone.

The marble Arc de Triomphe accepts the bodies of the general and the corporal, father and son, conservative and anarchist, have and have not. Declaring triumph, the marble arch stands solemn at ground zero of western civilization, presiding solid powerful and profound, absorbing and returning the adoration from the proud throbbing hearts and glistening eyes of the Grateful Nation, a community, still and always, organized for war.

Water, Wanderers, and Weddings

Going to Naples and to No Place

Jane Austen *needed* very little space, very limited material, to work with; asking for little seems immoderate to us. Given: a household in the country, then add its valuable neighbor—and there, under her hands, is the full presence of the world. As if coming in response to a call for good sense, life is at hand and astir and in strong vocal power. At once there is convenient and constant communication between those two houses. The day, the week, the season fill to repletion with news, arrivals, speculation, and fresh strawberries, with tumult and crises, and the succeeding invitations. Everybody doing everything together—what mastery she has over the scene, the family scene! The dinner parties, the walking parties, the dances, picnics, concerts, excursions to Lyme Regis and sojourns at Bath, all give their testimony to Jane Austen's ardent belief—which our century's city-dwellers find odd—that the unit of everything worth knowing in life is in the family, that family relationships are the natural basis of all other relationships.
("The Radiance of Jane Austen," *Eye* 6–7).

In "Moon Lake," Easter, Nina, and Jinny Love approach an old boat hidden in the vines in a forbidden part of the shore. To get to it they have to transgress a barbed wire fence, fight their way through fierce vines, and tromp through treacherous mud. As they near the boat they see a snake drop off into the water, perhaps another one swimming in it; even though she can't swim, Easter jumps eagerly into the old boat and trails her fingertips into the surface of the mysterious waters. Jinny Love is fearful: her "long oval face" goes "vacant" when she sees Easter, the boat, the lake: "I don't choose to sit myself in a leaky boat," she says: "I choose the land" (*Stories* 427), whereon she plants herself firmly, building a sand castle over her foot, keeping safe from the "stobs in the lake" that she fears would upset them if they take a boat ride (428). Nina works hard for the ride: "Firming her feet in the sucking, minnowy mud, [she] put[s] her weight against the boat" and pushes away from the shore, "determined to free it." The land struggles to hold her back: "Soon her legs were half hidden, the mud like some awful kiss pulled at her toes. . . . Roots laced her feet, knotty and streaming" (428). When she finally pushes the boat free, she and Jinny Love get in. Welty sexualizes the scene with the snakes, the stobs, and Nina's meditation on a pear, "beautiful, symmetrical, clean pears with thin skins . . . with snow-white flesh so juicy and tender that to eat one baptized the whole face, and so delicate that while you urgently ate the first half, the second half was already beginning to turn brown. . . . She even went through the rhyme, 'Pear tree by the garden gate, How much longer must I wait?'—thinking it was the pears that asked it, not the picker" (428–29). All three girls are on the verge of adolescence, Easter getting there ahead of Nina and Jinny Love, and the scene displays their varying attitudes toward the changes that are coming, the mixture of eagerness and anxiety. The scene closes when, all three in the boat, they discover that it is chained to the land: they are not yet ready to float free on the complex depths of adolescence and adulthood.

Moon Lake offers possibility, change, romance, escape: it's where Miss Moody, in a boat in the middle of the lake, goes to "hug" her dates. But it's also mysterious, treacherous: "If they let their feet go down, the invisible bottom of the lake felt like soft, knee-deep fur. The sharp hard knobs came up where least expected. . . . The alligators had been beaten out of this lake, but it was said that water snakes—pilots—were swimming here and there. . . . These were the chances of getting sucked under, of being bitten, and of dying three miles away from home" (415).

Mrs. Gruenwald warns the campers against letting "the stobs and cypress roots break your legs" and the girls with parents want "the orphans [to] go in the water first and get the snakes stirred up" (414). They swim under the careful supervision of ladies from Morgana and of Loch Morrison, their lifeguard. A rope separates their swimming area from the rest of the dangerous lake; beyond it lies "the deep part, some bottomless parts. . . . Here and there was the quicksand that stirred your footprint and kissed your heel. All snakes, harmless and harmful, were freely playing now; they put a trailing, moony division between weed and weed—bright, turning, bright and turning" (435). But their best efforts can't prevent Easter from nearly drowning after she is frightened and falls into the lake and Loch has to rescue her.

The scene with the boat is a paradigmatic one in Welty, almost iconic; it takes place in a liminal place where land and water merge, becoming both and neither, marking a transition as yet uncompleted and not likely to be, its muddy combination sucking us deep into its complications, both holding us and promising freedom. A number of Welty's stories turn crucially upon scenes set where land and water meet: Eugene MacLain and the Spanish guitarist come to a place called "Land's End" above San Francisco Bay; Ran MacLain and Maideen Sumrall take their abortive lovemaking to a shabby motel room near Vicksburg apparently cantilevered off the bank out over the Mississippi River; Mattie Will Holifield has a slightly more productive encounter with King MacLain on the banks of the Big Black. "At The Landing" begins with a Mississippi River flood during which Jenny gets raped and ends as she waits in a grounded houseboat for men to come in to her. The two strangers in "No Place for You, My Love" travel south of New Orleans also to "Land's End" over land increasingly below sea level, and Uncle Felix in "Kin" wants to meet Daisy at midnight at the river .

Delta Wedding makes the relationship between bodies of water and sexuality explicit in two scenes. In the first, Dabney, the bride-to-be, wanders on horseback around Shellmound contemplating the momentous step she is about to take into adulthood; she rides by the part of the river where there is a huge whirlpool. Her reactions to it reflect her profound agitation here on the verge of her marriage:

something made her get off her horse and creep to the bank and look in—she almost never did, it was so creepy and scary. This was a last chance to look before her wedding. She parted the thronged vines of the wild grapes, thick as legs, and looked in. There it was. She gazed feasting her fear on the dark, vaguely stirring water.

There were more eyes than hers here—frog eyes—snake eyes? She listened to the silence and then heard it stir, churn, churning in the early morning. She saw how the snakes were turning and moving in the water, passing across each other just below the surface, and now and then a head horridly sticking up. The vines and the cypress roots twisted and grew together on the shore and in the water more thickly than any roots should grow, gray and red, and some roots too moved and floated like hair. On the other side, a turtle on a root opened its mouth and put its tongue out. And the whirlpool itself—could you doubt it? doubt all the stories since childhood of people white and black who had been drowned there, people that were dared to swim in this place, and of boats that would venture to the center of the pool and begin to go around and everybody fall out and go to the bottom, the boat to disappear? A beginning of vertigo seized her, until she felt herself leaning, leaning toward the whirlpool. (*Novels* 211–12)

The second scene, later in the novel, after Dabney and Troy are married, is even more explicit: "Only she had not known how she could reach the love she felt already in her knowledge. In catching sight of love she had seen both banks of a river and the river rushing between—she saw everything but the way down. Even now, lying in Troy's bared arm like a drowned girl, she was timid of the element itself" (333–34). Shellmound, like most homes, provides many places for spouses to drown: on the property is a "Drowning Lake"; the river that runs by the plantation is the Yazoo, whose name means "River of Death."

Land, solid ground, is a known quantity, for better or worse, mostly for worse, as it's the way things are. It's where Loch drags Easter and brings her back to life after pulling her out of the lake; it's where heroic males "vaunt," where Mr. Nesbitt, "from the Bible Class," takes Easter by the arm and turns her around so that he can look at the breasts she has just started (*Stories* 418), where Mr. Voigt flashes Miss Eckhart's piano students. As an alternative to land, water is dangerous, to be sure, but can be negotiated by the courageous and adventurous. Less knowable and predictable, in spite of all its mysterious depths, water can neverthe-less become a measure of a character's capacity to span the treacherous boundaries between solidity and impermanence, security and indepen-dence, oppression and freedom, adolescence and sexual maturity. Thus Virgie Rainey, perhaps Welty's most self-confident, most completely and unashamedly sexual character, can swim unafraid naked in the Big Black river, at one with nature and with herself, unconcerned whether what brushes her knees is a fish or a snake (531). We can't help but re-member that the childhood lover Loch Morrison sees her with from his bedroom window in "June Recital" is a sailor or, more pointedly, that *The Golden Apples* ends as Virgie, the Fisher Queen, sits in the rain she has brought to the waste land of Morgana.

Danièle Pitavy-Souques describes the sea as a "symbole de vie éternel-lement recommencée" (*La Mort* 259) that provides "un espace de rupture, de c'est donc toujours une victoire le discontinu" (261). If her characters seem constantly in transition across the flux of earth and water, it is nearly always water that sets the journey in motion. It provides a rup-ture from the what is and offers hope, the lilt and expectation of the new, whether it's Niagara Falls, the lakes of Killarney, or fountains in foreign countries. It's the inspiration for thirsty lovers everywhere who seek nourishment.

Welty begins with the affirmation that of course love is possible; family is the bedrock fact that defines most people's lives, whether they are in it or out. But she goes profoundly further to face the reality that the very fact that we can and do love is precisely the cause of most of our everyday problems, that the problems caused by the ability to love are no less complicated than those caused by the inability, often because in our terrifying need to love and be loved we fail to give love the rest it must have in order to keep regenerating itself; we thus make of familial intimacy a ferocious and demoralizing thing. In "The Key," for example, a deaf-mute couple, Albert and Ellie Morgan, set out on a journey to find their lost love for one another in the restorative waters of life at Niagara Falls. As the observing narrator suggests, they've missed the train (or boat, if you will) long before now, however, because they think they can find their love outside themselves, at some place other than home. The narrator mostly blames Ellie for their problems because she seems hyper-anxious about everything, hovers over Albert with continual and unrelenting assurances of her love but has never given him the "powerful sign, that reassurance he so hopefully sought, so assuredly deserved." She wants more than anything to talk, to tell him of her love; she regards all silences, all privacies, all secrets, as "unhappiness lying between them, as more than emptiness. She must worry about it, talk about it" (*Stories* 44) and the narrator speculates that she will "sit and brood" over their having missed the train "as over their conversations together, about every mis-understanding, every discussion, sometimes even about some agreement between them that had been all settled—even about the secret and proper separation that lies between a man and a woman, the thing that makes them what they are in themselves, their secret life, their memory of the past, their childhood, their dreams. This to Ellie was unhappiness" (46).

The secret and proper separation that lies between a man and a woman—this seems to me the operative phrase in that story, perhaps in her work as a whole. Pitavy-Souques suggests that the phrase poses "la question du secret de l'âme, de la séparation qui doit exister entre les ep-oux, et du droit à l'inviolabilité de la personnalité" (*La Mort* 257). It allows for at least one meaning of the key, dropped so symbolically by the self-assured stranger, which Albert picks up and holds to his breast: an im-plicit admonition that separateness does, must, exist, and the acceptance of the fact that separateness can never be completely overcome. Love that doesn't recognize the separateness can sour and turn to desperation that relentlessly pursues its beloved, trying to penetrate into the remotest and most secret corners of the other's most private heart, hoping to escape its own loneliness and to find whatever reassurances it needs, in an actual union of the two human beings into one, which is of course impossible.

Sometimes escape takes forms other than travel. Indeed, as they wait, Albert sits with his head framed by a "wall poster, dirty with time, showing an old-fashioned locomotive about to crash into an open tour-ing car filled with women in veils." Although Albert "might seem . . . to be sitting there quite filled with hope," it doesn't take a very so-phisticated Freudian to understand that the poster suggests otherwise, might indeed argue that Albert is quite frustrated and angry at Ellie and at women in general, the veiled mystery of the other. Apparently, like Mr. Marblehall's fascination with *Terror Tales* and *Astonishing Stories*, Albert too fantasizes violence against women as a way out of his unhappiness. The fact that no one is "frightened by the familiar poster," its explicit depiction of impending male violence against women (38), may suggest that the possibility of violence is a commonplace of their lives, so common as to be beyond commenting on.

Familial violence against women, of course, takes many forms in Welty. In *Losing Battles*, the The Renfros, Vaughns, and Beechams demonstrate their hatred, their fear, of outsiders in their treatment of Gloria, who is problematic for them since although she is an outsider who pointedly refuses to be a Beecham, she is nevertheless Jack's wife and the mother of his daughter and so they must deal with her. They delight in the possibility that she may be Jack's first cousin because that would make her one of them even though their marriage would be thus legally incestuous. They initiate her into the family by forcing her face into an opened watermelon, a problematic ritual of play common in many southern and perhaps northern families too. Welty's language describes what the Renfro women do to Gloria as a sexual violation, a rape:

> a trap of arms came down over Gloria's head and brought her to the ground. . . .
>
> She struggled wildly at first as she tried to push away the red hulk shoved down into her face, as big as a man's clayed shoe, swarming with seeds, warm with rain-thin juice.
>
> They were all laughing. "Say Beecham!" they ordered her, close to her ear. They rolled her by the shoulders, pinned her flat, then buried her face under the flesh of the melon with its blood heat, its smell of evening flowers. Ribbons of juice crawled on her neck and circled it, as hands robbed of sex spread her jaws open.
>
> . . . they were ramming the sweet, breaking chunks inside her mouth. . . .
>
> "Come on, sisters, help feed her! Let's cram it down her little red lane! Let's make her say Beecham! *We* did!" came the women's voices. . . .

The aunts were helping each other to their feet. Gloria lay flat,
an arm across her face now, its unfreckled side exposed and as pale
as the underpelt of a rabbit.

"Why, you're just in the bosom of your own family," one of the rapists
says to her (*Novels* 706–7). It's a violent ritual that sugarcoats this vicious
celebration of "family." The only comfort she gets from her mother-in-
law, Miss Beulah, is brutal: "Gloria Beecham Renfro, what are you doing down on the dusty ground like that? Get up! Get up and join your
family, for a change. . . . go back in the house and wash that face and
get rid of some of that tangly hair, then shake that dress and come out
again. Now that's the best thing I can tell you" (708). By forcing her to
eat this particular fruit, her family feeds her, indeed, but violates her in
the very feeding. Part of the violation is that in so feeding her they hope
to close the family circle around her, to contain her alienness within it.

The Vaughn-Renfro-Beecham reunion is in all ways a sham: it
is a *re*-union, of course, which assumes dispersal and fragmentation,
and indeed except for Beulah Beecham Renfro, the family is scattered
throughout the state, many of them wanderers; their parents met mysterious deaths trying to escape from that family "place." Considerable
evidence suggests their ignorance, even illiteracy: apparently they do not
communicate throughout the year and no one writes a comforting letter to the family hero, Jack, while he is in Parchman, to let him know
when his beloved grandfather dies, much less makes the trek across the
state to visit him. Thus this family's "unity" is an illusion, an article of
faith rather than of substance, and all their fine talk a ritualistic paean
to a family structure that does not exist outside the talk. Beulah's land is
no biblical heaven but rather a land of smug insular self-righteousness.
Its communities call themselves Peerless, Wisdom, Upright, Morning
Star, Harmony, Deepstep, and Banner, which Miss Beulah calls the
"very heart" of Boone County (*Novels* 445); its citizens, so far as we
can tell from the Renfros, are none of these things. Across the river,
where Miss Julia Mortimer, the mortal enemy of their insularity and
ignorance, taught her school, is Alliance, a name implying the values
of true community that the Beechams, with all their talking, simply
lack. Connecting Banner and Alliance is a rickety and untrustworthy

bridge constructed about the time Miss Julia came there to teach. She, too, actually dies "in the road" trying to escape her literal imprisonment. The Boone County weekly newspaper is *The Vindicator*: clearly, the ritual story-telling of the reunion is an exercise in vindication—of themselves, or each other, of their state—and not a celebration of love. *Losing Battles* studies this family's single-minded, self-righteous insularity, and it stands as a devastating critique of Welty's native "place" and, not coincidentally, of the clichés of southern literary assumptions about family and geography.

In fetishizing home, we in southern studies have also fetishized place. I do not want to rehearse here the particulars of how badly we have mistaken Welty's ideas about "place" in fiction as a sentimentalization of accidents of geography, but it is, for my purposes, worth calling attention to Carol Manning's argument that *Losing Battles* is a parody of certain aspects of the southern tradition in literature: "parody . . . underlies the work as a whole. While the novel is first and foremost a convincing and amusing story about a particular family, on a second and subtler level it is a parody of values often called Southern and of conventional literary incidents which depict them. . . . Two objects of parody," she claims, "are the values of family devotion and unity" (143). The parody takes those values associated with the southern "place" to their logical extremes and shows what happens when a family—and any relationships radiating outward from home—makes fetishes out of those values, worships them as ends sufficient to themselves and so in effect hides behind them, hoping to stave off anything foreign and therefore suspect.

For Welty's characters, then, home and place are at worst traps, omnivorous insatiable enemies; at best they can be fluid, shifting, distant, by no means the stable constant reality of our mythologizing. "Place" in the first story of *The Bride of the Innisfallen*—the distinctive country south of New Orleans—is specifically *"No Place"* for love: but it is precisely the strangeness of that "place," its distinctiveness, its remoteness from their ordinary lives, and their capacity to discover it, that allows the two strangers a respite, a "Time Out" (*Stories* 561), from the complications that await them back home. There is likewise no "place" for love on the ship in "Going to Naples," none, perhaps, in any of the stories in this volume: No Place at all, except the journey itself. Naples, every bit as much a "place" as New Orleans, with its own unmistakable character, is here merely the end of the journey: "Going" is the operative word.

In *The Bride of the Innisfallen*, then, Welty demonstrates her admonition in "Place in Fiction" that "Human life is fiction's only theme" (*Stories* 793) through its almost complete divorcement from geographical place, from the numerous and cumbersome conventions of her southern and Mississippi place, its steadfast refusal to ring any of the standard southern bells. If in "Going to Naples," Welty operates at the furthest remove from the southern literary trappings, in "Kin" she moves directly into their heart; if in "Going to Naples" she eschews them as unessential to her work, in "Kin" she invokes them all, precisely, I would say, to demonstrate the extent to which those qualities we take to constitute "place" in Mississippi, in literature, are in fact merely constructs, an artifice, a combination of art and imagination. As Pitavy-Souques has convincingly shown ("Blazing Butterflies" 133–37), this is part of what Dicey Hastings discovers on her own journey back to her home "place," when she sees the strangers filling the old home waiting to have their pictures taken in front of a backdrop supplied by the itinerant photographer. It is, Dicey notes, "the same old thing, *a scene that never was*, a black and white and gray blur of unrolled, yanked-down moonlight" (674, my emphasis). She understands the significance of that phony "scene that never was" when, later, she meditates on the one painting in the old house, a "romantic figure of a young lady seated on a fallen tree under brooding skies," her great-grandmother, Evelina Mackaill:

> And I remembered—rather, more warmly, *knew*, like a secret
> of the family—that the head of this black-haired, black-eyed lady
> who always looked the right, mysterious age to be my sister, had
> been fitted to the ready-made portrait by the painter who had called
> at the door—he had taken the family off guard, I was sure of it,
> and spoken to their pride. The yellow skirt spread fanlike, straw
> hat held ribbon-in-hand, orange beads big as peach pits (to conceal
> the joining at the neck)—none of that, any more than the forest
> scene so unlike the Mississippi wilderness (that enormity she had
> been carried to as a bride, when the logs of this house were cut, her

bounded world by drop by drop of sweat exposed, where she'd died
in the end of yellow fever) or the melancholy clouds obscuring the
sky behind the passive figure with the small, crossed feet—none of
it, world or body, was really hers.

Dicey moves from this observation into an epiphany of sisterhood with
her great-grandmother, a bride, too, when she came to Mississippi's wilderness, as Dicey is a bride-to-be:

> *She* had eaten bear meat, seen Indians, she had married into the
> wilderness at Mingo, to what unknown feelings. Slaves had died in
> her arms. She had grown a rose for Aunt Ethel to send back by me.
> And still those eyes, opaque, all pupil, belonged to Evelina—I knew,
> because they saw out, as mine did; weren't warned, as mine weren't,
> and never shut before the end, as mine would not. I, her divided sister,
> knew who had felt the wildness of the world behind the ladies' view.
> We were homesick for somewhere that was the same place. (674–75)

Dicey and Evelina are sisters across the generations, both brides, both
travelers, one to, one from, the same place in Mississippi, one's journey
already long completed, the other's set to begin. Wherever that place,
wherever that "somewhere" that both Dicey and her great-grandmother
are homesick for, it has nothing to do with geography. With all of Mississippi surrounding them, all of that state in all of its placeness, Uncle
Felix's neighbors stand for their portraits in front of a representation of
a place that never was, hoping to locate themselves in time and in space
with whatever shabby representations of place itinerant photographers
can bring with them when they pass through.

Welty's work is amply peopled with outsiders, with rootless wanderers, hitchhikers, the lonely and inarticulate and frustrated, with the
unloved and the unlovely. But if in her work there are outsiders looking in, there are also insiders looking out (Price 61): Tom Harris, the
traveling salesman of "The Hitch-Hikers," sees the little nameless town
in which he finds himself as "none of . . . his, not his to keep, but be-
longing to the people of these towns he passed through, coming out of
their rooted pasts and their mock rambles, coming out of their time. He

himself had no time. He was free; helpless" (88), while the people who feel stuck in that same town look on him as something special, even exotic, colorful in comparison with their drab lives precisely because he seems to be so at home in the outside world: "It's marvelous," says one character of him, "the way he always gets in with somebody and then something happens" (86). A great deal of the energy of Welty's fiction derives from that moment of truth when the wanderer confronts the threshold, going in, or a family member confronts it, coming out. Most characters in one place want desperately to be in another place and expend a good deal of energy trying to get where they are not, even if they do not know where "there" is or what they hope to find when they get there.

In "No Place for You, My Love," two people, strangers to each other and strangers to the place, meet on a sweltering Sunday afternoon in New Orleans. They drive together in his rented convertible into the area south of New Orleans, on a route running parallel to the Mississippi River, until they reach the absolute end of the road. Welty tells us very little about them directly. His being "long" married makes him slip "into a groove" as he looks at her and believes that she is having an affair with a married man (561) and that he feels "more conventional" for thinking so. When she asks about his wife, he replies by holding up his "iron, wooden, manicured" right hand, which we take to signify his wife and their life together; she shifts her eyes from his hand to his face and he looks back at her "like that hand" (570). He is in New Orleans because his wife, back in Syracuse, is entertaining some college friends and does not want him "underfoot" (579). These hints lead us to suspect that there is very little or no passion in his marriage and that she is mostly indifferent to him, although he would have it otherwise.

She has a bruise on her temple, which she fears he will have to see when they dance (575). Perhaps she has merely bumped her head, but she feels that it sticks out "like an evil star," and her resentful hope that his seeing it will "pay him back . . . for the hand he had stuck in her face when she'd tried once to be sympathetic" (576) suggests considerable agitation over the real cause of the bruise and surely invites us to think that she has been struck by a man, perhaps her husband, perhaps the married man her New Orleans companion suspects her of having an affair with.

But the clearest indication of what is wrong back home in Toledo is that she is in New Orleans indulging herself in "deliberate imperviousness" (562). She has come to New Orleans to lick some wound that has hurt her deeply, to escape, for a while, the need to feel anything. This may be why she so resents her companion's rejection of her proffered sympathy with the wooden, rigid hand. "It must stick out all over me," she thinks, self-consciously, at their first meeting in Galatoire's, though what "It" is is left to the reader's imagination: "so people think they can love me or hate me just by looking at me. How did it leave us—the old, safe, slow way people used to know of learning how one another feels, and the privilege that went with it of shying away if it seemed best? People in love like me, I suppose, give away the short cuts to everybody's secrets" (561). "Deliver us all from the naked in heart," she later thinks (568).

On their drive southward they encounter hordes of crayfish and shrimp and terrapins and turtles and alligators, "crawling hides you could not penetrate with bullets" (565), that seem to her "respectable and merciful" (568). Both covet those thick hides, though the thousands of mosquitoes they do battle with remind us that they are not armor-plated, but rather two vulnerable and hurtable human beings.

They come to New Orleans, then, to retreat from unnamed, perhaps unnamable feelings at home. That is why it is "Time out" (561) in New Orleans, why they journey into such a queer place, down to "the end of the road" (570), to the "jumping-off place" (571), where, presumably, they could change their lives at home by stepping off the land, off of all that is solid, known and predictable, safe even if painful, and giving themselves to the water, all that is free, and dangerous. They are near Venice, Louisiana, a name that invokes its namesake city of islands within canals, neither water nor land, one of the fabled cities of romance and ad-venture. "Baba's Place," where they go to eat and dance, is close enough to the water that they can, if they choose, test their willingness and their capacity to step on to the water that would free them from home. They are here for a respite from the usual, the known, and for the afternoon they manage to escape not Time and Place so much as their own times, their own places, to which they know they must eventually return. But for now they are "immune from the world, for the time being," and at the end of the road they come together: dancing, they are "imperviousness in motion": "Surely even those immune from the world, for the time being, need the touch of one another, or all is lost. Their arms encircling each other, their bodies circling the odorous, just-nailed-down floor, they were, at last, imperviousness in motion. They had found it, and had almost missed it: they had had to dance. They were what their separate hearts desired that day, for themselves and each other" (576).

The area south of New Orleans is for him a "strange land, amphibious" (577), a land of insignificant towns that seems to him "like steppes, like moors, like deserts." But there is plenty of life there, happy and buoyant life, among the local people, who laugh boisterously everywhere. The "naked in heart," from whom she has prayed deliverance, abound: a naked baby, couples on porches—even a priest—in underwear; laughing, open faces, defenseless. Significantly, there is water "under everything," even under the tombs in the cemetery through which they drive. When they reach the end of the road he remarks, "If we do go any further, it'll have to be by water" (570). They allow themselves to feel nothing, not even for each other; they refuse to let happen what might happen: they spend the day together without ever really talking, never even exchanging names and actively resisting any impulse to get to know each other. At Baba's, at the extremity of their remove from their real lives, they dance as though "wearing masks" (576). Returning to New Orleans he stops the car and kisses her, but as though he feels obliged to, a perfunctory gesture; he doesn't even know whether he kisses her "gently or harshly" (578). They won't commit themselves to the journey completely; they do not want to grapple with its difficulties here, out of Place, out of Time. She grows thirsty; her lips dry, and at Baba's she asks for a glass of water, which Baba fails to bring to her. When they return to New Orleans, at the end of their day, her only comment is, "I never got my water" (579). The trip has failed to nourish her in any way.

The story ends on a note even stranger than the rest of it. As he drives through New Orleans to return his rented car, he hears partytime cranking up in the bars along the street and is reminded, almost as an epiphany, of his youth as a "young and brash" student in New York, when the "shriek and horror and unholy smother of the subway had its original meaning for him as the lilt and expectation of love" (580). His

past bemoans his present, where those high expectations seem so hope-
lessly and permanently frustrated.

The title of an early typescript of this story, "The Gorgon's Head"
(Marrs 36), suggests that these two people have turned to emotional
stone by something, some quality of experience, that they have looked
at while trying to deal with it, in their own homes. The present title,
which seems to me much more evocative of the experience conveyed in
the story, might be their mutual cry, an apostrophe to love, at the end
of their long afternoon. Perhaps too it is the cry of that "Something that
must have been with them all along [which] suddenly, then [at the end
of their trip], was not. In a moment, tall as panic, it rose, cried like a
human, and dropped back" (579).[1] Perhaps what that "something" cries
is the title of the story; if so, it is a cry of despair, of panic even: no place
for spouse in a complicated household? for lover because of spouse? for
you, here beside me, now, at this moment? for me, alone in a crowd,
thirsty in a rising tide? For these two there is no place, not at home, not
wandering free in a strange world at the bottom of the continent, for
love to thrive.

"The Bride of the Innisfallen," which treats a similar theme, is a piece of
comic magic. Its central character is a young American woman who if
not a newlywed is apparently a recently-wed. She is fleeing from her husband, we are told, leaving London without his knowledge, on the boat-
train to the coastal town of Fishguard, there to take the boat to Cork.
The London she leaves is a dark, rainy city during a "spring that refused
to flower"; it is a "black" 4 p.m. (596). We know little about her beyond
the fact that like the woman in "No Place for You, My Love" she is self-
conscious, waiting alone in the train's compartment, an early arrival, and
feels that her "predicament" is obvious. We do not know until the end of
the story anything about her "predicament," but the people who join her
in the compartment give us clues—a middle-aged woman in a raincoat;
a man from Connemara; a one-eyed Welshman who misses his station
three times in the Welsh night; two Irish sweethearts; a young pregnant

---

1. See also Welty's comments on that "something" in "Writing and Analyzing a Story" (*Eye* 107–15).

wife; a school girl; and a perfectly sullen little boy named Victor, who chews on the leather strap hanging at the door.

The story opens as the woman in the raincoat with "salmony-pink and yellow stripes" joins her in the compartment. She climbs aboard like a "sheltered girl" and indeed gets a "boost up from behind [which] she pretended not to need or notice" from a man we assume to be her husband; he is smaller than she, wears a wet black suit, and has a "doll's smile" on his face: she has a "stronghold of a face" (596). Though she is clearly the more competent of the two, she sits, the perfect wife, patiently enduring, obviously for the umpteenth time, his minutely detailed traveling instructions: " 'You don't need to get out of the carriage till you get to Fishguard,' the round man told her, murmuring it softly, as if he'd told her before and would tell her again. 'Straight through to Fishguard, then you book a berth. You're in Cork in the morning.'" She smiles sweetly, listening to him benignly: "She looked fondly as though she had never heard of Cork, wouldn't believe it, and opened and shut her great white heavy eyelids" (597).

She endures, as the other passengers enter and take their seats and perforce listen too, until the last possible moment. Even after he gets off the train they clasp hands through the window until the train actually starts to move. When he finally turns and starts to walk away, she repudiates him completely by sticking her tongue out at him and "at everything just left behind" (599). This action relieves the building tension and establishes the comic tone of the first part of the story. As soon as she can the lady opens a pack of cigarettes, picks out one that is partly burned down already—apparently one she has almost been caught smoking—and between puffs she holds it "below her knees and turned inward to her palm" (600), as though from long habit hiding her smoking from her husband.

The comic tone which their tender farewell helps launch does not undermine the seriousness of the problem the story treats. This man and woman clearly have problems, though he almost certainly doesn't know it—which is almost as certainly part of their problem. As they stand there in their endless farewell, they "shine in the face like lighthouses smiling" (599)—a complicated image which suggests that those faces, the individuals behind them, keep looking out, searching, seeking to illuminate what they are looking at, while they themselves remain behind the light, in the dark, essentially unseen and unseeable: mysterious and unknowable. But also, like lighthouses, their "shine" should perhaps warn those nearing of invisible dangers.

Everything that happens on this trip centers around things that come between husbands and wives. The incidents are many and come at us in wild and furious counterpoint; but I can mention only a few. Immediately we learn that Victor is returning to Ireland after having attended his brother's wedding in London, a wedding so "grand" (603) it has driven his poor mother to bed; that ceremony, the trouble and expense of it, stands in splendid ironical contrast to the problematic marriages of the story.

The one-eyed Welshman asks Victor whether, in his school, he studied French; Victor replies, "Ah, them languages is no good" (603). This in turn sets off an exchange between the Welshman and the man from Connemara over the relative merits of the Irish and English languages; the man from Connemara makes the exchange thematically important: *"Oh* my God," he says. "I have an English wife. How would she like that, I wouldn't like to know? If all at once I begun on her in Irish! How would you like it if your husband would only speak to you in Irish? Or Welsh, my God?" (604). His question of course is, finally, about the capacity of husbands and wives to communicate with each other. As he asks it he looks around at the young Irish sweetheart, sitting sweetly under the arched arm of her young man: she does not seem "to grasp the question" (605) because at this stage of her love she doesn't believe that anything can go wrong, that anything can come between herself and her sweetheart. The man from Connemara tells the Welshman about his former hobby of raising birds, particularly of one special talking bird, which died, he says, "Owing to conditions in England" (607); that condition, we later learn, is that English wife, who has apparently poisoned the bird, obviously in a rage because he has spent more time talking to it than to her (618).

Finally there are the ghosts, Lord and Lady Beagle, who haunt a Connemara castle, and who seem to represent some quintessence of the marriage bond, at least as the man from Connemara tells about them, in the cycles of romance and violence, permanently alternating: "First she comes, then he comes. . . . She comes first because she's mad, and he slow—got the dagger stuck in him, you see? Destroyed by her. She walks along, carries herself grand, not shy. Then he comes, unwilling, not touching with his feet—pulled through the air. By the dagger, you might say, like a hooked fish. Because they're a pair, himself and herself, sure as they was joined together—and while you look go leaping in the bright air, moonlight as may be, and sailing off together cozy as a couple of kites *to start it again*" (608, my emphasis). The sweethearts, the innocents, again cannot understand, and they are simply amazed.

On board the *Innisfallen*, the boat from Fishguard to Cork, after having traveled in close quarters on the train, the travelers disperse, and quiet prevails. The larger compartment for the third-class passengers is a "vortex of quiet, like a room where all brains are at work and great decisions are on the brink." Old men, "lost as Jesus's lambs," wait for the bar to open. The young pregnant wife, who has already told everybody how anxious she is, how much she hates traveling over water, is "as desperate as she'd feared." She "saw nothing, forgot everything, and even abandoned Victor, as if there could never be any time or place in the world but this of her suffering." The man from Connemara sprawls out asleep, though at one point he looks up to see the American girl "pinned to her chair across the room, as if he saw somebody desperate who had left her husband once, endangered herself among strangers, been turned back, and was here for the second go-round . . ." (619–20). He may be right. She simply stares back at him, motionless, lost in her own thoughts.

The next morning finds them near journey's end, on their way up-river to Cork City, after crossing "a far, wide sea, very deep and treacherous" (611). In contrast to the rain and gloom of the London they left, and to the dark and foggy night of Wales they have traveled through, in Ireland it is bright, "a world of sky coursing above, streaming light." And if in London spring "refused to flower" (596), in Cork City it has flowered brilliantly: "Boughs that rocked on the hill were tipped and weighted as if with birds, which were really their own bursting and almost-bursting leaves. In all Cork today every willow stood with gold-red hair springing and falling about it, like Venus alive. Rhododendrons swam in light, leaves and flowers alike; only a shadow could separate them into colors" (623).

This is the end of the journey, a new beginning, the edge of experience, the jumping-off point—a new time, a new place, bright with expectation, blossoming with possibility. As the boat pulls into the dock someone shouts "There's a bride on board" (621), though the shouter apparently doesn't know that there is more than one "bride"; this one, though, seems to symbolize all the bright promise of that glorious Cork morning and clearly stands in subtle contrast to the old married folk we have encountered in the story. Welty's description of the bride is gently satiric: she stands "by the rail in a white spring hat and, over her hands, a little old-fashioned white bunny muff. She stood there all ready to be met, now come out in her own sweet time. Delight gathered all around, singing began on board, bells could by now be heard ringing urgently in the town" (621).

Significantly, though, she is alone in her anticipation, waiting to be met. We do not see *her* off the boat and we will not know whether anyone meets her. But we do see what happens to the others: the woman in the raincoat, in a beautifully understated scene, is met by a "flock of beautiful children" and a man bigger than herself, whom she is extremely glad to see. Welty refuses to explain which, if either, of the two men—the one here or the one who put her on the train in London—is actually her husband, and we can easily conclude, if we want to (and I certainly do) that the woman in the raincoat somehow leads two lives, one in London, another in Cork, like Mr. Marblehall, perhaps, or, in view of the children in Cork, more like a Remarkable Mrs. Pennypacker. Doubtless she will soon be as ready to leave Cork as she was to leave London, and will again stick out her tongue in repudiation, this time of Cork. The man from Connemara disappears mysteriously into the streets with his cap set on his head at a "fairly desperate angle." Sadly, the young pregnant wife is met by "old women in cloaks" and three young men who are apparently her brothers: which helps to explain why she has been so quietly desperate during the trip; it does not appear that any of the three young men is her husband.

The American woman, on whom the final paragraphs of the story focus, of course meets no one and does not want to: that is why she has come to Cork. She spends the glorious spring day wandering the streets, completely free and exhilarated. But at the end of the day her real life, her "predicament," catches up with her; it begins to rain. She thinks of her husband and starts to wire him. "England was a mistake," she writes, then scratches it out, taking back "the blame but without words." We surmise that she and her husband had gone to London, possibly from America, and apparently at her instigation, like Albert and Ellie Morgan hoping that different surroundings might nurture, reaffirm, their love for one another and make their lives together smoother; but it obviously has not done so. The problem, apparently, is not a loss of love between them, but rather "Love with the joy being drawn out of it"—"that was loneliness," she thinks, there in London with her husband and all their complications—not "this" (623), here in Cork, where she knows nobody. We do not know clearly what her trouble is, but it seems to be an inability to communicate some excess of joy, which she therefore has to stifle to keep from getting out of hand. She cannot tell him her "secret": perhaps, like Ellie Morgan, she tries too hard, cannot let it rest; perhaps she speaks to him in her own equivalent of Irish, a language he cannot understand. Perhaps he is indifferent to her. Her trouble, he has told her, is that she "hope[s] for too much" (624)—from him, perhaps, from herself, from their marriage, from life. And so she has found London, too, stifling. "*I* was nearly destroyed," she thinks (623).

Her trip to Cork, another place, but without her husband, has released her from her building pressures at home; she is exhilarated, wants to wire home "Don't expect me back yet." As the story ends she enters a pub, a "lovely room full of strangers" (624)—a room full of people who don't know her and whom she doesn't know, and who therefore cannot either expect things of her or put limitations on her. It is an ending very much like that of "No Place for You, My Love," in which the man, after his wandering, remembers his youth in New York and the crowds and the shrieking clash of the subway as the "lilt and expectation of love": the bright promise, for both of them, of openness, of possibility, of freedom, of love without complication.

The more serious subtext of "Kin" concerns the mysterious events of Kate's and Dicey's barely remembered childhoods at Mingo, the old family home—especially one event which they treat comically as a family legend while the two of them and Kate's mother, Dicey's Aunt Ethel, visit and reminisce. On Aunt Eva's wedding day, Sister Anne "fell" into the well. Kate believes she fell "on purpose" to make her "contribution to Cousin Eva's wedding celebrations, and snitching a little of *her* glory" (651). Sister Anne has remained an old maid and "Eva's Archie Fielder got drunk every whipstitch for the rest of his life" (652), Aunt Ethel says, maintaining the comic tone of the family legend but perhaps intimating that something more serious was at work than "southern" eccentricity. Given the juxtaposition in the telling, we might infer a connection between her "fall" and Uncle Archie's drinking, a connection that allows us to speculate that Sister Anne might have jumped in, in sorrow, for something, some love, some disappointment that perhaps had passed between her and Archie. Did she try to commit suicide over losing him? The story provides no answer, of course, but rather suggests a darker alternative to the family history still current as Dicey comes "home" for a final visit before she gets married. There seem to be other suppressed narratives: there always are.

Kate and Aunt Ethel treat Sister Anne with great disdain for being country and "vulgar"; she's "the remotest kin in the world" (649), "a remote cousin of Uncle Felix's, to begin with. Your third cousin twice removed, and your Great-aunt Beck's half-sister, my third cousin once removed and my aunt's half-sister . . ." (650), Aunt Ethel tells Dicey, before Dicey doesn't want to hear any more and stops her. She's a "buzzard" (648) Kate says, describing how she just "insists" her way into the family (648). She can't cook or sew or "cultivate her mind" (654) and, of course, she is lazy, though she certainly doesn't seem lazy in the latter part of the story at Mingo, where she appears very busy indeed. But Sister Anne has been the only one of the family, remote as she is, to have come to Mingo to take care of the ailing Felix. She claims to have seen no other family members and, tellingly, claims not to have seen "a living soul in fourteen days." They patronize her as "*poor* Sister Anne" (652) because she isn't married: "She just hasn't got anybody of her own, that's her trouble. And she needs somebody" (654): they simply can't understand why, at age forty, Sister Anne left a man standing at the altar (650). Dicey meanspiritedly tells her that Aunt Ethel hasn't been out because "she just can't abide you" (676), even though it seems clear that Aunt Ethel is now bedridden herself. Apparently Dicey thinks

Sister Anne is invulnerable to such insults. She sees Sister Anne putting rosebuds into a vase with "unscratchable hands" (663) but soon after notes with "reluctance" that her "fingers were bleeding from the roses" (665). Sister Anne is clearly more vulnerable than any of them think. Such details allow us to wonder whether there's a connection of any sort between her episode in the well, Eva's wedding, and her maiden life.

Perhaps she's not the only vulnerable one. During her seventeen years of widowhood, Aunt Ethel has not been able to "bear to hear the name of her husband spoken, or to speak it herself" (652), we do not know whether from love and grief or from anger and shame, though it's a curiously protective reaction that seems to call for some speculation. Dicey snidely insinuates that Kate will probably be an old maid by claiming that she, Dicey, was not going to be one (647). She's "already engaged up North," but hasn't yet set a date for some reason, a fact that may indicate either eagerness or reluctance to go through with it.

Water, besides that in the well, plays a recurring role in "Kin." It begins in Sister Anne's report on Felix, which she writes on the old-fashioned gilt-edged "correspondence card," to let them know that she must watch him day and night and that she has to drop water on his tongue so he can speak (648). Aunt Ethel thinks it "just isn't fair to have water dropped on your tongue" (653), but doesn't spell out what she thinks is wrong with that, especially when he apparently can't speak at all without it, or speculate what illness or condition keeps him from drinking it by the glassful, especially now that Mingo has indoor plumbing. At Mingo, Kate and Dicey discover that Anne has shunted Felix into a little crude cubbyhole of a room for the day while a photographer takes pictures in the parlor; in the room is a "water pitcher that did not look cold, and a spoon," with which Kate pours some water onto his tongue (669). At lunch on the old breezeway, they are "so lightly enclosed there" that it is "as though we ate in pure running water" (670): Dicey continues to romanticize Mingo, through an association of water with all that remains of her memories of her visits here as a child. In Uncle Felix's cubbyhole she finds the stereopticon that she had loved, with which she and Uncle Felix had visited romantic lands. He was apparently obsessed with being or seeing some place else, she thinks, because it "was as though, while he held the stereopticon to his eye, *we* did not see *him*" (671); he becomes virtually an ostrich, hiding from the present world, which is less gentle and inviting than what the stereopticon offers: "Sand-pink cities and passionate fountains, the waterfall that rocks snuffed out like a light, islands in the sea, red Pyramids, sleeping towers . . . volcanoes; the Sphinx, and Constantinople; and again the Lakes"—the Lakes of Killarney (671). Plenty of passion here, a dream of change to challenge and engage the desire for other worlds. Unlike Uncle Felix, Dicey has lived in one of those "picture cities" (671), and she may understand the desire always to be someplace else, especially if for any reason one is unhappy at home, even as she meditates on the painting of her pioneer Great-Grandmother Evelina Jerrold, "her divided sister": "We were homesick for somewhere that was the same place" (675). That's perhaps why she's shaken when Uncle Felix, just before they leave, hands her a cryptic note with a mysterious message: "River—Daisy—Midnight—Please" (675).

Neither she nor Kate understands the message, though Dicey pretends to. It seems clearly a reversion to the past, like his equally cryptic oral reversion to what seems his time as a drummer boy in the Civil War (667–68). Some have suggested that Uncle Felix confuses "Daisy" with "Dicey," but there's no evidence that anybody actually says "Dicey" in his presence and he seems far too enfeebled to remember her from her childhood visits. But Dicey is shaken, she tells Kate, by the word "Please" (678). Kate is adamant that Felix means Beck, his wife, and that he wants her "to meet him in Heaven" (675). But Dicey believes, with a "secret pang," that Uncle Felix had been cheating, or wanting to, perhaps begging to: "I know I did feel the cheat he had found and left in the house, the helpless, asking cheat. I felt it more and more, too strongly" (679). Why she feels this "too strongly" we are left to speculate. She has remembered Uncle Felix as quite a gentleman, responding to his roses as they approach the house. Now, seeing his Cape Jessamines "all in bud," she seems "to reel from a world too fragrant" (678). Perhaps, as Quentin Compson suffocates from the smell of honeysuckle, which he associates with his sister's sexuality, so does Dicey suffocate from the fragrance of the Cape Jessamines—a discovery of illicit passion, even betrayal, where she least expected it; or perhaps she discovers not passion so much as its absence where it should be, a check on love where she had always assumed it thrived. As she thinks how the "please" hurts her, she puts "the old iron ring over the gate and fasten[s] it" (678), locking away all those unsettling feelings. "Kin" ends as she and Kate drive home, getting farther and farther away from those feelings, to where she can again face the future, thinking "of my sweetheart, riding, and wonder[ing] if he were writing to me" (681). It presents itself as an ending like the endings of "No Place for You, My Love" and "The Bride of the Innisfallen," but it lacks the intimations of joy, the lilt of expectation, in memory, in expectation, that those characters feel.

Why her certainty that Felix has wanted to cheat on his wife? She "reels from a world too fragrant," just, she says, as Aunt Ethel "had reeled from one too loud" (678). Has Aunt Ethel refused to hear or mention her husband's name for all these years because he, too, was unfaithful? Did Sister Anne and Archie cheat on Eva? As she leaves the old home, Dicey turns for one more look and notices the old house, "floating on the swimming dust of evening" and looking to her like a "safe-shaped mass darkening" (680). This is a phrase worth pondering: home, all that it means to the memory, to the past, all its accumulated meanings as our source, all of its power to sustain us, becomes, as she looks, an undifferentiated mass against the evening, a mass shaped vaguely like safety but darkening into the unknown, the alien and dangerous. "Home," the idea of home, is our location in time and space, but it is also the fata morgana, the "desert illusion" of all those things that "home" ought to mean but so seldom, in Welty's fiction, actually does mean. The four small words of Uncle Felix's elliptical note have undone Dicey's family history, unmoored the permanently fixed characters and incidents by the suggestion of marital betrayals. Uncle Felix, lost like an ostrich in the Lakes of Killarney and other romantic places contained in the stereopticon: was he too escaping from an unhappy marriage? Did he cheat on Aunt Beck? Did Aunt Beck cheat on him, or simply deny him sufficiencies of water, as Sister Anne does? Did Sister Anne leave her fiancé at the altar for the same reasons? Will Dicey's husband betray her? Has he already?

That's Dicey's house darkening in front of her. Whyever she came to Mississippi for this visit, whatever fears and anxieties about marriage she brought with her, she will take them back with her, increased by the loss of the home she had remembered.

As Dicey and Kate prepare to leave Mingo Dicey turns to see all those gathered there to have their photographs taken "posed there along the rail, quiet and obscure and never-known as passengers on a ship already embarked to sea. Their country faces were drawing in even more alike in the dusk, I thought. Their faces were like dark boxes of secrets and desires to me, but locked safely, like old-fashioned caskets for the safe conduct of jewels on a voyage" (680). "Going to Naples," the story immediately following and the final story in *The Bride of the Innisfallen*, literalizes her metaphor.

"Going to Naples," along with "The Bride of the Innisfallen" and "Circe," stands at the furthest remove of any of her stories from her home territory, yet at the same time it masterfully encapsulates many of the themes and characters Welty had dealt with in the "Mississippi" fiction: thematically it is very familiar territory, though considerably darker. If "The Bride of the Innisfallen" and "No Place for You, My Love" end on notes that invoke the memory of love's happy expectations, "Going to Naples" dramatizes the darkness at the heart of domesticity: youth's urge toward sexual freedom in courtship and marriage—precisely love's expectation—and family strictures against it. It ends on a darkening note consonant with the end of "Kin."

It begins very simply, "The *Pomona* sailing out of New York was bound for Palermo and Naples" (*Stories* 682), by naming the journey's origins and its destination and identifying the story's "place" in its first three words—"The *Pomona* sailing"—as not just the physical ship but rather its motion through markless oceanic space. The *Pomona's* place, then, may rather be time itself than anything geographical: the view from the *Pomona's* rear deck is of the ship's wake, its evanescent path, the fading record of where the passengers and crew have come from; the view from the front deck, until they reach sight of the European shore, is empty of all save water and sky. It is a "warm September" (682), and the crossing intersects the autumn solstice, a conjunction of water, sky, time, and storm that frees Gabriella, if only momentarily, from her overbearing mother and from the young man, Aldo Scampo, with whom, but for her mother, she might fall in love.

Two scenes merit attention. The first is a record of Gabriella's and Aldo's burgeoning love:

> The long passage through the depths of the ship . . . seemed made for Gabriella and Aldo. True, it was close with the smell of the sour wine the crew drank. In the deepest part, the engines pounding just within that open door made a human being seem to go in momentary danger of being shaken asunder. It sounded here a little like the Niagara Falls at home, but she had never paid much attention to *them*. Yet with all the deafening, Gabriella felt as if she and Aldo were walking side by side in some still, lonely, even high place never seen before now, with mountains above, valleys below, and sky. The old man in the red knit cap who slept all day on top of that box was asleep where he always was, but now as if he floated, with no box underneath him at all, in some spell. Even the grandfather clock, *even the map*, when these came into sight, looked faceless, part of a landscape. (693; second emphasis mine)

In this marvelous passage, Gabriella and Aldo's love creates its own magical landscape, its own romantic "place," out of the sour smells and loud mechanical clanging of a physical setting perhaps indebted to O'Neill's *The Hairy Ape*. The "faceless" grandfather clock suggests that this is Time Out for them too, as New Orleans and the land south of it is for the strangers in "No Place for You, My Love," thought they are never very far from time, as the solstice and the old people remind her.

"Going to Naples" is a dark allegory of the voyage from the New World to the Old, from childhood into sexual play if not yet into sexual experience, into independence and maturity, then directly into old age and death, the destined "place" of all travelers. One older man is going past Naples to Genoa, the city, he says, of the most beautiful cemeteries in the world. Numerous old women on the trip, introduced early, form a significant part of the story's metaphorical understructure. Their faces haunt Gabriella: they are always "the same black shawls, the same old caps, backed up against the blue [of the sky]—faces coming out of them that grew to be the only faces in the world, more solid a group than a family's, more persistent one by one than faces held fast in the memory or floating to nearness in dreams. On the best benches sat the old people, old enough to be going home to die . . ." (684).

As the *Pomona* leaves New York harbor, Gabriella waves to one woman, the Statue of Liberty, saying goodbye, in effect, to the freedom and liberty of her childhood; she has already waved goodbye, even if she doesn't know it, to the romantic waters of Niagara Falls, the quintessential destination, the "place" of honeymooning lovers; but she, having never been in love before, has never paid much attention to the falls. On board she and Aldo explore no known landscape at all but rather a universal landscape, the universal place, of romantic love, which she has also never seen before. Landing in Naples harbor, she says hello to another woman, her grandmother, whom she and her mother have traveled to visit. Nonna sits, significantly, "almost in the center of everything." Like the old women on the boat, she is a "little, low, black figure waiting. It was the quietest and most substantial figure there, unagitated as a little settee, a black horsehair settee, in a room where people are dancing" (716). This description reminds us of Gala Night on board, during which the old ladies preside over the moment of her independence, the moment when she discovers that she can dance alone—and, indeed, even prefers to dance alone, though her freedom from time, when it comes back "in" at their landing in Naples, is completely illusory, a flailing at her realities, from which there really is no Time Out. It would be lovely to think, with Dawn Trouard, that in her dance Gabriella accepts and even celebrates her aloneness as the condition of her existence (cited in Kreyling, *Understanding* 186). Perhaps she does for this brief moment. But the solstice during which Gala night occurs changes nothing. Time is never really Out, and Gabriella must, like all escapees, yield to reality. These old women, going home to die, are auguries of her future, and Nonna, already in Naples, also in black, waiting for Gabriella, makes one with them, ominous, portentous:

> And there was Nonna, her big, upturned, diamond-shaped face
> shimmering with wrinkles under its cap of white hair and its second
> little cap of black silk. . . .
>
> Nonna drew Gabriella down toward all her blackness, which
> the sun must have drenched through and through until light and

color yielded to it together, and to which the very essence of that smell in the [Naples] air . . . clung. . . . She gave Gabriella an ancient, inviting smile. (716–17)

Mama Serto has the story's closing line. It's something of a non sequitur, for nothing in the story's language prepares us for it; but emotionally, thematically, it is stunningly appropriate. She hears the church bells "in the still-hidden heart of Naples" (722) and exclaims: "And the nightingale . . . is the nightingale with us yet?" We stop short of an automatic response—"Yes: *already* with us"—for the magical flourish upon which the story ends so abruptly strikes us with wonder: suddenly we are in yet another place, the specifically literary place of Keats's "Ode to a Nightingale," whose melancholy preoccupation with easeful death informs the whole story, especially in its elegiac closing pages.

Yet perhaps we react too soon from Keats, since the story supplies no answer and the question comes from Mama's pretty certain sense that indeed the nightingale is *not* with them. But it doesn't seem likely that Mama is looking for poetry to redeem her from this world where "youth grows pale, and spectre-thin, and dies." For Keats the nightingale, the "immortal Bird," represents the freedom attained through poetry that outlives mortal humanity; he associates the bell that tolls him "back from [the bird] to [his] sole self," the self that must bear unhappiness and die, with the word "Forlorn." But her question comes from a voice "beseeching" (722) apparently to her mother, whom she follows through the gate. Perhaps she wants an answer from her mother that she can't give to her own daughter: When will I be happy? When will I be free?

Just prior to the bells, Mama witnesses a heartbreaking goodbye between Aldo and her daughter: Gabriella "reached out her hand and with her fingertips touched his cello," which Welty sexualizes into the phallus she is likely never to caress: "—or rather its wrinkled outer covering, at once soft and imperious. It was like touching the forehead of an animal" (721). As they watch Aldo's back pass through the gate and out of Gabriella's life, Mama begins to cry. "*She* was being the daughter—the better daughter" (722)—better, apparently, than Gabriella, though we are not sure why. Nonna stands up to go lead them home: she stands "perfectly straight, and could have walked by herself, though Mama, with a cry of remembrance, seized hold of her" and they move toward the gate. What does Mama remember when she touches Nonna? Her own youth of bright expectation, which the ungainly Gabriella has already, on board, used up? Is Mama the "better daughter" because she had a family? Perhaps she weeps for all that Gabriella will not have, even though she herself is the agent of her not having it. In a line they march toward the bells that toll for them. Nonna leaves the port first, though none too firmly; Gabriella's mother follows and "Gabriella [takes] her place a step behind" (722), following in their footsteps. "See Naples and die!" Aldo shouted at Poldy as they walked down the gangway (714): Gabriella surely will, if she is not dead already.

Nearly all the traveling in Welty's fiction is intimately connected with family; dissatisfaction at home inevitably generates escape, from parents or spouse, a search somewhere else for what home is supposed to provide but doesn't, and when it does it often does so in strangling portions that leave us even more unsatisfied, needy, and lonely. Family is the locus in Welty for all that simultaneously gives us life and robs it from us; for all that feeds us and terrifies us, like the pigeons Laurel Hand remembers from her visits to her grandmother's mountain home in West Virginia, who stick "their beaks down each other's throats, gagging each other, eating out of each other's craws, swallowing down all over again what had been swallowed before: they were taking turns. The first time, she hoped they might never do it again, but they did it again next day while the other pigeons copied them. They convinced her that they could not escape each other and could not themselves be escaped from. So when the pigeons flew down, she tried to position herself behind her grandmother's skirt, which was long and black, but her grandmother said again, 'They're just hungry, like we are'" (*Novels* 969).

We're all hungry, we all want to feed and be fed: that essential and repetitive intimacy—feeding and eating, "swallowing . . . what had been swallowed before"—lies at the core of Welty's families, creates problem in the very act of giving and needing, the understandable attempts to be close that give to intimacy a quality of despair, the more because "family" *means* comfort and stability but is so easily upset precisely because the intimacy itself so often throws things out of balance. In "Acrobats in the Park" a family of acrobats delicately balances itself on each other's arms and legs in intricate and artful patterns, until one of them becomes pregnant and they can no longer hold together: what nourishes life often destroys structure or at least alters the structure in ways that demand new ways of understanding it, or adapting. But the old structures cling tenaciously to their unity, their traditions; they struggle desperately to survive through memory that willfully misrepresents the past and defrauds the present and, too often, through violence. It's a careful balancing act indeed that can handle the stress that change inevitably brings without crumbling, without sending children and spouses outward from a center that cannot, or at least does not, hold. As Welty describes them, Jane Austen's families could maintain that balance. Welty's don't seem to be able to.

The Landscape of Alienation in "Old Mr. Marblehall"

I n its own way, "Old Mr. Marblehall" is as much a tour-de-force as William Faulkner's "Carcassonne"—richly poetical, densely imaged; cooler and more detached, but just as calmly deliberate, as totally confident in its power to shake and move and tantalize, and no less stubbornly reluctant to yield itself to us completely. Despite its manifest modernity, however, it resonates powerfully with two curious but equally enigmatic nineteenth-century short stories that may provide at least one way of getting at its riches. Like "Old Mr. Marblehall," both Edgar Allan Poe's "The Man of the Crowd" and Nathaniel Hawthorne's "Wakefield" are narrated by observers who find something anomalous in the behavior of a denizen of a crowded city, a citizen otherwise indistinguishable from those thronging around him in the streets.

Poe's narrator does not pretend to be a writer but claims merely to be an interested observer of human types. His story begins in a London coffee house, through the window of which he watches the streets while recuperating from a bout of ill health. He observes that it was "well said of a certain German book" that "it does not permit itself to be read": "There are some secrets which do not permit themselves to be told. Men die nightly in their beds, wringing the hands of ghostly confessors, and looking them piteously in the eyes—die with despair of heart and convulsion of throat, on account of the hideousness of mysteries which will not *suffer themselves* to be revealed" (388).

As he watches the great blur of humanity walk past his window, this narrator arranges them into categories according to their appearance and demeanour—clerks, gamblers, jew pedlars, pickpockets. Close to nightfall he notices in the midst of the mob an old man sixty-five to seventy years old, approximately Mr. Marblehall's age, who has a

> countenance which at once arrested and absorbed my whole attention, on account of the absolute idiosyncracy of its expression. Any thing even remotely resembling that expression I had never seen before. . . . As I endeavored . . . to form some analysis of the meaning conveyed, there arose confusedly and paradoxically within my mind, the ideas of vast mental power, of caution, of penuriousness, of avarice, of coolness, of malice, of blood-thirstiness, of triumph, of merriment, of excessive terror, of intense—of supreme despair. I felt singularly aroused, startled, fascinated. "How wild a history," I said to myself, "is written within that bosom!" (392)

The narrator, wanting to "know more" of this man's life, follows him for the next twenty-four hours, in the pouring rain, in and out of London's richness and its desolation, as he seeks crowds to be among, seeming first to have a destination or a purpose, and then not to. As the next evening looms, the fatigued narrator gives up his secrecy, steps in front of the man, stops, and looks him full in the face. The man does not notice him at all, decides he cannot "read" this character, gives up the chase, and concludes the narration by calling the old man *"the man of the crowd,"* re-invoking the nostrum with which he began, that some books, and some people, cannot be read.

Hawthorne's "Wakefield" is a more striking analogue to "Old Mr. Marblehall." Mildred Travis suggested in 1974 that it could be an actual source for Welty's story. Travis is correct, I think, in ways that go considerably beyond the number of narrative and thematic parallels she draws in her note and which in some ways anticipate Danièle Pitavy-Souques' reading of "Old Mr. Marblehall." In "The Man of the Crowd," Poe's narrator spots his hero because something in his face sets him apart; the hero of Hawthorne's story begins as a character—"let us call him Wake-field" (290), the narrator says, as Melville's asks to be called Ishmael—in "some old magazine or newspaper" that the narrator "recollects" (290) having read. The story was reported as truth, he claims, of a man who left his wife and home one day in London, established his own residence one block away in another street, lived there secretly for twenty years unbeknownst to his wife, who assumed he was dead, and then just as suddenly and unexpectedly returned and lived his remaining years at home as "a loving spouse" (290). Poe's narrator believes that some lives cannot be read; Hawthorne's is equally sure that that fact need not deter one from the pleasures of imposing a "reading," even upon a "person" appearing as a character in a newspaper story.

Intrigued with this bare bone of an incident, Hawthorne invites readers to construct their own narratives about this curious man or to follow him as he constructs one. The substance of "Wakefield," then, is a fiction-writer's speculations on how one might build a fiction out of such putatively "factual" materials, working, as Ellen Westbrook sug-gests, "within the range of the probable," and, by implication, asking readers to consider where narrative truth lies (4). He thus anticipates by eighty-six years Virginia Woolf's demonstration in "An Unwritten Novel" of how ceaselessly a fictive mind works to impose upon the ob-served world or to deduce from it such assignments of character and motive and circumstance as help explain it or *make it interesting.*[1]

Hawthorne's narrator then summarizes Wakefield's life during these twenty years so near to yet so far from his former life. He speculates about Wakefield's relationship with that former life, describing the times he ap-proaches his old home, spies upon his wife in her domestic surroundings, and flees again to his own apartment. The narrator constantly sets him, like Poe's Man of the Crowd, against the busy London streets; he believes that he must "follow close at his heels" to keep up with Wakefield, "ere he lose his individuality" (292) in the crowd, since there is nothing to distin-guish him from the crowd except the narrator's interest, and ours, which has been piqued by something very strange that Wakefield has *done,* not

---

1. In 1944 Welty reviewed Woolf's posthumous *The Haunted House,* and paid particular attention to "An Unwritten Novel."

by anything special that he *is*: "Poor Wakefield!" he writes. "Little knowest thou thine own insignificance in this great world! No mortal eye but mine has traced thee" (292). Welty's narrator similarly asserts, in a Mississippi idiom, that "nobody gives a hoot about any old Mr. Marblehall. . . . Nobody cares. Not an inhabitant of Natchez, Mississippi, cares if he is deceived by old Mr. Marblehall" (96), but obviously the narrator, like Poe's and Hawthorne's, who may or may not be an inhabitant of Natchez, cares a great deal about him and his deception—as, thanks to the observing narrator, does the reader.

Like Old Mr. Marblehall, Wakefield enters the crowd precisely *to be discovered*. He becomes Poe's Man of the Crowd, but without his desire for anonymity: as Hawthorne depicts him, he imagines footsteps following him and a far-off voice calling his name. But he cannot escape his own insignificance because he cannot force acknowledgment from someone external to himself. Indeed, after ten years' separation, one day he jostles against his wife in a crowded street; they stand face to face, but he is so much a face in the crowd that though they stare directly into each other's eyes, even she does not recognize him (296).[2] The narrator makes one minor incursion into the mind of Wakefield's wife, to observe that she, "without having analyzed his character, was partly aware of a quiet selfishness, that had rusted into his inactive mind—of a peculiar sort of vanity, the most uneasy attribute about him—of a disposition to craft, which had seldom produced more positive effects than the keeping of petty secrets, hardly worth revealing—and lastly, of what she called a little strangeness, sometimes, in the good man" (291).

The narrator assumes that such a person as Wakefield would be characterized by a "certain sluggishness," by an intellect given to "long and lazy musings, that tended to no purpose"; his thoughts are "seldom so energetic as to seize hold of words. Imagination, in the proper meaning of the term, made no part of Wakefield's gifts" (291). A bit later he tells us, more bluntly, that Wakefield's behavior is "characteristic of a feeble-minded man" (293).

---

2. An ironist might suspect that she in fact *does* recognize him and refuses to admit it, but there is no evidence of such irony in the text—which is a very good reason to believe that the narrator, like our author, is a male! But it is pleasant to a modernist to suggest that she may believe herself well rid of him.

At least three compulsions work on Wakefield, as the inventing narrator constructs it for us, though it is not completely clear whether these compulsions are simultaneous and therefore contradictory and troubling to Wakefield or whether Hawthorne's narrator offers them simply as clearly distinct possible motives for his behavior. The first is that unlike Poe's man, but very much like Mr. Marblehall, Wakefield desperately wants to be discovered, to be observed, so that he will signify something: he is, he thinks, doing something "singular," something that lifts him out of the crowd, out of the blur of the quotidian, out of the ordinariness of domesticity. But of course in his thinking he cannot be singular unless some observer authenticates him as such; his desire to be seen as singular, then, in effect cancels itself out. The second compulsion is to put himself in danger of discovery, from which situations he constantly re-enacts his escape from insignificance, ritualizing it into patterns that impose significance. The third compulsion is more perverse. He refuses to return home, because he has been "rendered obstinate" by "the *inadequate sensation* which he conceived to have been produced in the bosom of Mrs. Wakefield. He will not go back until she be frightened half to death" (294; my emphasis), until he has seen some evidence of her mourning for him, mourning that would give him proof that he does indeed signify something in her life and therefore in his own, proof that she obviously cannot or will not give him.

He uses his absence, then, to manipulate a reaction, to force from his wife a reaction consistent with his need to have his own significance confirmed; he does not want to abandon his life but rather to live at a distance from it, to construct that unlived life as a reflection of his wife's response to his absence. He wants to gain a life by a fantastic triangulation between his present life, his wife's responses, and what he imagines his former life *might have been* if he were there to live it, although to be sure the narrator assures us that "imagination" is not one of Wakefield's strong suits. In this way Wakefield perhaps hopes to gain some control of his life that he might not otherwise have had, to feel not so completely anonymous and helpless as a man of the crowd.

Wakefield's narrator does not position us in Wakefield's mind, but, from his observer's distance, merely speculates about his self-imposed twenty-year exile. The narrator of "Old Mr. Marblehall" moves freely and fluidly in to and out of Marblehall's mind in ways that make it difficult to determine the story's point of view—or difficult at least to describe it in traditional narrative terms. The narrator begins by describing Mr. Marblehall as a representative "old" person, as someone here singled out because he never did anything, never even got married until he was sixty, and who has a peculiar relationship with the inhabitants of Natchez, where he is both known and unknown: known in his external *place*, unknown in his interior life. The narrator knows, but apparently nobody else does, that Mr. Marblehall has two wives, two children, two houses, two lives that are perverse reflections of each other. But he too begins as part of a crowd; the narrator, after speaking of him, after waiting for him to make his appearance on the street, points him out: "*That's* Mr. Marblehall." He is "preciously . . . made," or thinks he is, as old people do, who walk "like conspirators, bent over a little, filled with protection. They stand long on the corners but more impatiently than anyone, as if they expect traffic to take notice of them. . . . He looks quaintly secretive and prepared for anything, out walking very luxuriously on Catherine Street" (111; my emphasis).

In successive paragraphs the narrator describes, perhaps a bit too snidely, Marblehall's wife, his smallish ancestral home on the shaling banks of the Mississippi, and his son, all of which set Marblehall firmly in a place, a social and historical context: as he walks back toward his small mansion, the narrator suggests that "you have to merge him back into his *proper blur.*" He is so much a man of the crowd that even the narrator asks, "Why look twice at him?" (113; my emphasis)—to which the answer is, because there are two of him. To demonstrate, the narrator follows him into his *other* life, his life as Mr. Bird; his double life is his claim on our attention.

However mystified and intrigued by character and by problems of fictional representation, Poe's and Hawthorne's narrators in these stories appear to take for granted some things that Welty does not. For Poe's and Hawthorne's narrators, there *is* a perceivable, describable world, a comfortable world, which they invoke simply by setting their stories in London, a signifier which bestows an external world—a character, a geography, a history—upon the story, and which they therefore do not feel obliged to represent.

Welty's narrator undertakes something quite different. Like London, Natchez has its own well-established signification, in some ways more potent and evocative than that of London because more particular, more historically singular. The Natchez setting is deliberate and significant precisely because of Natchez's purchase on history, because of its literary "placeness." Welty firmly fixes Marblehall in Natchez—among its antebellum houses, its Mississippi River banks, its antebellum past, and its pretentious Daughters of the American Revolution and United Daughters of the Confederacy aristocracy—partly because readers do have an image of Natchez, even if they've never been there, which they impose upon this story. Welty specifically invoked Natchez's "southernness" when in her revision of the *Southern Review* version for *A Curtain of Green*, she added the "United Daughters of the Confederacy" to the list of Mrs. Marblehall's social activities.

But after so firmly and deliberately fixing Marblehall in Natchez history and culture and geography, the narrator immediately proceeds to stress his very modern alienation from it and the alien nature of Natchez itself. Indeed, Natchez protects itself from the ravages of its geographical constant, the Mississippi River, by a "box maze" which sits on the river's "edge like a trap" (112), so that "Natchez," as historical place, as Pitavy-Souques has suggested ("Blazing Butterfly"), exists only to be deconstructed; in this story it is as illusory and problematic as Old Mr. Marblehall's double life.

Hawthorne, reminding us that Wakefield is a fictional construct, abandons verisimilitude in the very act of making us aware of it. Wakefield and Poe's man are not attached to London though they are in it: it is for all concerned merely a big city in which to get lost. Welty insists upon the verisimilar; she goes to lengths that Poe and Hawthorne do not to set Mr. Marblehall in a specific social and historical and geographical context. Mr. Marblehall, on the other hand, is a fixture in Natchez—his home is "ancestral" (112)—and his people have been in Natchez since 1818 (113), right after Mississippi became a state, when an ancestor came as an actor, to play a role on stage. Perhaps his status as a member of such a family helps account for the curious collocation of attitudes toward him, for the town's various degrees of awareness of him, and for why the narrator can claim on the one hand that "nobody gives a hoot about any old Mr. Marblehall" (113) but on the other hand that everybody seems to maintain an almost preternatural consciousness of his Marblehall/Bird life.

The narrative voice is both closer to and farther away from Mr. Marblehall than that of "Wakefield," and the "voice" is a disorienting composite of voices—sometimes it's a gabble of the language of local gossip—which are never completely separable. I propose that the voices emerge from Mr. Marblehall's own highly self-conscious projections onto the town of those things he would think about himself if he were in a position to watch himself as the town is. Thus the narrative is generated out of Marblehall's desperate self-consciousness, his need to be observed. Like Wakefield, and like his Marblehall actor-ancestor, all he does is something to be viewed, something designed to produce a satisfying reaction, a standing ovation, say, as if only in being an object of somebody else's gaze can he affirm his own significance.

He may double his life but he does not make it any more eventful or significant. Indeed, he behaves the same way in each life, lying in bed reading *Terror Tales* and *Astonishing Stories*. Mr. Marblehall's debilitating self-reflexivity, self-consciousness, may remind us of the man who dreams that he is a butterfly and then, waking, isn't sure whether he is a human being who dreamed he was a butterfly or a butterfly now dreaming he is a man. Thus Mr. Marblehall may at one and the same time be storing up life, doubling it, and also killing time: his daring and extraordinary double life does not itself afford him any discernible pleasure, much less invest him with significance. His double life, like Wakefield's, merely gives exposure its own chance to affirm him. But Marblehall goes Wakefield one better, by engendering a second child, creating a child precisely to follow him to his first home, discover him, and paint his singularity on a fence for all to see. Thus Marblehall may be a "great blazing butterfly" imaginatively bursting from its cocoon and exploding magnificently upon the world, and at the same time be "stitching up a net" (118) for his own capture; his double life does not afford him taste or pleasure or freedom from the quotidian. He hopes his double life will free him from dailiness but in fact it merely repeats it, more firmly grounds him in it.

Welty's narrator tells us that at age sixty-six Mr. Marblehall has finally discovered the secret to life, "what people are *supposed* to do." They are, he thinks, supposed to "endure something inwardly—for a time secretly; they establish a past, a memory; thus they store up life" (117; my emphasis). Mr. Marblehall has done this and more: he has "multiplied his life by deception" and, having done so, he "speculates upon some glorious finish, a great explosion of revelations" which, apparently, will reveal him to all eyes. But these glorious revelations will be in the future and in the meantime he has to find a way "to kill time, and get through the clocking nights." Apparently he kills time by staying awake: "*Otherwise* he dreams that he is a great blazing butterfly stitching up a net; which doesn't make sense"(118; my emphasis).

Indeed it doesn't "make sense." But very little in this astonishing story makes "sense," narrative or linguistic or logical; it seems *not to permit itself to be read*. Its language stands opposed to the story it is trying to tell: its sentences don't always cohere, its comparisons do not always compare, its pronouns too frequently float free of antecedents, its modifiers do not merely modify but cancel out or obstruct. Practically the only thing that makes interpretable, readable, "sense" is Mr. Marblehall's double life, but it does so only in broad outlines: the closer we get to the story's smallest component parts, the more nearly sense ravels out into a series of questions raised by verbal structures, descriptions and images, that don't quite compute, that don't yield themselves completely even after repeated readings. What are the "parlor-like jaws of self-consciousness" (111) that Mrs. Marblehall has spent her life trying to escape? What does it mean that she has "a voice that dizzies *other ladies* like an organ note" but "amuses *men* like a halloo down the well" (112; my emphasis)? How does the clock that measures the time Mr. Marblehall kills get a "fruity bursting tick, to get through midnight" (115)? Why is it that "when time is passing it's like a bug in [Mr. Marblehall's] ear" (115)? And what does it signify that in Mr. Marblehall's yard there is a very curious statue which the narrator describes as *the* "stone figure of the pigtailed courtier mounted on the goat" (117)? The narrator can't figure out what Mr. Bird is doing, bending over to stare at his odorless zinnias because it's "twilight, all amplified with locusts screaming; [and] nobody could see anything" (115), but in the paragraph's first sentence he "can easily be seen" (114) and two sentences later, he is again "quite visible" (115).

Sentences and paragraphs start in one direction, lop suddenly off, and move in another direction: before he figured things out, the narrator tells us, for example, Mr. Marblehall "didn't know what to do. Everything was for all the world like his first party. He stood about, and looked in his father's books"—we seem about to get some useful interpretative information, a pathology of family dysfunction perhaps, but almost as soon as this story gets started, the narrator disrupts it and jumps to a summary conclusion that deflects us away from Mr. Marblehall's childhood, toward something completely different, evasive: "and long ago he went to France, but he didn't like it" (114). The prose is throughout opaque and fragmented; its joints don't always join. It has an oddness that keeps frustrating its own attempts to tell the story, all the while maintaining a tantalizing and evocative power that chips away at the boundaries of traditional narrative just as inexorably as the Mississippi River chips away at the base of the high bluff the Marblehall family mansion sits on.

The story's language, in all its shimmering fragmentation, thus operates as an objective correlative to Mr. Marblehall's constant nightmare reenactment of his life—for nightmare it is, with nightmare's own language of disruptions and evasions and substitutions, which both conceal and reveal, which both alienate one from oneself and reveal one to oneself, if one knows how to read the language. "Old Mr. Marblehall" is the most brilliant rendering in American fiction of nightmare's dreamwork that I know of save only for the original version of Faulkner's *Sanctuary*, which Welty of course could not have read in the late thirties.[3] Mr. Bird's life is a nightmare's crystallization of his Marblehall life to its horrific essences, which reveals to us its psychic realities.

The dreamwork begins as a simple reversal-substitution of his ancestral mansion on the river for one of the identical anonymous galleried houses at the other end of town where, after getting there, "you find yourself lost." "Nobody ever looks to see who is living in a house like that." Inhabitants of this part of town are people who in the evening "after they sit on the porch . . . go back into the house, and you hear the radio for the next two hours." The radio "seems to mourn and cry for them" (114),

---

3. Originally written in 1929, Faulkner revised it heavily in proof before its publication in 1931.

voicing a kind of misery that becomes more intense as the dream moves to describe Mrs. Bird, a nightmarish version of his Marblehall wife. Mrs. Bird is "worse than the other one," standing on the "night-stained porch" and screaming things to a neighbor about what he does in bed, which obviously does not satisfy her. "She is more solid, fatter, shorter, and while not so ugly, funnier looking. She looks like funny furniture—an unornamented stair post in one of these little houses, with her small monotonous round stupid head." Sometimes she becomes the very picture of a "woodcut of a Bavarian witch, forefinger pointing," a picture accompanied in his vision by the telling detail of "scratches in the air all around her," which would be the artist's static rendering of her violent motion in casting spells—even though Mrs. Bird herself is "so static she scarcely moves, from her thick shoulders down past her cylindered brown dress to her short, stubby house slippers" (115). From the porch, after screaming to her neighbors about his reading habits, she "rolls back into the house as if she had been on a little wheel." Their little nightmarish son has always "supposed that his mother was totally solid, down to her thick separated ankles" (116), but her legs, apparently, remain always close together.

Mr. Marblehall transfers his worst nightmare vision of his wife to this little Bird son. Mrs. *Marblehall*, with her "electric-looking hair" that on any occasion she dresses into a "unicorn horn," sings "O Trees in the Evening" in a voice "full of a hollow wind and echo, winding out through the wavery hope of her mouth." Her "untidy head trembles in the domestic dark." This neurotic, pretentious woman, with her own needs—she is "servile, undelighted, sleepy, expensive, tortured" (111–12)—becomes, in the nightmare, Mrs. Bird, all of whose "devotion is combustible and goes up in despair" (115). But the little boy's vision transmogrifies her into a hellish figure, the abiding Gorgon of Mr. Marblehall's nightmare: "But when she stands there on the porch screaming to the neighbors, she reminds him of those flares that charm him so, that they leave burning in the street at night—the dark solid ball, then, tongue-like, the wicked, yellow, continuous, enslaving blaze on the stem" (116). Hair becomes tongue becomes "enslaving blaze."

Thus Old Mr. Marblehall is also a petrified man: his name is almost a palindrome, at the center of which is "Mr. Marble". He is caught between two Medusas, both of them perhaps creations of his imagination.

He is no Perseus to slay either of them, but clearly he fantasizes about doing so, spending his time in bed, in both lives, reading in *Terror Tales* and *Astonishing Stories* "about horrible and fantastic things happening to nude women and scientists. In one of them, when the characters open bureau drawers, they find a woman's leg with a stocking and a garter on" (115). No wonder neither woman is satisfied.

The Bird son "knows what his father thinks" (116) because he, Marblehall, is that son, the self that the self creates, the self that is aware of the self. Mr. Marblehall believes he can have a life only if he can be observed having it; he seeks confirmation of his self through the gaze of an Other, even if he has to create that Other to do the gazing. Thus his imaginatively- or biologically-engendered son will, he fantasizes, follow him through the Natchez streets, like Hawthorne's and Poe's gazers, to try to read "the wild mystery" in his bosom. This modern man of the crowd, then, creates his own self-observing eye that will narrate his terrible singularity, shock the Natchez world with the dynamic mystery of his inner life, and so free him from the enslaving flames of his own despair. The great blazing butterfly of his dream may well be Welty's nightmarish genuflection to its more delicate cousin in Hawthorne's story "The Artist of the Beautiful," a fabulous, delicate mechanical reproduction of nature which a child's joyful touch destroys just as completely as the cynical hands of pragmatism have destroyed its predecessor. Marblehall's butterfly is an imaginative, wish-fulfilling explosion from his cocoon, an ecstatic release from his marble bonds, which even in his dreams he nevertheless knows he will experience some time "in the future" but *not now*. For now, he is John Marcher, waiting for experience, meaning, significance, to fall on him from somewhere else. For now, he is J. Alfred Prufrock, afraid to assert himself against his own meaninglessness. He, the blazing butterfly who would be free thus keeps stitching up the net of his own containment. The narrative voice of "Old Mr. Marblehall," then, is Mr. Marblehall himself and the net he keeps stitching up is the net of language, which always fails him at the verge of articulation, refuses him the ecstatic release that full articulation would allow.

Welty's southern "place" is, then, an *interior* place, whatever else it is, and she can get into the nooks and crannies of our most secret places with more sharpness and clarity than anybody I know. Old Mr. Marblehall may be, following Hawthorne and Poe, a man of the crowd, and he is exactly that, of course, when you see him within his "proper Natchez blur." He is not, however, merely an "everyperson," but is sharply, terrifyingly, personalized. Like Poe's Man of the Crowd, Old Mr. Marblehall's breast contains "mysteries which will not suffer themselves to be read." His modernness lies in his compression of those mysteries into a nightmare narrative that simultaneously begs and refuses to be read. Welty's narrator assumes, like Poe's, that there is a "wild history" in her characters' bosoms, a history inscribed in violent fantasies of escape from the meaninglessness of his Natchez life, from the despair of his marriage. Alas, however, it will not be his lot, like Poe's man, to die soon "with despair of heart and convulsion of throat" while "wringing the hand of a ghostly confessor." That is not for this modern man, who must continue to endure what he has stored up. "Old Mr. Marblehall"'s final paragraph is a pithy and chilling, an astonishingly intimate and personal invocation of modern alienation and despair: "Old Mr. Marblehall! He may have years ahead yet in which to wake up bolt upright in bed under the naked bulb, his heart thumping, his old eyes watering and wild, imagining that if people knew about his double life, they'd die" (118).

Mr. Marblehall is both a man of and a man alienated from the Natchez crowd. His geographical and historical place grant him nothing of identity; except for the narrator's grace in placing him in language he would be as empty a signifier as any character in American fiction. Unlike Wakefield, he indeed does seem able to "seize hold of words," but in the problematical world of modernist fictional language, the very words he seizes are often as empty of coherent signification as he is. Like Poe's Man of the Crowd there are indeed wild mysteries written in his bosom; but they are written in a language emerging from the modern unconscious, which is indisputably the predominant landscape of Welty's old-fashioned Natchez, Mississippi.

Domestic Violence in "The Purple Hat," "Magic," and "The Doll"

I want to get a running start for a reading of Welty's odd story "The Purple Hat" by backing up to two very early stories, "Magic" and "The Doll." The first is an exact contemporary of its more famous sibling, "Death of a Travelling Salesman." Both were accepted by *Manuscript* on 19 March 1936 and published in the summer and fall issues of the same year; "The Doll," published in *The Tanager* in June 1936, was not far behind. All three concern women dabbling in pleasure.

"Magic" is a grim little story about a grim defloration. Myrtle Cross, on her way home from her afternoon shorthand class, encounters her boy friend Ralph, a singularly dull young man, in front of the Western Union office where he works in downtown Jackson. They confirm their date for the evening and their understanding that the date will include their first sexual experience; their conversation reveals that this decision has involved some negotiation about both marriage and where they will go to do this thing that he is clearly nervous about (though being a male he'd never admit that he is) and that she is "scared" (3).

Myrtle prepares for their date at home, in a room lighted by a single naked bulb that casts shadows all over the room. She looks intently at herself in the dim mirror, not sure of whom she sees—she smiles "like Marlene Dietrich" (5)—but wanting to capture herself, as she was before the change. As she leaves the house with Ralph she looks at her family's living room with a glance, "as if to arrange and harden the already well-moulded scene" (6). Romantic dreams mark the shabby scene: her mother reads "Dream World" and on the piano sits the sheet music for "Girl of My Dreams." Clearly such cultural fantasies have shaped her notions of love—of pleasure, of expectation. From an ad in a movie magazine, and for a dime, Myrtle has ordered off for a "Magic Love Philtre," which arrived contained in a "small, lustreless phial with a gilt sticker," which she keeps hidden—significantly—under the skirt of her kewpie doll; to complete her toilet, she takes the phial from under the doll's dress and anoints herself with the Magic Potion. When Ralph arrives, she "fixes" "an expression of anticipation on her face" (5).

As they walk down the street toward their destination, she looks for the romantic moon. Ralph tells her that she's looking for it in the wrong direction, though he has no idea how ominously right he is. Through an open window of a house on the corner a radio plays Hawaiian music, the "grovelling sweetness of the guitars" (6) evoking the faraway romantic islands. They listen for a moment; she whispers, "Ain't that beautiful?" and they get romantic, their arms about each other. But the music accompanies a startling image: "The chorus was played over and over. In the room they could see a family sitting under a fringed lamp, their heads sunk as though all their necks had been broken" (6).

Immediately Ralph wants to get on with the evening, suggests that they move on to the nearby cemetery, the agreed-upon point of their assignation, and they do, having sex on a grave. Afterwards, Ralph says to her: "If you don't like it, shut up . . . I know plenty women that do." He is lying, of course, and he turns over and begins to cry in great big heaping sobs. For her part, Myrtle is mostly unmoved by the experience; she knows the moon has risen but "feels no need" to turn and look at it. "That had been it," she thinks: "It was over. That had been the thing" (7). When a man in a black hat looks over the hedge at her, laughing soundlessly, she screams and runs out of the cemetery, past the house where they had heard the music, and back to her home, where she takes the phial of Magic Love Philtre and drops it out the window into the flowerbed, rejecting the "magic" of it all but not the phallic reality: it arrives in the flower bed erect, sticking up "on end . . . like another stem, rising up to grow" (7).

I am transfixed by the image of the family sitting in their living room, "their heads all sunk as though all their necks had been broken": a scene not of violence so much as violence imposed in the seeing of it on what should have been a scene of domestic harmony; it virtually explodes off the page as a terrifying cautionary vision of Myrtle's future. The domestic order and security that she tried to memorize before she left the house seeking her own desire has been transmogrified, in their vision through that window on the domestic, into an emblem of domestic death, swathed still in the "grovelling sweetness" of romantic myth, just as the love, the desire, the pleasure she sought has itself been crudely tied to death, in their having sex on the cold wet grass of a grave. The image of that family is powerful, I think, and full of resonances: a vision, even if but a glimpse, which has the power to define and control.

"The Doll," somewhat more complex, has at its climax a similar incident. Marie and Charles have gotten engaged the night before and she now drives down town with no particular agenda except perhaps to drop in on him at his office in a tall building. She has stopped at a church bazaar and bought a little rag doll in a white dress that becomes for her, as the kewpie doll does for Myrtle, an emblem of domesticity, of her capacity to be a mother, to have a family. She wears a curious hat, which we may connect to that later purple one, "a leghorn hat with the red cloth apple on it" (11). As if the apple were not symbol enough, Welty explains Marie's awareness that this hat "will stand for me and for the words I said last night" (11): obviously she had tempted and been tempted and marriage is the negotiated doorway to her pleasure. She wants to see Charles, but more particularly she wants him to "look down" from his office and "recognize" her by that hat that stands for herself and her words. She wants him to be conscious of her at all times, as she is conscious of him, thinking of him as "sitting leanly at his desk above . . . his long hand to his head, thinking about problems of law: a chained myth when he was not with her" (11). She wants his vision to contain and define her as she wants to contain and define him by hers. But instead of his seeing her from up above, she spies Charles walking in the streets, perversely exercising his capacity to exist on his own terms, outside her controlling and defining vision: "He was so calm. He spoke to no one. He was there, he was bared to her eyes, he was displayed, he had taken off his coat and lost his hat; she stared at him, but it was impossible not to know that he was wrapped in a cloak of himself which he thought unobserved" (12). She has the impulse to run to him and say "I saw you" (12), apparently to reassert her observing control over their intimacy, which is directly linked to her own selfhood, but she cannot do so. Instead she leans back in her car and lapses into a Weltian meditation: "Who was the more hidden, the more hiding, she thought, pressed against the cushion. Again he walked in his slow, obscure way up the street: she was watching him in the driving mirror" (12). She gives way to weeping: "Charles? He was another person. He was not herself, and yet neither was he any of the others in the street. . . . She was sickened with some perception of mystery" (13).

That evening, her sense of his alienation, his separateness from her works to problematize their time together. There is some uncomfortable dialogue, some weeping, and she finally shows him the rag doll, which she holds by its "unelbowed arms" and makes it glide across the table. She wants to engage him in some sort of baby talk by getting him to tell her why the doll is smiling. The sound of a fire siren breaks into the growing tension and they laugh, "suddenly snatched from their aloneness and projected into the world." They get in their car and chase the fire engine to a burning house. The scene is of a piece with the scene in "Magic" when Myrtle and Ralph see the family with broken necks:

> They stood side by side watching. Separately, and then slowly together as if hypnotized they saw the long, red scarves of flame part and disclose a little square window, and there, standing with stick arms raised like a doll, a woman waiting to be rescued; then, lowering their gazes, which were twisted together into one strand, they saw the ladder and the fireman in his helmet ascending. It was like the crude action of opera, they felt, and then, their arms tightly touching, believed gradually, as the man climbed, that indeed they were the ennoblers as well as the helpless projectors of this fiery danger, this cheap rescue pantomime: they were the music of the opera, the reason for this compulsion and crudity; and in tumultuous peace and self-worship at last they threw themselves with haste into each other's arms, hiding their eyes from the glare of the burning house in the shadows of each other. (14)

In this crudely revealing passage two lovers, alienated in and by their love, become one again by triangulating their anxieties off of someone else's very real danger and then presuming to be the cause and the effect of the danger, a melodramatic and cheap reading of the scene. They want to believe that they cause the danger and, by observing, "ennoble" it: they think their watching raises it into something artistic, even tragic. The "Doll" of the title, then, is first the rag doll that Marie bought to symbolize their fertile union; it becomes the woman in the window trapped in a burning house and "waiting to be rescued": we're not told that it is a bedroom, but I'd bet you a phial of Magic Philtre that it is. They go back to their car feeling a "throbbing pride" and drive over the city for a while, "feeling like precious jewels, not like people who might be afraid again. They were in horror of speaking" (14).

Like Myrtle and Ralph, Marie and Charles leave the domestic scene in union, go back to the house where they don't make love but rather talk. Charles wants to talk about how two people can be so close and so much in love, and still seem thousands of miles apart. She shushes him from such talk, even while rejoicing to hear that he too has such anxieties and to understand that she can therefore "desert her fear for his own" and so can comfort him. The doll, of course, is also Marie, who has thus orchestrated her own rescue from her separateness, no less metaphorically than literally. Violence, impending violence, even violence that she participates in only vicariously, has allowed her to bring her own raging fears under control.

"The Purple Hat" is a considerably more sophisticated and powerful treatment of these themes, both more and less direct. It's a curious story that has mystified us all: even Welty has expressed uncertainties about it.[1] In a bar, the rumbling New Orleans sky outside, a fat man narrates, to a practically wordless bartender and a nervous young man who drinks to steel his nerves for something, a very strange story about the middle-aged woman he has watched for thirty years from his high

---

1. Though to be sure she might have simply been being playful and evasive, as she often was. She told Charles Bunting, "I wish I hadn't written that story. . . . It was just an odd story I wrote in an odd moment, about something I don't know much about: gambling. But I really meant it to be no more than a kind of ghost story. . . . I meant it to be a ghost story, a playful ghost story. I wasn't trying to be allegorical or anything else" (Bunting 63).

position on the catwalk above the gambling tables at the Palace of Pleasure. She is a ghost, he thinks, because he has seen her killed twice—the
first time by being shot in the face, the second by being stabbed with a
giant needle she keeps in her purple hat. But she always returns, every
evening, to keep her appointed rounds at the crap tables, from five till
midnight, always in the company of a young man, perhaps the same
one, perhaps a different one, to whom at midnight she says goodbye
and leaves.

In his narration he maintains the same sort of cool distance from
his subject as he does as an observer from his catwalk in the dome of
the Palace of Pleasure. He speaks along with the "calm roll of thunder" (268) outside the bar that validates his implicit claim to godlike
omniscience and objectivity: "I can see everything in the world from
my catwalk" (271), he claims; "somehow all that people do is clear and
lucid and authentic there, as if it were magnified . . ." (270). He can
see but cannot hear what the patrons say; but what he sees is enough
to allow him to create a straightforward cultural condemnation of this
woman. He could, of course, be telling a simple cautionary tale for the
young man at the other end of the bar; more likely, however, he wants
to provoke the young man into a pre-emptive strike that will serve his,
the narrator's, purposes.

His story, then, is a cultural narration of women's lives, and is anything but objective. He speaks to the accompaniment of the thunder,
he is "fat . . . cosy and prosperous" (268), and believes he knows exactly
what he sees; what he cannot hear he infers with supreme confidence.
She is "one of those thousands of middle-aged women who come every
day to the Palace, would not be kept away by anything on earth. . . .
Most of them are dull enough, drab old creatures, all of them, walking
in with their big black purses held wearily by the handles like suitcases
packed for a trip. No one has ever been able to find out how all these
old creatures can leave their lives at home like that to gamble . . . what
their husbands think . . . who keeps the house in order . . . who pays . . . "
(269). For him, the young men are her victims: "She finds them, she
does. She picks them. Where I don't know, unless New Orleans, as I've
always had a guess, is the birthplace of ready-made victims" (270). "I am
sure she speaks to him, in a sort of purr," he says, "the purr that is used

for talking in that room, and the young man does not know what she seeks of him, and she is leading him on, all the time. What does she say? I do not know. But believe me . . ." she leads him on . . ." (272–73).

He likewise dismisses as irrelevant her sexual needs, even the possibility that she could actually have sexual desire. She is middle-aged and "disgusting." Her purple hat, clearly her genitals, is a grotesque display, as the narrator sees it, of her open and public sexuality (she should be home with her husband, keeping house). It's "quite a hat. A great, wide, deep hat such as has no fashion and never knew there was fashion and change." It is trimmed with "old plush flowers . . . —roses? Poppies? A man wouldn't know easily." Women's needs never change, never go out of style. At "some point in the evening, she takes the hat off and lays it carefully in her lap, under the table" and the young man of the evening becomes "enamoured" of it: she "lays it down below the level of the table there, on her shabby old lap, and he caresses it" (271–72). The narrator doesn't think this is the strangest form of love in New Orleans. The young man seems to be caressing a "little glass vial with a plunger [that] helps decorate the crown" (271) because he does not seem to know that "by spinning the brim ever so easily as it rested on the lady's not over-sensitive old knees, it would be possible to remove the opposite ornament," a hatpin she uses to keep the hat on her head and which, the narrator claims, two other young men have used to kill her. The "little glass vial with a plunger" could contain Myrtle's "magic philtre"; more likely, given its position on the hat, it represents her clitoris, which the young men stroke so publicly, if under the table, before, for some reason, they discover the hatpin and, for some reason, slip it "between [her] ribs and [pierce her] heart" (273). But the narrator's story doesn't have to be logical for it to work on the young man the way the narrator, the culture, want it to.

Not surprisingly, most of the sparse commentary on "The Purple Hat" has followed the narrator's line in assuming that the woman is the victimizer. It apparently never occurs to him or to anybody else that since she is the one being murdered she might actually be the victim. No one, certainly not this "fat . . . cosy and prosperous" narrator, has suggested any number of other possibilities for her behavior: that she goes every evening to the crap table to be alone, to escape domesticity, that what she says to the various young men, her escorts for the evening or several, is something like "Leave me alone. I came here to get away from the grovelling sweetness of Hawaiian guitars on the radio and sitting around my living room with my husband like our necks had been broken." Or, perhaps more, borrowing from Freud the idea that hats are genitals and, more specifically, from Marie the suggestion that her hat "stands for herself" and, even more specifically, if we can assume that Myrtle's Hollywood phial of Magic Love Philtre has been transplanted to the garden of this flowery purple hat from the flowerbed just outside Myrtle's window where she threw it; if we can make these perhaps tenuous connections, then perhaps what this middleaged woman is saying to her young men is, simply: "Play with me, fondle me, touch me, caress me, gamble with me: give me pleasure—why else would I come here to the Palace of Pleasure?—*and then leave me alone.*"

But these are words, of course, which the "fat . . . cosy and prosperous" male narrator can never hear or even allow himself to imagine a woman saying. From his exalted position on the catwalk in the dome of the Palace of Pleasure, high above the sweat and travail of the actual gambling, he mostly condemns what he sees: "I am the man whose eyes look out over the gambling room. I am the armed man that everyone knows to be watching, at all they do" (270). As he describes his position, he sounds very much like the observer in Jeremy Bentham's Panoptican prison, of which Michel Foucault makes so much in *Discipline and Punish*: a prison in which all prisoners are visible to a central observer who may or may not actually be observing them at all times; but it is enough to insure order and discipline that prisoners think they are being observed at all times, whether they are or not. Marie's Charlie throws her into an emotional tailspin when he dares act as though she is not observing him, and women who in the Palace of Pleasure act as though they are not watched threaten to throw the entire cultural suppression of female pleasure into disarray.

The narrator, then, is an agent of social control: a superego if you will, self-appointed to be sure, but working in the service of the culture to insure that women who take themselves alone to the Palace of Pleasure do not do so without suffering for it. Moreover, the "fat . . . cosy and prosperous" folks in the catbird seat or even on the catwalk above it all are the ones who get to tell the story and to do the punishing, arrange the facts to fit the codes, and arrange a punishment appropriate to what they have decided is the crime.

"I have seen this old and disgusting creature in her purple hat every night, quite plainly, for thirty years, and to my belief she has been murdered twice. I suppose it will take the third time" (271), he tells the bartender elliptically, but he clearly means that he thinks it will take the third time to make sure she is really murdered and will stay dead and be forever out of the way, incapable of pursuing her own pleasure. His narration in this little bar thus has a direct and immediate purpose, not, as has been supposed, to warn the nervous young man at the other end of the bar to stay away from the woman but rather to manipulate him into killing her—to make him serve the culture's purposes by punishing her for her freedom, for not being where she ought to be, at home doing the domestic. He warns the young man to be wary of her: "After a certain length of time goes by, and love has blossomed, and the hat, the purple hat, is thrilling to the touch of your hand—you can no longer be sure about the little vial. There in privacy you may find it to be empty. It is her coquettishness, you see. She leads you on. You are never to know whether . . .". Welty's ellipsis suggests that the narrator, seeing the young man rise from his seat and disappear into the street for his five o'clock appointment with destiny, doesn't need to finish the sentence with either whether "you will fall in love" or whether "she will betray you." So he warns the young man: get her before she gets you.

The narrator pulls out a big wad of bills and pays both tabs, leaving a generous tip, his purpose accomplished: "Up on the catwalk you get the feeling now and then that you could put out your finger and make a change in the universe," he says, with great satisfaction. "Is she a real ghost?" the bartender wants to know. The narrator pauses while the authoritative thunder rolls, and says, "I'll let you know tomorrow" (274–75)—after, he confidently assumes, the third murder has taken place and things can be peaceful again: "The only good of shooting her was, it made a brief period of peace there," he says earlier (271).

Violence, real or imagined, is a staple of Welty's fiction. She does not depict it as dramatic or even particularly tragic, as do Faulkner and, say, Flannery O'Connor. But to present it as tragic or dramatic would make it an unusual occurrence, something outside the normal. Violence in Welty is, to the contrary, so normal a part of women's every day experience as to be practically unnoticeable, so normal that we have for years simply folded it into, perhaps hidden it behind, the larger picture we have been pleased to call her essentially comic vision. But violence is everywhere in her work; it forms the mortar which holds a good deal of everything else together. It seeps into everything else through incident, through language—she frequently describes even the most common occurrences of family life in metaphors of violence—and through narrative vision, which works violence so completely into the fabric of feminine normality that we who operate from "fat . . . cosy and prosperous" catwalks may not notice how omnipresent it, or the threat of it, is in women's lives especially.

In an early interview, Welty remembered that one of the first stories she wrote began, "Monsieur Boule deposited a delicate dagger in Mademoiselle's left side and departed with a poised immediacy" (Van Gelder 3), a line that claims a place among the seminal tropes for her work. It's thus all right there at the beginning: the language which both diminishes the act of violence—"delicate dagger" indeed!—and at the same time posits the systemic nature of the impunity with which Monsieur Boule can murder her and remained "poised," unconcerned. "*Boule,*" of course, is French for "ball," and though *Monsieur* is singular, it doesn't take much cleverness to see him and his other avatars in all their plurality, so that one of her first lines of fiction introduces a precursive Mr. Balls, in all his testosteronic splendor, as he commits an act of violent aggression against a woman.

The Ponderable Heart

*T*he *Ponder Heart* is Eudora Welty's oddest book. Every line, every illustration, seems to scream "Laugh! Laugh! Laugh, damn you!"—and yet I never feel quite like laughing, never quite feel like taking the book seriously enough to laugh either at it or with it. It always seems too slight, indeed too silly, to be the work of a major writer. Perhaps because I don't have an uncle just like Edna Earle's Uncle Daniel, *The Ponder Heart* seems to me a deliberate collection of every tawdry cliché of Southern literature, of small-town rural life, a collection so thick I'd like to think of it as a parody of that tradition. But it doesn't feel like parody, if only because it does not protect itself through the distances of irony that we have come to expect of modernist narratives; it feels more like a yielding, an obeisance, to that tradition, an exploitation of those clichés for audiences, including those sophisticated readers of the *New Yorker*, where it first appeared, who always seem ready, eager, to believe the worst about the South but who if not handed the worst are just as happy to accept the silliest, especially if it seems vaguely, even preposterously, redemptive.

What I offer here doesn't completely redeem *The Ponder Heart* for me, and perhaps it doesn't need redeeming for you. But I want to get to it by way of a scene from one of Welty's earliest stories. "Magic" is an exact contemporary of its more famous sibling, her first major publication, "Death of a Travelling Salesman." Both were accepted by *Manuscript* on 19 March 1936 and published in the summer and fall issues of the same year (Polk, *Bibliography* 435).

Myrtle Cross's evening begins in a lower-class home awash in romantic dreams: her mother reads "Dream World"; on the piano is the sheet music for "Girl of My Dreams," and as she makes herself up in the mirror Myrtle smiles "like Marlene Dietrich" (5). Clearly her notions of love—of pleasure, of expectation—have been molded by such cultural fantasies. A single naked bulb casts shadows all over the room and in her mirror. On their date, she and Ralph pass a house on the corner and hear through the window Hawaiian music on the radio, the "grovelling sweetness of the guitars" (6) that evoke the faraway romantic islands, and she whispers, "Ain't that beautiful?" But immediately they see through the window a startling image: "Listening, they began to move aimlessly around under the open window, their arms about each other. The chorus was played over and over. In the room they could see a family sitting under a fringed lamp, their heads sunk as though all their necks had been broken" (6).[1]

I propose that image of the family in their living room, "their heads all sunk as though all their necks had been broken," as a sort of epicenter in Welty's depiction of family: a scene not of violence so much as of violence imposed in the seeing of it on what should have been a scene of domestic harmony. It virtually explodes off the page as a terrifying cautionary vision of Myrtle's future and of families to come throughout Welty's career. The cheesy, manufactured domestic order and security of Myrtle's home has been transmogrified in her and Ralph's mutual vision of domestic death swathed in the "grovelling sweetness" of romantic myth, just as the love, the desire, the pleasure she seeks with Ralph is crudely tied to death when they have sex on the grave. Though Welty did not collect "Magic," it nevertheless stands as a kind of introduction to her treatment of family themes throughout her fiction, wherein violence, the appearance of violence, or the language of violence, upon

---

1. For a slightly fuller treatment of "Magic," see "Domestic Violence in 'The Purple Hat'" in this volume.

the body or bodies of the beloved are so often the norm that we hardly notice how much of it she uses—or how much we ourselves use it. *The Ponder Heart*, for all its comedy, all its apparent light-heartedness, is very much a part of that thematic—the romantic illusion of domestic love trapped in bodies whose necks, the connection between mind and body, appear broken: domestic death become literal. Perhaps indeed sheer boredom has overtaken this family, their heads leaning forward in sleep or apathy, which would be bad enough. But Welty's language, registering Myrtle's and Ralph's response, raises the scene's stakes for them as observers and for us as readers.

At the center of *The Ponder Heart* are two married bodies: Bonnie Dee Peacock Ponder's less-than-five-foot, ninety-eight-pound petite one and Uncle Daniel's gargantuan one. The short novel calls attention to Bonnie Dee's petite stature a couple of times directly and less directly to Daniel's size on a number of occasions: he eats calorie after calorie of fattening foods at Edna Earle's table at the Beulah Hotel;[2] Edna Earle calls attention to his huge hat several times, as well as to his big head; Bonnie Dee tries to make a skirt out of one of his pants legs (398); and when he faints and falls to the floor, he is too heavy for Edna Earle, Narciss, and Dr. Ewbanks to lift him up (401).

So, far from being the slim aristocrat played by David Wayne on Broadway and by Peter McNicoll in the more recent film of *The Ponder Heart* or the trim character in the first edition's illustrations, Daniel is clearly considerably overweight. Likewise, far from being the generous, good-hearted openhanded philanthropist Edna Earle depicts him as, he is a grossly self-indulgent, spoiled, manipulative, in some ways sociopathological leech who gets away perhaps literally with murder by buying his way out of any possibility that he might have to face the consequences of his actions. At home, he is the same kind of tyrant his father was: when you want something done, Edna Earle says, you just tell Uncle Daniel "how many Negroes" the project will need, and

---

2. "He'd point out what he'd have on his plate—usually ham and steak and chicken and cornbread and sweet potatoes and fried okra and tomatoes and onion-and-egg—plus banana pie . . ." (364). "He ate me out of house and home . . ." (365), Edna Earle says.

he "hollers them in . . . out of the fields, and they come just like for Grandpa" (366). After he kills Bonnie Dee and is about to have to face up to that fact, he, fat old Uncle Daniel, "hitche[s] both arms around his knees" (415)—that is, assumes the pre-natal position, an obvious retreat to a safeplace. Daniel is then, quite simply, an aging child, a brat, a monster, with no sense of responsibility.

Perhaps I paint too harsh a picture of Daniel, perhaps not. But perhaps we can more easily accept this portrait by remembering that his only model for male behavior is his tyrannical father, Edna Earle's Grandpa Ponder, the irascible, club-wielding plantation-running patriarch who drove all of his children to run away from home—all save Daniel, his youngest, whom he spoils by providing him no limitations whatever, apparently hoping to retain at home at least one Ponder to carry on the family name and the family tradition of bullying. We may easily understand Daniel's corpulent body, then, to be symbol and product of his father's, and that tradition's, aggrandizing will to control and consume.

Edna Earle is at least a second cousin to the narrator of "Why I Live at the P.O.," also part of a dysfunctional family and doing her best to escape. *The Ponder Heart*'s Edna Earle deploys her considerable narrative talents to hold together what fragments of the family remain, herself and Daniel, and to keep the family head held high. If the earlier Edna Earle's narration is an exercise in self-justification, this one's is an exercise in self-erasure, a denial of her own story in favor of Daniel's, partly because she is conditioned by a traditional sense of "family" that works to betray her even as she defends it so vigorously. Indeed, Edna Earle is scion of an inheritance that she will never get because Daniel literally gives it away right out from under her even while she is defending him in court. Of course she accepts that betrayal as the most natural thing in the world; we, she, might expect nothing more of her family.

Edna Earle and Daniel are the last of that family: the Ponders and their problematic heart are as nearly historical dead meat as Faulkner's Compsons are. The same Grandpa Ponder who in his fierce imperious wisdom decided that Daniel needed to get married for his own good also decided that Edna Earle should not get married, also for Daniel's good. But of her own prospects, she defends her grandfather: "Poor Grandpa!" Edna Earle exclaims. "Suppose I'd even *attempted*, over the years, to step off—I dread to think of the lengths Grandpa would have gone to stop it. Of course, I'm intended to look after Uncle Daniel and everybody knows it" (350), she admits, in a self-justifying evasion of her own needs. She has her own hopes for family though; she knows that Daniel is never likely to have any children and is hyper-conscious of her own impending old-maid-hood and barrenness. She just can't get that travelling salesman Mr. Springer to pop the question but she clings to the fading hope that she will one day have children of her own; she accepts the pinches and pats of Judge Tip Clanahan, an old family friend, because she believes that the minute men stop pinching her she will be foredoomed to spinsterhood. She is, then, a woman thoroughly trained by her culture's expectations of women; she quietly mourns her own inability to get married even as she accepts her role as the stereotypical southern spinster. As proprietor and manager of the Beulah Hotel, she is housemother and homemaker to family members and strangers alike.

The Ponders are *the* old established family in Clay, in the entire county for that matter, even if Edna Earle is in reduced circumstances and having to run the Beulah Hotel. Her grandfather raised her and Daniel as siblings, nearly, after Daniel's brother, Edna Earle's father, and all of the other uncles, aunts, and siblings left home for reasons that Edna Earle doesn't explain, because she is still afraid of Grandpa, long after he is dead: "Papa for one," she tells us, "left home at an early age, nobody ever makes the mistake of asking about *him*, and Mama never did hold up—she just had me and quit" (342). Even so, her mama's one accomplishment is to write a "pageant"—a Tom Thumb wedding, for which, obviously, no script could be more clearly already written before she ever laid hand to paper (347, 354), a cultural pæan to the matrimonial grand narrative that has treated her so badly. Though Grandpa Ponder raises her and Daniel as siblings, Grandpa shows Daniel considerable favoritism: he has no control over him—he's allowed to skate on the dining room table, for example—and Edna Earle gets confirmed in the tradition that says the Ponder women's first responsibility is to look after the Ponder men. Grandpa thinks that any marriage but his own is "a show of weakness of character" (350) and he claims to prize "character" and discipline above all else: but his failure to teach Daniel any discipline makes a monster of him.

Edna Earle thus takes Daniel as her responsibility when Grandpa Ponder dies of a heart attack, an apoplectic fit, upon discovering that Daniel has proposed to one Bonnie Dee Peacock, daughter of a white trash family from way out in the country, but now clerking at Woolworth's, and has been accepted on *trial*, a trial that lasts for more than five years (362) before she decides that she doesn't want to be married anymore and takes off back home to live with Mama for a while. Bonnie Dee's "trial" marriage becomes a trial indeed for Daniel, Edna Earle, and the town of Clay: marriage as trial—and tribulation: it is, for Bonnie Dee, a very dangerous place—becomes a working, if submerged, metaphor for the book.

From one point of view *The Ponder Heart* is almost as silly as the courtroom scene that forms its second half. Most sympathetic critics have tended to treat it as a kind of genial fable about what happens to unaffected goodness in the world. Ruth Vande Kieft, one of Welty's earliest and most influential critics, suggests that Daniel "has a Dickensian sort of eccentricity. His particular 'humour' is his over-generosity: the compulsion to give away which springs from his enormous, 'ponder'ous heart." She concedes that the "incongruity of [Daniel's] nature is that this out-sized heart has no balancing counterpart of rational and moral intelligence," but goes on to concur with Edna Earle that even though he lacks "the wisdom of the serpent" and is "foolish as a dove; lacking a trace of 'common sense,'" and even though "he borders on insanity"; even so, she argues, the novel's moral center lies in the "clash" between Daniel's "wisdom" and the "'foolishness' of the ordinary world of selfishness and calculation" (69–70). We have thus traditionally taken a decidedly uncritical view of Edna Earle as a first-person narrator, even though she is demonstrably tainted by her own needs, biological, cultural, and economic.[3]

As we have seen, however, there is plenty of evidence, discernible through the cracks of Edna Earle's telling—indeed, in her outright lies on

---

3. Kreyling (*Understanding*) is a notable exception to this generalization; his arguments about this novel's "subtexts" anticipate and complement my own. Baris, too, though her interests in *The Ponder Heart* are significantly different from my own.

the witness stand—that allow us to construct a story quite different from the one she tells. She gives us all we need to discover in Daniel's "generosity" a pathology based in a reaction against his father: to buy the love he did not get at home (indulgence, after all, is not love) and to be the center of attention, he gives away things his father has bought. Even Edna Earle recognizes that "all he wanted was our approval" (419), though in fact there was almost certainly something else he really wanted.

Several questions about Bonnie Dee's death get begged because Edna Earle lies on the witness stand and because Daniel, reverting to old habits, begins giving money away, again to buy the town's affection, precisely at the point in the trial where he is about to admit his culpability and be held accountable. As always, his giving diverts attention from something lacking in his own character. We can't reconstruct from the testimony in court what actually happened to cause Bonnie Dee's death, though we might work our way through Edna Earle's lies on the witness stand to discover what did not happen. One lie is Edna Earle's elaborate story of the lightning ball that she describes as scaring Bonnie Dee to death. But she didn't see any fireball at all: she picks that up from Narciss's testimony that she saw one, though Narciss couldn't have seen one either because she was hiding under the bed at the time, if she is telling the truth (391). Edna Earle then elaborates a tale in which a lightning ball comes down the chimney and works its way around the parlor and the living room before exiting through a window. But since she has already testified that Bonnie Dee was dead when she and Daniel arrived, clearly she is lying about at least *one* of these instances and probably about both. Edna Earle is making Daniel's defense up as she goes along, trying to construct something plausible out of the implausible, the impossible (Kreyling, *Understanding* 160).

Nor can we reconstruct completely very much about Daniel and Bonnie Dee's marriage, why she leaves or why she comes back and then sends Daniel to the Beulah to live, but we can speculate. Edna Earle thinks that Bonnie Dee should be grateful for marrying well above her class to a prominent wealthy man. But Daniel leaves her all alone out at the Ponder place, which even Grandpa Ponder finally understood was "lonesome" (360), while he comes to town every night to "tell about how happy he was" (362). He thus makes in narrative a reality that doesn't exist in life. After Bonnie Dee returns and sends *him* packing, he is "happy" to be separated from her, secure once again with surrogate mother Edna Earle. Why does she leave in the first place? We can't know for sure, though we might note her youth (she is seventeen) and his age.[4] One could also make the case that Daniel is a sex maniac: hence his dalliance at the county fair with Intrepid Elsie Fleming, the female motorcycle rider who wears such a tight suit; also at the fair he traps Edna Earle in the ferris wheel so he can escape to the tent where the scantily-clad ladies are dancing. Edna Earle constantly warns her interlocutor that Daniel will probably not be able to keep his hands off of her, but that she shouldn't mind that; we do not know anything about the details of his marriage to Teacake Magee, either, except that she scares herself with the vehemence of her "No" when the prosecutor asks her if under any circumstances she would want Uncle Daniel back (389). Though he claims to look for and pine after Bonnie Dee when she leaves, he is at the same time looking for Intrepid Elsie Fleming (365). Even while he's giving away money at the end of the trial, he stops long enough to importune Johnnie Ree, pulling at her skirt and asking her to go riding (421). Michael Kreyling has suggested that Daniel is a domestic version of King MacLain: there is no evidence that he ever actually *scores* with the women he chases, but he is King MacLain down to his white panama hat and suit (Comments).

Bonnie Dee returns five years later; though Edna Earle claims she still looks seventeen, she is older and apparently somewhat wiser. Within a few minutes of her return Daniel phones Edna Earle: "Make haste! She's fixing to cut my throat!" Edna Earle finds him on top of the dining room table, apparently the one on which he skated as a child. Narciss greets Edna Earle's arrival with "Hallelujah! . . . Prayers is answered," a response that suggests that she also thought Daniel was in danger. But Bonnie Dee enters, "sashaying around the table with her little bone razor wide open in her hand." She "commence[s] to lather his face" and to shave him. She dismisses Edna Earle by saying, curiously, "*Court's*

---

4. He is in "his forties" when he marries Miss Teacake Magee, and we do not know how long after that he married Bonnie Dee or how long he spent in the Asylum; Bonnie Dee comes to town while he is in the asylum (346, 352).

opened"—her play on their "trial" marriage and a suggestion that she, razor in hand, is about to convict Daniel of some terrible crime or at least to threaten him with certain consequences if he repeats it. She speaks "bossy," Edna Earle says. Edna Earle leaves, but returns when Narciss summons her to call Dr. Ewbanks. She re-enters the room to find Daniel "stretched" out on the floor; she then explains what has happened without having seen it and so obviously, as she does in the courtroom, makes it up or relies on what Bonnie Dee tells her. Bonnie Dee, she tells us, "came real close to his eye with that razor, biting her tongue as she came, [and] he'd pitched right out of his chair" (369–70). Clearly Bonnie Dee has warned him, razor in hand, how he is to behave with her or face the consequences. Just as clearly, Daniel has taken her seriously: when Dr. Ewbanks arrives after Bonnie Dee's death, Daniel and Edna Earle both notice an "awful-looking knife sticking out" of the fish-bait can he has brought with him: Daniel faints, a residual effect of his fear of Bonnie Dee's razor (401).

How Bonnie Dee dies is, of course, the great hole at the center of Edna Earle's narrative. After testifying first that Bonnie Dee was dead before they arrived, then that she had died of fright from the fireball, she finally claims that she died from Daniel's incessant tickling, and that she "died laughing" (415); this is clearly a cockamamie story which she contradicts twice before she tells it. We don't know what really happens, though Daniel almost tells us in his testimony: "I went to hug my wife and kiss her . . . but you might hug your wife too hard," he says. When Gladney asks him to demonstrate, he hedges: "But that time I didn't. . . . I went to hug her, but I didn't get to." Gladney asks why he "didn't get to," and Daniel stops cold, frowning, while Gladney continues to press: "When you ran into the parlor to hug her—only you didn't get to—did Bonnie Dee speak to you?" Daniel, taking the clue, allows that yes indeed she did: she said she was afraid of the lightning, and then started falling. His own lawyer interrupts this line of testimony to try to get into the court record the fact that Daniel is crazy, had been institutionalized in the asylum, but he is shouted down by Daniel and then by Edna Earle, who tries to tell the court her tale of death by tickling. Immediately Daniel begins giving away money—what's left of Edna Earle's own inheritance. He thus disrupts and closes the trial, apparently creating a mistrial, and there's no indication that he will ever be tried again for Bonnie Dee's death (411ff).

From this suppression of testimony, we may well understand that in fact Bonnie Dee didn't die of tickling or from fright, but of more sinister means that Daniel and Edna Earle are trying to protect Daniel from and that Edna Earle is complicit at least in her narration here and on the witness stand. Did Daniel simply crush the life out of her petite body by lying on top of her? Dr. Ewbanks tells the court that Bonnie Dee died of what he calls "Misadventure," which he defines as an "act of God. Like when the baby gets the pillow against its face, and just don't breathe any more" (397). Kreyling suggests that Bonnie Dee died from Daniel's attempt to rape her (Comments). Did Daniel in fact murder Bonnie Dee, as the prosecution claims—perhaps to protect himself from her razor? If so, if that is even a possibility, then *The Ponder Heart* is a dark fable about an abusive husband who murders his wife, all packaged, and for generations read, as a lighthearted fable about a generous if eccentric heart gone topsyturvy.

But even granting the seriousness of all these questions that go begged, *The Ponder Heart* still doesn't feel like a tragedy or even like a very serious book, though to be sure that seriousness or lack of it lies precisely in Edna Earle's telling, which makes it feel like a comic fable of generosity gone awry. But Eudora Welty is very clever. As noted, most critics and readers have assumed the "Ponder heart" to be Uncle Daniel's generous one. But in fact the only times Edna Earle discusses a heart is to show it in crisis: Grandpa's, whose apoplexy kills him; Bonnie Dee's, whose heart fails her; and even Daniel's "aging" heart, which "races" (370). It would seem more likely, then, that the "Ponder heart" of the title is not Daniel's pathologically and problematically generous one but rather precisely that heart in a crisis of expectations and on the verge of collapse, a heart that needs to control and to acquire, a heart that believes it can buy contentment, a heart too rigid or too weak to continue beating through a family crisis—the sort of heart that must escape or cave in, or in any case break.

Even if *The Ponder Heart* is nothing more than a farce, the cultural narrative about family that underlies Edna Earle's story is nevertheless crucial to its humor. The novel voices some sense of family values that lie in our language of love, which we often accept as merely language but which more often than not define who we are and what we believe about ourselves and our institutions. The prosecuting attorney builds his case from a message that Daniel sent to Bonnie Dee: "I'm going to kill you dead, Miss Bonnie Dee, if you don't take me back" (397–98). The prosecutor takes those words literally and it is part of the defense's method to get us and the jury to understand that we should take such language as exaggeration, not as literal intention. He didn't mean that literally, Edna Earle says on the witness stand, when asked whether she ever heard words like that in the Ponder household. She has grown up with such talk, in a "perfectly normal household" where "[t]hreats flew all the time." The prosecutor asks whether she considers this a "perfectly innocent remark," so that "in your estimation it meant nothing like a real threat?" "Meant he got it straight from Grandma," Edna Earle says. "That's what it means. She said 'I'm going to kill you' every other breath to him—she raised him. Gentlest woman on the face of the earth. 'I'll break your neck,' 'I'll skin you alive,' 'I'll beat your brains out'—Mercy! How that does bring Grandma back" (398).

Welty undercuts the apparent comedy of such exchanges with some grimmer realities about family violence: while giving this testimony Edna Earle silently remembers Williebelle Kilmichael who means such words at least to the extent of shooting her husband in the britches with buckshot and she remembers that even the prosecutor Gladney's wife has also famously peppered him with buckshot on more than one occasion. Very near the end of the book, Edna Earle reflects on the brutal sense of family relationships that our culture not just tolerates but accepts as givens:

Oh, . . . I wished that Uncle Daniel had just whipped out and taken a stick to Bonnie Dee—out of good hard temper! Of course never meaning to kill her. And there *is* temper, on Grandpa's side. Uncle Daniel was just born without it. He might have picked up Grandpa's trusty old stick hanging right there on the hatrack where Grandpa left it, and whacked her one when she wasn't glad to see him. That would have gone down a whole lot easier in Clay. (422)

This is a pretty grim, even jarring note for a farce, until we understand it in the context of Clay's family values. Thus we perhaps understand how Grandpa had dealt with disobedience among his children and why they all left home. Edna Earle, lying about so much, may also lie about whether Daniel has a temper (Daniel even threatens to "beat" her if "she dont stop" giving him counsel during the trial [409]); she certainly lies about how Bonnie Dee died.

What does it all mean? the judge asks Edna Earle. Don't mean a thing, she says, "except love, of course. It's all in a way of speaking,"—a line that reflects *Delta Wedding*'s more complicated statement, that families often speak "of killing and whipping . . . in the exasperation and helplessness of much love." Perhaps it's love, perhaps it's more exasperation and helplessness. If it's love, we may permit ourselves to wonder what kind of love manifests itself with Grandpa's trusty old stick or with language that laughs at it. We might even wonder how much of the language of our own households is the language of threat, of violence. We might also usefully compare *The Ponder Heart*'s language with the language and actuality of violence in Dorothy Allison's *Bastard Out of Carolina*, where violence appears almost as a direct objective correlative to the language the family uses.

Eudora Welty could not have known at mid-century what we now know about the enormity of domestic violence—the statistical horror, I mean, the extent of the misuse and abuse of women and children. Even so, readers today can't help but wince or shuffle uncomfortably in our seats when we read such language, especially perhaps when a woman uses that language to accept or justify the cultural conditions that allow such attitudes to prevail and, more especially, when the language, the telling, insists—or perhaps merely hopes—that we will laugh at it and so be complicit with those conditions. What Welty did know, in the fifties, is that language does in fact mean something, that it carries all the weight of our traditions, for good and for ill. She knew that language, the language of fiction, the language of narrative, the language, even, of love, often both hides what it wants to express and expresses what it wants to hide. Perhaps she knew that the language of comedy is the only way for prisoners to deal with their grim realities.

Welty names deliberately. The Lockharts of "At the Landing" and *The Robber Bridegroom* become here rather the ponderous heart, the ponderable heart. A locked heart is a ponderable one and this family's name is an invitation, indeed an instruction, for us to think seriously about this organ—the literal core of our corporeal selves, the metaphorical core of our spiritual and emotional selves—and to wonder why the Ponders, with all their acquiring and holding, are dying out, dispersed and fragmented by the tyrannical will of him who wanted to be the patriarch totem around which the Ponders would all cohere while the lower-class, even white trash Peacocks, whom the class-conscious Edna Earle disdains, proliferate and flourish in joyous profusion.[5] The real Ponder heart is more nearly Grandpa's Ponderous one—rigid, pre-emptive, and ruthless. If families sit around the parlor of an evening with their necks broken, it is almost certainly their hearts that broke first.

The Ponder heart is not the generous and loving, if eccentric, "heart" of our need and our mythology but rather a dark and complicated place, perhaps the heart of the heart of a domestic darkness no amount of electricity or lightning either can illuminate.

---

5. "Old lady Peacock wagged in first . . . all of them behind her—girls going down in stairsteps looking funnier and funnier in Bonnie Dee's parceled-out clothes, and boys all ages and sizes and the grown ones with wives and children, and Old Man Peacock bringing up the rear." "*They're* not dying out," Edna Earle notes, admitting that the Ponders are (384). In *The Optimist's Daughter*, Laurel Hand must feel the same way, observing the profusion of Dalzells in the hospital and of Fay's family at the funeral.

WORKS CITED

Aaron, Daniel. *Writers on the Left: Episodes in American Literary Communism*. New York: Harcourt, Brace & World, 1961.

Allison, Dorothy. *Bastard Out of Carolina*. New York: Dutton, 1992.

Baris, Sharon Deykin. "Judgments of *The Ponder Heart*: Welty's Trials of the 1950s." *Eudora Welty and Politics: Did the Writer Crusade?* Ed. Harriet Pollack and Suzanne Marrs. Baton Rouge: Louisiana State UP, 2001. 179–201.

Barthes, Roland. *Mythologies*. Tr. Annette Lavers. New York: Hill and Wang, 1975.

Bleikasten, André. "'Cet affreux goût d'encre': Emma Bovary's Ghost in *Sanctuary*." *Intertextuality in Faulkner*. Ed. Michel Gresset and Noel Polk. Jackson: UP of Mississippi, 1985. 36–56.

_____. "Terror and Nausea: Bodies in *Sanctuary*." *Faulkner Journal* 1 (1985): 17–29.

Blotner, Joseph. *Faulkner: A Biography*. New York: Random House, 1984.

Bunting, Charles T. "'The Interior World': An Interview with Eudora Welty." Welty, *Conversations* 40–63.

Butler, Judith, *Gender Trouble: Feminism and the Subversion of Identity*. New York: Routledge, 1990.

Butterworth, Keen. *A Critical and Textual Study of Faulkner's* A Fable. Ann Arbor: UMI Research P, 1983.

Coffee, Jessie McGuire, *Faulkner's Un-Christlike Christians: Biblical Allusions in the Novels*. Ann Arbor: UMI Research P, 1983.

Cowley, Malcolm. *The Faulker-Cowley File: Letters and Memories, 1944–1962*. New York: Viking, 1966.

Crane, Joan St. C. "William Faulkner to Eudora Welty: A Letter." *Mississippi Quarterly* 42.3 (1989): 223–28.

Faulkner, William. *Absalom, Absalom!* 1936. *Novels 1936–1940*. 1–315.

_____. "An Innocent at Rinkside." *Essays, Speeches & Public Letters*, 48–51.

_____. "Appendix: Compson: 1699–1945." *Novels 1926–1929*. 1125–41.

_____. *As I Lay Dying*. *Novels 1930–1935*, 3–178.

_____. *Collected Stories of William Faulkner.* New York: Random House, 1950.

_____. *Essays, Speeches & Public Letters.* 1966. Revised edition. Ed. James B. Meriwether. New York: Random House, 2005.

_____. *A Fable.* 1954. *Novels 1942–1954,* 665–1072.

_____. *Faulkner in the University.* Ed. Frederick L. Gwynn and Joseph Blotner. New York: Random House, 1959.

_____. *Faulkner: Novels 1926–1929.* New York: Library of America, 2006.

_____. *Faulkner: Novels 1930–1935.* New York: Library of America, 1985.

_____. *Faulkner: Novels 1936–1940.* New York: Library of America, 1990.

_____. *Faulkner: Novels 1942–1954.* New York: Library of America, 1994.

_____. *Faulkner: Novels 1957–1962.* New York: Library of America, 1999.

_____. "Foreword" to *The Faulkner Reader. Essays, Speeches & Public Letters,* 179–82.

_____. *Go Down, Moses.* 1942. *Novels 1942–1954,* 1–281.

_____. *The Hamlet.* 1940. *Novels 1936–1940,* 727–1075.

_____. *If I Forget Thee, Jerusalem [The Wild Palms].* 1939. *Novels 1936–1940,* 493–726.

_____. *Light in August.* 1932. *Novels 1930–1935,* 399–774.

_____. *Lion in the Garden: Interviews with William Faulkner, 1926–1962.* Ed. James B. Meriwether and Michael Millgate. New York: Random House, 1968.

_____. *The Mansion.* 1959. *Novels 1957–1962,* 327–721.

_____. *The Marionettes.* Ed. Noel Polk. Charlottesville: UP of Virginia, 1977.

_____. "Mississippi." *Essays, Speeches & Public Letters,* 11–43.

_____. *Mosquitoes.* 1927. *Novels 1926–1929,* 257–540.

_____. "My Grandmother Millard and General Bedford Forrest and The Battle of Harrykin Creek." *Collected Stories,* 667–99.

_____. *Requiem for a Nun.* 1951. *Novels 1942–1954,* 471–664.

_____. *Sanctuary: The Original Text.* Ed. Noel Polk. New York: Random House, 1981.

_____. *Selected Letters of William Faulkner.* Ed. Joseph L. Blotner. New York: Random House, 1977.

_____. *The Sound and the Fury.* 1929. *Novels 1926–1929,* 877–1124.

_____. *The Town.* 1957. *Novels 1957–1962,* 1–326.

_____. *The Unvanquished.* 1938. *Novels 1936–1940,* 317–492.

Fussell, Paul. *Wartime: Understanding and Behavior in the Second World War.* New York and Oxford: Oxford UP, 1989.

Godden, Richard, and Noel Polk. "Reading the Ledgers." *Mississippi Quarterly* 55.3 (2002): 301–59.

Godden, Richard. "A Fable . . . Whispering about the Wars." *Faulkner Journal,* 17.2 (2002): 25–88.

Gresset, Michel. "From Vignette to Vision: The 'Old, Fine Name of France' or Faulkner's 'Western Front' from 'Crevasse' to *A Fable. Faulkner: International Perspectives: Faulkner and Yoknapatawpha, 1982.* Ed. Doreen Fowler and Ann J. Abadie. Jackson: UP of Mississippi, 1984. 97–120.

_____. *Fascination: Faulkner's Fiction, 1919–1936.* Durham: Duke UP, 1989.

Harvey, Benjamin. Interview. September 14, 2006.

Hawthorne, Nathaniel. "Wakefield." *Nathaniel Hawthorne: Tales and Sketches.* New York: Library of American, 1982. 290–98.

Hinkle, James, and Robert McCoy. *Reading Faulkner: The Unvanquished*. Jackson: UP of Mississippi, 1995.

Huxley, Aldous. *An Encyclopaedia of Pacifism*. London: Chatto & Windus, 1937.

Jehlen, Myra. Class *and Character in Faulkner's South*. New York: Columbia UP, 1976.

Koestler, Arthur. *The Invisible Writing*. London: Collins, 1954.

Kreyling, Michael. Comments in discussion at the International Welty Conference in Rennes, France, October 2002.

_____. *Understanding Eudora Welty*. Columbia: U of South Carolina P, 1999.

Lyons, Eugene. *The Red Decade: The Stalinist Penetration of America*. Indianapolis: Bobbs-Merrill, 1941.

Manning, Carol. "*Losing Battles:* Tall Tale and Comic Epic." *With Ears Opening Like Morning Glories: Eudora Welty and the Love of Storytelling*. Westport, CT: Greenwood P, 1985. 137–62.

Mark, Rebecca. *The Dragon's Blood: Feminist Intertextuality in Eudora Welty's* 'The Golden Apples.' Jackson: UP of Mississippi, 1994.

Marrs, Suzanne. *The Welty Collection*. Jackson: UP of Mississippi, 1988.

McHaney, Thomas L. Interview. September 14, 2006.

_____. Review of Walter Sullivan, *A Requiem for the Renaissance*. *Mississippi Quarterly* 30.1 (1976–77): 185–88.

Morell, Giliane. "The Last Scene of *Sanctuary*." *Mississippi Quarterly* 25.3 (1972): 351–55.

Peckham, Morse. "The Place of Sex in the Work of William Faulkner." *Studies in the Twentieth Century* no. 14 (1974): 1–20.

Pitavy-Souques, Danièle. "A Blazing Butterfly: The Modernity of Eudora Welty." *Welty: A Life in Literature*. Ed. Albert J. Devlin. Jackson: UP of Mississippi, 1987. 113–38.

_____. *La Mort de Méduse*. Lyon: Presses Universitaires de Lyon, 1992.

Poe, Edgar Allan. "The Man of the Crowd." *Edgar Allan Poe: Poetry and Tales*. New York: Library of America, 1984. 388–96.

Polk, Noel. "The Artist as Cuckold." *Children of the Dark House*, 137–65.

_____. *Children of the Dark House*. Jackson: UP of Mississippi, 1996.

_____. *Eudora Welty: A Bibliography of Her Work*. Jackson: UP of Mississippi, 1994.

_____. "Faulkner at Midcentury." *Children of the Dark House*, 242–72.

_____. *Faulkner's* Requiem for a Nun: *A Critical Study*. Bloomington: Indiana UP, 1981.

_____. "Introduction." *The Marionettes*, ix–xxxii.

_____. "The Landscape of Illusion in Eudora Welty's 'The Wanderers.'" *Southern Landscapes*. Ed. Tony Badger, Walter Edgar, and Jan Nordby Gretlund. Tübingen: Stauffenburg-Verlag, 1996. 236–42.

_____. "Ratliff's Buggies." *Children of the Dark House*, 166–95.

_____. "Water, Wanderers, and Weddings: Love in Eudora Welty." *Eudora Welty: A Form of Thanks*. Ed. Louis Dollarhide and Ann J. Abadie. Jackson: UP of Mississippi, 1979. 95–122.

_____. "Woman and the Feminine in *A Fable*." *Children of the Dark House*, 196–218.

Price, Reynolds. "The Onlooker, Smiling: An Early Reading of *The Optimist's Daughter*." *Shenandoah* 20 (Spring 1969): 60.

Schwartz, Lawrence H. *Creating Faulkner's Reputation: The Politics of Modern Literary Reputation*. Knoxville: U of Tennessee P, 1988.

Travis, Mildred, "A Note on 'Wakefield' and 'Old Mr. Marblehall.'" *Notes on Contemporary Literature* (1974): 9–10.

Trilling, Diana. *Reviewing the Forties*. New York: Harcourt, 1978.

Trouard, Dawn. "Eula's Plot: An Irigarayan Reading of Faulkner's Snopes Trilogy." *Mississippi Quarterly* 42.3 (1989): 281–97.

_____. "X Marks the Spot: Faulkner's Garden." *Faulkner in Cultural Context: Faulkner and Yoknaptawpha, 1995*. Ed. Donald Kartiganer and Ann J. Abadie. Jackson: UP of Mississippi, 1997. 99–124.

Van Gelder, Robert. "An Interview with Eudora Welty." Welty, *Conversations*, 3–5.

Vande Kieft, Ruth. *Eudora Welty*. 1962. Revised Edition. Boston: Twayne, 1987.

Watson, Jay. "Writing Blood: The Art of the Literal in *Light in August*." *Faulkner and the Natural World: Faulkner and Yoknapatawpha, 1996*. Ed. Donald M. Kartiganer and Ann J. Abadie. Jackson: UP of Mississippi, 1999. 66–97.

Welty, Eudora. *Acrobats in a Park*. Northridge, CA: Lord John P, 1980.

_____. "Author Gave Life to Fictional County." *Washington Post and Times-Herald*. 7 July 1962, 2-C.

_____. *The Bride of the Innisfallen*. 1955. *Stories*, 557–722.

_____. "The Bride of the Innisfallen." *Stories*, 596–624.

_____. *Complete Novels*. New York: Library of America, 1998.

_____. *Conversations with Eudora Welty*. Ed. Peggy Whitman Prenshaw. Jackson: UP of Mississippi, 1984.

_____. *Delta Wedding*. 1946. *Novels*, 88–336.

_____. "Department of Amplification." *New Yorker* 24 (1 January 1949), 41–42.

_____. "The Doll." *The Tanager* 11 (June 1936), 11–14.

_____. *The Eye of the Story*. New York: Random House, 1979.

_____. "Going to Naples." *Stories*, 682–722.

_____. *The Golden Apples*. 1949. *Novels*, 313–556.

_____. "Kin." *Stories*, 647–81.

_____. *Losing Battles*. 1970. *Novels*, 425–879.

_____. "Magic." *Manuscript* 3 (September–October 1936), 3–7.

_____. "No Place for You, My Love." *Stories*, 561–80.

_____. *The Optimist's Daughter*. 1972. *Novels*, 881–992.

_____. "Place in Fiction." *Stories*, 781–96.

_____. *The Ponder Heart*. 1954. *Novels*, 337–424.

_____. Review of Faulkner's *Selected Letters*. *Eye*, 212–20.

_____. Review of Virginia Woolf's *The Haunted House*. *Eudora Welty: A Writer's Eye: Collected Book Reviews*. Ed. Pearl Amelia McHaney. Jackson: UP of Mississippi, 1994. 25–29.

_____. *Short Stories*. New York: Harcourt, Brace, 1950.

_____. "Some Notes on River Country." *Stories*, 760–72.

_____. *Stories, Essays, & Memoir*. New York: Library of America, 1998.

_____. "The Wanderers." *Stories*, 515–56.

Wyatt-Brown, Bertram. *Southern Honor: Ethics and Behavior in the Old South*. Oxford: Oxford UP, 1982.

Index

Welty, Eudora: community in, 19; and
critics, 7–8, 191, 195; family in, 137,
139–40, 141, 161–62, 187, 189, 195–96,
197; home in, 156; interaction with
Faulkner, 6–7; intimate vs. epic, 8–9;
language in, 171–72, 175, 185, 197; love
in, 137–38, 141, 147, 152, 158, 159, 180,
197; love and hate in, 13, 17, 18; narrative voice in, 168, 170; "place" in, 140,
141–42, 169, 174; and southern literature, 19; violence in, 139, 180, 184–85,
187, 196, 197. *See also individual works*

Wernick, Robert, 104
Westbrook, Ellen, 165
Wharton, Edith, 32, 33
"Why I Live at the P.O." (Welty), 189
Wilson, Edmund, 6
Wilson, Woodrow, 102
women writers, 5, 8
Woolf, Virginia, 165
World War I, 36, 37, 111, 112
World War II, 111
Writers on the Left (Aaron), 92
Wyatt-Brown, Bertram, 48

www.ingramcontent.com/pod-product-compliance
Lightning Source LLC
Chambersburg PA
CBHW060358030726
47497CB00003B/769